Yoga for Daily Life

Published by :
Lotus Press Publishers & Distributors

Yoga for Daily Life

Krishan Kumar Suman
M.A. B.T., Yogacharya, Ayurveda Ratna
Chief Editor: Yoga Manjari

4735/22, Prakash Deep Building
Ansari Road, Darya Ganj,
New Delhi - 110002

Lotus Press : Publishers & Distributors
Unit No. 220, 2nd Floor, 4735/22, Prakash Deep Building,
Ansari Road, Darya Ganj, New Delhi- 110002
Ph.: 41325510, 098118-38000
• E-mail : lotuspress1984@gmail.com
www.lotuspress.co.in

Yoga for Daily Life

ISBN: 978-81-8382-303-6

Printed & Published by : **Lotus Press Publishers & Distributors,** New Delhi-02

Dedication

I dedicate this work in humily to Swami Shivananda Saraswati who initiated and enlightened Swami Satyananda Saraswati and many more disciples who dedicated their lives serving the mankind through Yoga.

Preface

"There is no dearth of books on yoga in the market. But there are only a few which really fulfil the purpose." Generally, yoga is being taken as a set of physical exercises needed to eradicate a number of diseases and keep one physically fit. Where as yoga is a treasure of knowledge about the human body, mental make up, physic and the soul. In fact it aims at achieving a healthy union between an individual soul and Universal Super Soul. It is like an ocean where most of the unseen world lies at the bottom which is unseenable as well as unreachable and the Science of Yoga which is a unique approach to lead an ideal human life gives its best to reveal and bring to surface the hidden secrets which the modern Science has failed to grasp and deal with. It is for this reason we say that the philosophy of yoga starts from the point where the knowledge of Science ends. So writing a book on yoga is not so an easy job. A realized 'yogi' has a vivid picture of the human life and the hidden godhood in him, the inner of inner-self the abode of 'Divine Energy'. As a result of his long experience and a whole life practice of complete yoga also termed as 'Ashtanga Yoga' he has in his mind a vivid picture of the three subtle 'nadis' viz. ida, pingla and sushumna and the seven plexus the power centres stationed on them in a very mysterious manner. The activation of these power centres, producing sympathetic vibrations, making them harmonically vibrant to suit a rising of the divine energy from the lowest focal point to the top most roof of the human body is not an easy job.

To transfer and communicate all these vivid pictures from the mind and implant them to the highest degree in the mind of the readers is a gigantic task that requires a lot of skill, labour and a command over the vocabulary for embedding appropriate words, the best suited, to get in to fulfil the need for an ideal transportation of images from one mind to the other.

An ideal narration is just like the placid flow of water in a stream with a musical humming note soothing and impressing the mind of the reader quietly pouring in the sacred knowledge like the divine nectar to arouse in him a blissful experience.

Apprehending and grasping in this elixir of life and then practising the same with an unlimited patience under the supervision of a competent yogacharya leads the practicer to a state of perfection of human life that one dreams of. An ideal practice of yoga is a wonderful experience felt by an individual. It brings in a proper functioning of various systems is the human body establishing a perfect balance in secretion of juices or chemicals by prominent glands setting in a blissful rhythm to produce a best possible co-ordination between the body, mind and the soul. The reward can well be experienced in rendering of all worldly duties and deportments assuring in unique achievements and successes. In short one becomes a master of one self gifted with powers of a perfect control on all his thoughts, utterances, deeds and actions.

Today every single item of food is adulterated, and contaminated. The air we breath is a mixture of smoke, dust and poisonous gasses. Over population and noise has further worsened the living conditions. The poison spreading every where has adversely affected the elementary organs the liver, lungs, kidneys and the heart making people victims of various curable and incurable diseases. The author of the book aims at equipping the readers with more and more knowledge of yogic Science to enable them tone up the bodily systems with yogic postures, clear the lungs with practice of pranayama and wash away the poisonous and undigested food from the stomach and improve the functioning of glands for proper secretion of juices in the body. He is confident that a practicer of yoga can survive well living under most adverse conditions of the surroundings and environment in metropolis like Delhi. He believes that one can increase the span of his life by atleast 10 years living a rational yoga way of life. Longevity here does not mean a prolongation of helpless feeble old age but a continuance of youthful active life. No doubt this ancient Science that was confined to the Indian ascetics has proved to be a boon to the mankind and has been made available even to the common man. Through practice of yoga one can keep healthy and strong and can enjoy the amazing state of blessedness of the lasting youth. He can maintain a perfect miraculous balance between physiological and mental faculties. Well tuned body, mind and soul all working in a rhythm is an ideal state for the human being.

It has now become a firm conviction that yoga is not a mere physical culture but is a thing of 'Universal Utility' a Scientific approach to an ideal life ensuring an all-round development of body, mind and soul. A concious endevour on the part of a practicer can equip him with powers of perfect control on his emotional urges. Admittedly surrounded by spirit of asceticism and practised by Indian sages of the past it carries a quality of adaptability to cope up with the needs of the modern man.

The author of the book has been known to me since the year 1967 when we had first met in Nainital a hill station in India during summer holidays in an educational tour. Because of a virtuous unique personality, a true human being I had always been tempted to be with him in a bid to learn more and more, continuously till the date. His life is a tale of tireless efforts made while passing through different phases of life. He has immensely practiced yoga and has been in the company of outstanding 'yogis' of repute. He has comprehended every single aspect of Ashtaang Yoga. He is well versed in the study of Gita and has materialized in his own life the teachings of the holy scripture. He has mastered and delved to the very depth of so called spiritual achievement. The present book is an outcome of his life long experience and knowledge and I congratulate him for producing such a unique treasure of knowledge of yoga which would prove to be of utmost value and importance to the aspirants, to the students of yoga and the common man.

As for me I have observed while going through every word of the book that the author has tried his best in exposing the vast treasure of the 'divine knowledge' of what we say with a sense of pride the science of yoga to his esteemed readers, the elite class of the society. I hope this book will be immensely useful in creating an awareness among the masses about the utility of yoga in day-to-day life.

Uma Parshad Kaushal
Retd. Vice Principal,
Govt. NCT, Delhi
Editor 'Yoga Varsa'
A Popular Hindi/English
Quarterly Magazine.

About the Book

"The Quantum of the subject-matter exhaustively dealing with the Art of yoga has been divided with into 11 chapters in the book with emphasis laid for a routine daily practice by the readers.

In **Yoga a way of life** the word yoga has been defined with its aims and objectives as the only way of passing a perfect life devoid of diseases and disorders.

In **Yogic Discipline** the emphasis has been laid on leading a chaste and pure life without falling a prey to any of the social evils. We must observe the path of truth in our thoughts words and deeds. Study of Yama and Niyama deals with everything in details.

Yogic Postures are of six kinds with five types of movements based on seven principles. 'Yogasanas' can be chosen as per needs of the striver. They also help in awakening of the serpentine power (Kundalini) the mystic energy reservoir.

Controlling the Life Force: This deals with the 'Prana' the art of breathing. Although a very common thing, the intake of oxygen and release of carbon dioxide but in fact it is a reservoir of energy and control over 'Prana' grants you not only a perfect control over life but also bestows eternal peace and Bliss. It is a key to open the lock or a treasure of mystic powers. It deals with existence of subtle body, the three locks, the mudras and the 'asanas' involved in practice of pranayamas. It tells how it effects in 26 ways. The precautions and 16 types of pranayamas have been dealt in details with the helps of diagrams.

Role of Bandhas: It tells about the three locks and their utility for the human body.

Know about Mudras: Method of practising 20 mudras and their benefits have been given in details.

The Six Purificational Practices: Taking a dip in the Ganges or a holy river or taking a bath in our home does not purifus is a common saying until we don't change ourselves and become chaste, truthful and innocent. Here in this chapter you come to know how cleaning of inner organs is carried out the yogic way which has repercussions to your well-being.

What is Concentration: Concentration is a must for deriving good results. Concentrating the sunrays through a lens can burn a piece of paper. The 26 advices given here tell how great benefits can be derived by achieving power of concentration.

Psychic Centres: The seven plexus, the chakras, the power centres and making them vibrant to release immense energy from the lowest one the mooladhara to make it rise to the top, the roof of the human body, the Sahastrar situated in the head is the dream of the Yogins. It is strange to read it and every one would love to practice for the same.

Bhagwat Kriya Meditation: It is a seven days programme which has been discussed in details in this chapter.

Yoga in Office: Tension and Tension in the office at home and elsewhere and how it effects our efficiency and working capacity and how to manage and control and get rid of the same something so beneficial has been narrated in this chapter.

There are 226 figures and coloured photos on 16 pages in this book to understand the theme easily. There 66 Yogasanas, 14 Pranayamas, 4 Bandhas, 20 Mudras, 6 Purificational Kyias and 7 Chakras have been described beautifully. This book is a good guide for the Yoga Sadhakas to get deep experiences and live a yogic happy life.

K.K. Suman

Author

Contents

1

Yoga A Way of Life

Yoga is not just performing yogasana and or Pranayama. It is a way of life. Yoga is the science of right living. Yoga works on all aspects of a person; the physical, vital, mental, emotional, psychic and spiritual. It is the most valuable inheritance of the present. It is the essential need of today and the culture of tomorrow. Yoga is our Indian cult and way of spiritual life which claimed to endow perfect physical and mental health along with inner force to its practitioner.

What is yoga?

"Yoga is the true union of jivatma and parmatma"

"Jivatma parmatmaikyavastha yogah."

Shandilyopanisad

According to the Kathopanisad—

"yadapancavatisthante jnanani manasa.

Budhisca na vicest tamahuh paramam gatim"(5/10)

When the five senses of perception lie still with the mind in the self, when even the intellect not works, that supreme state, that firm control of the senses and mind is known as yoga. Yogi becomes free from all vagaries of mind.

Yoga is the path that bridges the conscious with the unconscious mind.

"Yoga ensures unity and harmony of the body, mind and soul, a well integrated personality which is at peace with itself and with society", says Shri B.K.S. Iyengar.

According to Maharishi Patanjali, "yoga means Samadhi." In his classical work of 'Yoga Sutras,' he explained yoga as the control of thought waves in the mind.

Yoga-Citta-Vrithi nirodhah.(Y.S.1,2)

With the help of only four words, he has masterly defined the essential nature of yoga, implying the process as well as its culmination is explained here with. The meaning of the four words at depth, Yoga in Sanskrit language has many meanings, but as it is derived from the root "**Yuj**" which means to join, the idea of joining runs through all the meanings given to the word yoga. Yoga means any effort of the individual self to merge with the Universal self and also the final merger with the Self. **Chitta** is a Sanskrit word derived from the term "**cit**" which means consciousness and broadly speaking corresponds to mind of modern psychology, but it has a more comprehensive field of functions. It is the internal power which cognises, wills and retains, that is, the whole of the psychic apparatus. **Vritti** is a term derived from the root **vrit** which means a way of existing, including the modifications and states of a thing. In the yoga system the **vritti** has been used technically to imply cognition of the conscious mental states. It implies the knowing states of the mind, each **vritti** being a piece of knowledge. It has been translated as modification because the mind is modified by the knowledge brought in by the sense organs and each one of these changes or fluctuations in the state of the mind is called a vriti. **Nirodha** means restraint, control, inhibition, and all those meanings are applicable to the practice of Yoga. Restraint is involved in the initial stages, control in the more advanced stages, inhibition or complete suppression in the last stage.

Goals of Yoga

The ancient scriptures all insist that the ultimate goal of spiritual independence is the only worthwhile achievement, but human nature being what it is, few if any of its seekers approach anywhere near the complete union which is yoga. To achieve some of the goals of yoga are—

1. Peace of mind,
2. Developing the inner faculties,
3. Control of mind and body,
4. Super Natural powers,
5. The power of concentration,
6. Control of behaviour,
7. The quest for truth,
8. Psychosomatic control,
9. To get rid of the diseases,
10. Balancing the life forces,
11. Relaxation of stress, and
12. Control of the senses and emotions.

Types of Yoga

There are many streams of yoga as— Rajyoga, Gyanayoga, Bhaktiyoga, Layayoga, Hathayoga, Astangayoga, Kundaliniyoga and Karmayoga. One can choose any stream according to one's interest and capacity. Combination of Hatha, gyana, bhakti and Karmayoga is very beneficial but Astangayoga is a very systematic way to live a yogic life.

How to live a yogic life?

Kriyas of yoga is the way of life, life is a journey through a never ending road of relationship, conflicts, materialism and feelings with its ups and downs through smiles and frowns, through sweet-smelling.

- Yama and Niyama are the basic foundation of living a yogic life. They provide character and discipline,

There are five **Yamas.**	There are five **Niyamas**.
1. Non-violence (Ahimsa)	1. Physical, mental, external, internal cleanliness. (Shaucha)
2. Truthfulness (Satya)	2. Satisfaction (Santosa)
3. Non-stealing (Asteya)	3. Austerity (Tapas)
4. Celibacy (Brahamcharya)	4. Study of Self and scriptures (Swadhyaya)
5. Non-acquisition (Aparigraha)	5. Surrender to the Lord (Ishwarapranidhana)

- Follow this tradition—early to bed and early to rise which makes a sadhaka healthy and wise.
- Cleanliness is next to God. Though Satkarmas clean the body from outer and inner. These kriyas are neti (sutra neti and jala neti), Dhauti-(kunjala, agnisara, shankha prakshalana), Nauli, Basti, Kapal bhati and trataka.

- Practise yogasanas daily according to your capacity, situation and interest. To improve health, to maintain health, to cure certain types of pains in the body, to overcome tiredness, to increase the power of resistance, to cure the minor ills, to remove the stress, to increase vitality and promote a feeling of well-being, to improve the circulation of blood and to make the body flexible Asanas and pranayamas are the very useful sadhana. You can be smart and active the whole day.
- Simple, balanced but Satvic food is necessary for a sadhaka. Milk, fruits, juices are good in meals. Drink daily, about ten glasses of water and must observe weekly fast.
- Relax your body through Shavasana, shithilasana, yoga nidra and pranayama.
- Massage your body while you take bath, with oil of mustard or coconut oil.
- Work with interest, surrender its fruit to the God. *Gita* says, 'yoga Karmsu kaushalam' do all the karmas efficiently and in accordance with Karmayoga. Keep a balance while working.
- Meditate daily atleast for half an hour. Increase it upto the stage of Samadhi.
- Take a sound sleep or about six hours. Go to bed at about 9.30.P.M. Do introspection, prayer then perform Shavasana.
- When you get extra time study the holy scriptures like *Ramayana, Gita, Upnisadas, Vedas* etc.
- Be positive, think positive and do positive deeds.
- Selfless service is the important sadhana to purify the mind, chitta and to remove the ego.

- With abhyasa and vairagya control your senses and mind.
- Enjoy the humour and comedy. Laughter is the best medicine. It helps our healing process. It relaxes us quickly and makes us sportive.
- Transform sexual, physical and mental energy into spiritual force through pranayama, certain asanas, mudras, bandhas, complete relaxation, mantras and meditation on chakras. The inverted postures, such as vipritkarani, sarvangasana, sirshasana, yogamudra are very useful in this sadhana.
- According to yoga, the main obstacles in the development and evolution of our latent forces are as follows—illness, languor doubt, carelessness, laziness, attachment to sensory pleasures, false perception, lack of concentration and instability. Remove these obstacles with the help of willpower, introspection, prayer and practice.
- Adopt a correct attitude towards the situations created by our relations with others, control your emotions.
- Keep mauna for some time daily and for 4 to 8 hours weekly you can save your energy and can develop your concentration power, control your speech and say only what is useful, necessary or indispensable.
- Be polite, keep a calm tone of voice.
- Avoid hurting or wounding others.
- When others are over excited and quarrelling remain quiet and undisturbed, seeking ways to appease them.

- Ignore gossip and harsh criticism of others
- Know your own nature and your ambitions. Assess your both positive and negative qualities. Accept your faults and mistakes you might have committed. Don't repeat them again.
- Organize your work, plan it properly for the whole year, considering seasonal changes, festivals, holidays and family functions among relatives. Use the planner.
- **'Samatvam yoga uchyate'** says *Gita*. A sadhaka should adopt equanimity in profit and loss, honour and insult, hot and cold, achieve a sthitpragya state.

This is a yogic way of life, a life which provides bliss and moksa the liberation from all bondages.

◆ ◆ ◆

2

Yogic Discipline

Introduction

Discipline is a very essential qualification in all walks of life. The modern age is however considered to be the most indisciplined race and the root cause is hunger for material objects. The lust for material objects makes the mind impure and unfit for higher ideals of life.

Ethical discipline is very necessary for success. Ethical discipline is the practice of right conduct in life specially in the yogic field. Maharishi Patanjali laid emphasis on first two limbs of Astanga yoga (Rajyoga). You will have to tame your mind, you will have to control your mind. This is all you have to do, control your senses, calm your mind. Goodness and discipline make life a blessing. These will bring sure success and prosperity.

A yogi diligently applies the principles of 'Yama' and 'Niyama' in his life for yogic discipline. They are the basic rules and steps of self-realisation. The practice of Yama and Niyama helps in self-control. Yama are the rules of morality. They require firm determination to abstain from doing wrong. Niyama are resolution to control and guide actions of the body and mind to do the right.

Uprooting bad habits (Sanskara) is Yama and developing good habits is Niyama. Unless we get rid of bad habits, we cannot enjoy the fruits of good habits. Daily meditation, Swadhyaya, positive thinking, good company, inspiring books, observance of yama and niyama greatly help in the cultivation of good habits.

Yama and Niyama are inter connected. Introspection helps us to remove our shortcomings. The practice of yama and niyama helps in practice of other limbs of astaangayoga and their practice strengthens observance of yama and niyama which in turn leads one to a life in harmony with God and Nature. Yama and Niyama form the foundation of a balanced life.

One should be resolute on one's intentions to practise 'Yama and Niyama'. It is better to live by the difficult principles of yama and niyama for lasting peace and harmony than by sensual pleasures which give temporary satisfaction, but which are forever in conflict with the self.

Yama

Yama means right thinking, social discipline to give up, abstinence, moral hygiene, restraint and conditional yogic behaviour, both social and personal. It is ethical discipline. As a part of Rajyoga, Patanjali laid emphasis on Yama, which is a symbol of social and ethical discipline, self-purification and abstinence. Yama enables one to achieve command over speech, mind, body and emotions.

The main stages of discipline for a sadhaka for God realization are as under:

1. Non-violence (Ahimsa)

To inflict any injury on an innocent is violence. Worry, jealousy, hatred, anger and similar negative emotions of all kinds are also a violence. Ahimsa means freedom from pain, fear and loss. Ahimsa means a mighty spirit full of love and energy. The spirit of non-violence can be acquired through right education and practice of yoga. Yogic education brings calmness and peace to the human mind. A disciplined and systematic life guides man to do right things.

2. Truthfulness (Satya)

Truthfulness is avoidance of falsehood. Guru Nanak described truthful living as the surest path to Godliness. Mahatma Gandhi laid emphasis on satya, King Harish Chandra was the symbol of truthfulness. Truthfulness is one of the three attributes of God, the other two being bliss and consciousness. Truthfulness has to be Chaste, observed in speech, thought and action.

3. Non-Stealing (Asteya)

Stealing brings unhappiness to the person who steals. When a person practise Asteya, wealth comes to him of its own, but he may not accept it. It does not mean only taking away a thing that belongs to somebody also. Wealth should be befittingly used for public purposes. One should use money as a divine gift. If we do not allow our surplus money to serve others in distress, it means we are stealing it from God. Don't have a greed of others property. Stealing is a sin and is therefore to be discarded at all cost. Satisfaction will help in non-stealing.

4. Chastity (Brahmacharya)

Celibacy is a necesity for the practice of yoga. It demands complete abstinence from sex in thought, emotion and practice. Brahmacharya is the master key for opening the realm of health and happiness. It also consolidates vigour and strength, ensuring good health, peace and a long life. Excessive sexual activity destroys intelligence, and capacity for self-development. Celibacy is the main source of kundalini awakening.

5. Non-Possession (Aparigraha)

Aparigraha means non-covertousness to keep control over one's needs. One should not desire things that are not necessary to one's life. One should cut down one's possessions and requirements to the minimum, says Patanjali. Accumulation disturbs the mind and is the root cause of all unhappiness. Disinterest in worldly possessions and detachment to luxuries render the mind pure and fit for higher and nobler ideas. Simple living is the best policy for yogic discipline. Donations to the needy is a very helpful habit to gain detachment from holding the things.

In addition, seven rules are specified by other scriptures and texts. These are faith, charity, modesty, sound mind. Japa of mantras, vrata and forgiveness.

Niyama

It is second limb of eightfold yoga. Niyama has five forms of discipline according to Patanjali Yogadarshan. Yoga lays a clear cut emphasis on purity. Niyama is a higher discipline. It has positive aspect. It belongs to inner rules. It is an attitude sublimated to yogic norms. Niyama which helps to discipline the body and subtle faculties. The niyama is personal and internal hygiene. The niyama helps to train the subtle faculties by winning the temptations of passion (kama), anger, gread, infatuation, pride, malice and envy.

Niyama is the logical follow-up of yama. These rules are prescribed for personal observance. Niyama is individual discipline, self-purification and observance of peace, both inward and outward. Higher discipline has also five main stages which should be adopted for self-improvement and God realization. The kinds of niyama are as under:

1. Cleanliness (Shaucha)

Purity and cleanliness are very important for those who want to practice yoga. Cleanliness is next to God, it is a proverb, cleanliness is one of the divine character. This cleanliness is of the external and internal parts of the body. Shaucha is the cleanliness of the impurities of mind. It is the restraint of the sense organs. There are six process of eliminating impurities. It is known as shatkarma (six fold process). These six processes are—Neti, Dhauti, Basti, Nauli, Trataka and Kapalbhati.

The second variety of purity consists of keeping the whole mind free from six enemies. These are lust, anger, avarice, temptation, pride and vanity.

2. Contentment (Santosha)

Contentment is a great quality of mind. It is adjusting the mind to accept whatever is available at a particular time. It is to free the mind from all kinds of desires and longings when contentment comes everything that belongs to this world becomes insignificant. It is the most superior of all the possessions of mankind. Always remember that the richest man in the world is one who is satisfied with his lot. Contentment gives one a poised mind which results in the attainment of pure happiness.

3. Austerity (Tapa)

Tapa/penance has been defined as equanimity of the mind towards hot and cold, honour and humiliation, happiness and misery, loss and gain, victory and defeat. Austerity is the conquest of all worldly desires or sensual pleasures by practising in thought, speech and action. Fasting on auspicious days, to have brotherly feeling and humility towards all and to control the senses is austerity. To utilise one's speech in proper manner and in the praise of the God is austerity of speech.

Austerity helps one remove the impurities of the body and mind and guides him towards the mastery over the senses. Yogic postures and breathing control lead to purity which inturn propels the sadhaka of yoga towards the attainment of perfect bliss. Tapas helps in the purification of the mind to achieve higher level of individual realisation. It burns all evil and bad tendencies, controls the body and helps develop one's will power.

4. Steadiness of Self (Swadhyaya)

Regular study of religious and yogic literature in search of truth and self-realisation is swadhyaya. Yoga sadhaka, should have both theoretical and practical knowledge of yoga and be familiar with the literature covering its different aspects. Know your good and bad habits and get rid of all the bad habits and sanskaras. Sit for introspection before going to bed. Proper study is very important for self-development and to dispel illusions and false mental constructs. Study the biographies of saints and yogis. Study yourself through meditation.

5. Surrender to God (Ishwarapranidhana)

Bhagavad Gita says,"whatever you do, eat and sacrifice. Whatever your mortification you undergo, commit each unto Me by surrendering to me." A true sadhaka feels that God is supreme and that he is only an instrument in his hands. He has bestowed up on us by His grace and mercy. To remain aloof and to perform all actions as an offering to God is pure devotion. Devoid of desires, the sadhaka attains unity with God and becomes one with God.

In addition to the above mentioned rules the Hathayoga Pradipika and Yogopanisad lists few more disciplinary rules are these Dhrti (steady intellect), Daya (compassion), Arjava (straightforwardness), Mitahara (moderation in diet) and listening to established doctrines etc.

Before we can control our mind we must first establish self-control दम (damas). This is the mastery over selfishness, anger and fear. Control of breathing through pranayama, control of Nadies (Ida-Pingla and Susumna) and Tattvas are helpful in maintaining the discipline. Awareness, selfless service, law of karma, faith in God, abhyasa and vairagya, regularity, are also helpful to achieve the discipline and perfection.

◆ ◆ ◆

3

Yogic Postures

Introduction

Yogic posture (yogasana) is a system of physical culture. Asanas are an instrinsic part of Astanga yoga and Hathayoga. Yogasanas are necessary for healthy living. Yogasana practice comes first in Hathayoga texts such as **Hatha Yoga Pradipika.**

In one of the Upanishads, or ancient vedic writings, we find the confirmation or source of Patanjali's statement regarding a "simple postur". Quoting from Upanishads.

"Any posture in which one can remain still without discomfort is known as a comfortable posture. Such a posture may be utilized by persons who can't practice a regular posture".

There are 84 main asanas which are practised by yogis in India and abroad. Maharishi Patanjali says in yoga sutra" स्थिर सुखम् आसनम् (Sthira Sukham Asanam). He said only meditative postures. In Hathayoga various poses are described which are for integral living, attainment of wholesome health and happiness.

Three stages in Yogasana

During the performance of the yogasana one undergoes three stages.

1. **Sthira:** Stability of the physical body.
2. **Shoonya:** Vaccum state of the mind, thoughtlessness.
3. **Sukham:** Bliss (when one starts enjoying the stability without any thought) and relaxation.

The victory over an asana is called **'Asanasiddhi'** which is achieved when a person stays for 2.40 hours without movement in the asana. Keeping the steady rhythm of breath. This condition is for meditative asanas.

Types of Yogasanas. There are six types of yogasanas:

1. Standing
2. Sitting
3. Kneeling
4. Lying on back
5. Lying on abdomen
6. Inverted poses.

Five basic movements:

1. Contraction and stretch
2. Twisting
3. Forward bending
4. Backward bending
5. Sideways bending.

Yogasanas based on principles

1. **Gravity:** The inverted postures such as the Sarvangasana, Sheersasana and vipreetakarini and the reverse postures take advantage of gravity to increase the flow of blood to the desired part of the body as in the brain, thyroid and gonads.
2. **Organ Massage:** The position of the asana causes a squeezing action on a specific organ or gland, resulting in the stimulation of that part of the body

stretching muscles and ligaments. This movement increases the blood supply to the muscles and ligaments as well as relaxing them. It also takes pressure off nerves in the area.

3. **Deep Breathing:** While holding the yogic posture we breathe slowly and deeply, moving the abdomen only. This increases the oxygen and prana supply to the target organ or gland, thereby enhansing the effect of the yogasana.
4. **Right Posture:** If we perform the right posture, we can get the full benefit.
5. **Staying in the Posture:** After performing the final posture one should stay for long time according one's capacity. Increase the staying gradually. We can get much benefits staying in the final pose.
6. **Concentration:** As well as breathing slowly and deeply, we also focus our attention on the target organ, chakra or gland. This brings the mind into the kriya. Where there is mind the prama flows there and blood also runs there. If there is pain in a particular organ, the concentration removes that.
7. **Relaxation:** It is very necessary to take rest between two asanas and in the last. Shavasana is the best way to relax. If you are not well then avoid practice.

Origin of Asanas Names

Many of the asanas have animal names such as the fish, lion, cobra etc. Yogis observed how animals relaxed. This is because yogis devised their asanas, partly by observing how animal instincts work in the wild life.

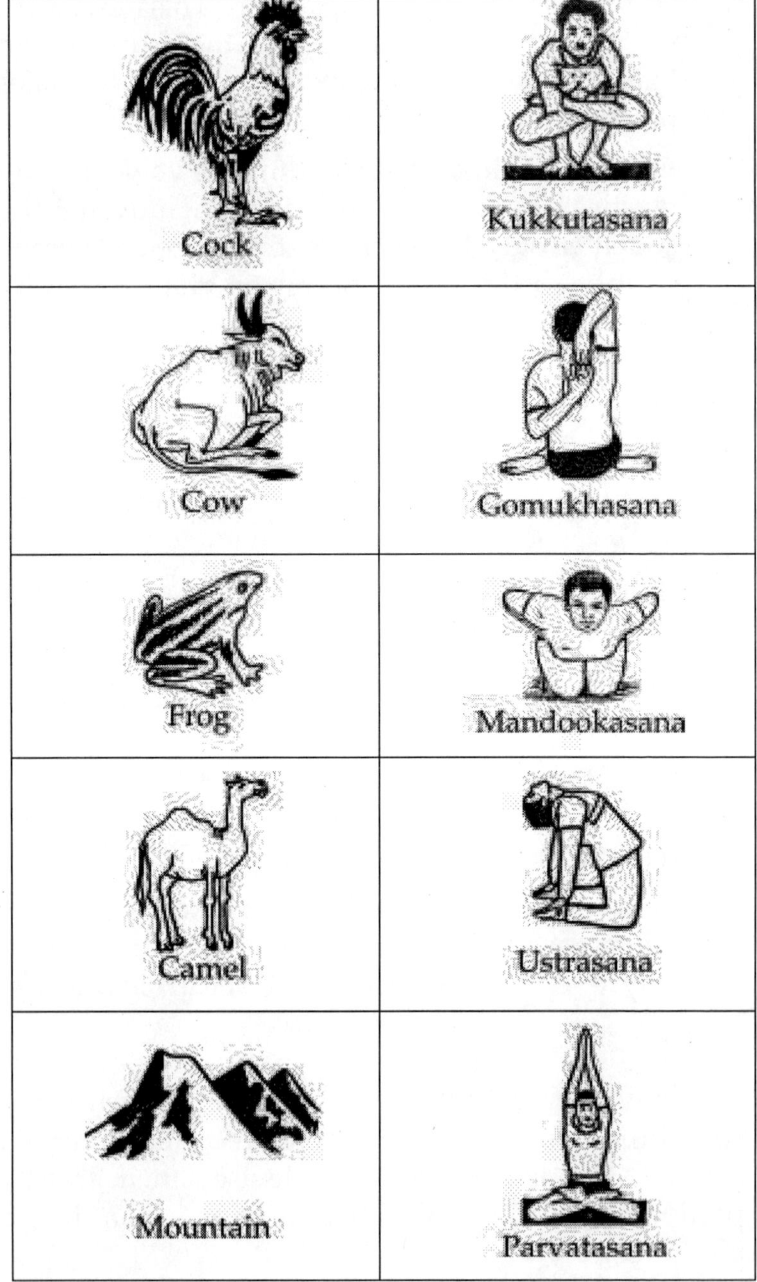
Cock
Kukkutasana
Cow
Gomukhasana
Frog
Mandookasana
Camel
Ustrasana
Mountain
Parvatasana

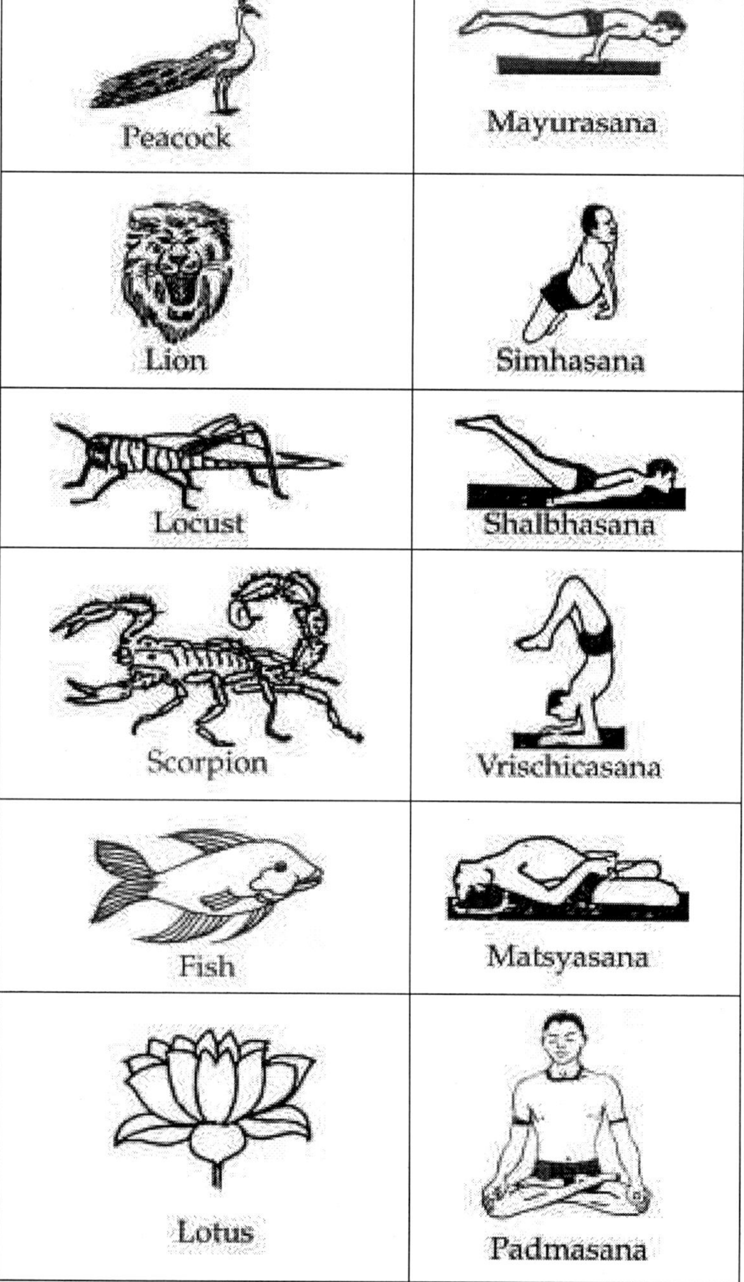
Peacock
Mayurasana
Lion
Simhasana
Locust
Shalbhasana
Scorpion
Vrischicasana
Fish
Matsyasana
Lotus
Padmasana

Select your Asanas

There are three groups of yogasanas; beginners intermediate and advanced. It is not necessary to practise all the yogasanas in a particular group. For a regular practice of a balanced programme tailored to individual needs, capacity, time and aspects, such as standing sitting, on the belly, on the spine and twisting postures.

Instructions for the Practice of Yogasanas

The following instructions should be thoroughly understood before practice. Yogasanas become more efficacious and beneficial when performed in the proper manner after correct preparation.

1. **Place:** Any well ventilated place, free from noise and distractions for the mind to be well suited for the practice of yogabhyasa. The garden is the best place for yogabhyasa.
2. **Time:** The morning hours from 4 A.M. to 6 A.M. and evening hours from 6 P.M. to 8 P.M. are most suitable. But one should adjust according to one's daily schedule. You should practice atleast once a day.
3. **Dress:** Your dress must allow freedom in all flexible movements of the body. Don't wear tight dress.
4. **Asana:** Spread plastic sheet first. Then spread carpet or rug mat and blanket. Spread white sheet of cloth in the last.
5. **Bathing:** It is better to bathing before performing the yogasanas or after half an hour of the practice.

6. **Breathing:** Always breathe through the nose. Try to coordinate the breath with the asana practice.
7. **Sequence:** After performing shatkarma, asanas should be done followed by pranayama. Begin your yogabhyasa. With 'om chanting' by repeating prayer, Gayatri mantra and conclude your yogabhyasa with prayers for peace and harmony in the world. Fill your mind with positive and elevated thoughts for yourself and for humanity.
8. **Mental attitude:** When you maintain a pose for a longer duration, you can practise repetition of Divine name, or your mantra mentally with feeling and devotion. Free your mind of all negative thoughts of fear, hatred, jealousy, greed, and uncontrolled desires. Fill your mind with the positive thoughts of universal love, truthfulness, purity, and wisdom.
9. **Be Regular:** Choose a set of yogasana, and practise them every day. Off and on practice delays your progress. If you practise yogasanas regularly with patience, faith, and perseverance, you will evolve quickly.
10. **Be Moderate:** In sleep, food, sport, entertainment, walking, working and everything that life needs, learn to be moderate. In a rhythmic moderation, there lies the key to success and spiritual advancement.
11. **Counterpose:** This concept of counterpose is necessary to bring the body back to a balanced state. Specific counterposes are recommended for certain asanas.
12. **Empty Stomach:** The stomach should be empty,

while doing asanas. They should be practised three or four hours after food.

13. **Closed eyes:** In the early stages of the practice of asanas, it is better to open the eyes to check the posture and can correct the pose. When the eyes are closed, the mind becomes calm and one can look inward and concentrate mainly on the benefits of the asana.
14. **Diet:** A vegetarian diet consisting of milk, wheat vegetables, nuts, fruits, nutritious vegetarian products, is ideal for Hathayoga. As you continue the practise of Hathayoga exercises, you will be less inclined to nonvegetarian types of food. Avoid stimulants, intoxicants, smoking and any indulgence, to hallucinogenic drugs for quick results. Eat always sattvic food.
15. Don't aim at perfection in the very beginning.
16. To relieve stress and strain, take up shavasana in the beginning only, which helps every cell, nerve fibre limbs get deep relaxation and reduces pain in the body.
17. Perform asanas in slow motion, maintaining the rhythm of breath, posture, co-ordination of muscles with joints, as per the capacity of your body.
18. The body must not shake when in asana.

Abdominal Group (Spine Poses)

This group of yogasana is related to abdominal or digestive system. This group is useful in digestion, excess of wind, lack of appetite, constipation, acidity, diabetes, disorders of the reproductive system and varicose veins. It removes energy blockages in the abdominal region.

Concentrate on breathing movement, mental counting, the muscles stretching and abdominal pressure. A short rest should be taken between each yogasana until the breathing returns to normal. Choose one practise at a time. Be aware of physical limitations and don't take strain.

Avoid these yogasanas if you are suffering from serious heart problems, high blood pressure, sciatica and slipped disc or soon after abdominal surgery.

These yogasanas are performed on the spine and sitting position.

1. Padottanasana (Leg Raising)

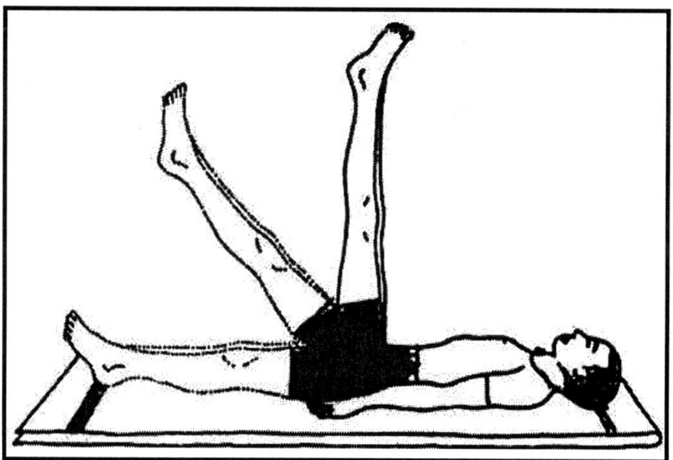

Method: Lie on the spine with feet together, keep your palms beside the thighs, facing the ground. Inhale and raise the right leg at 90° or as much as possible, without bending the knee. Hold this position for some time. While exhaling bring the leg down slowly then repeat the asana with the left leg and relax. This may he repeated raising both legs together.

Benefits

1. This asana strengthens the abdominal muscles and massages the organs.
2. It strengthens the digestive system lower back, pelvic and perineal muscles.
3. It helps correct prolapse.
4. This asana removes the pain in the lumber region due to wrong posture or pressure.
5. It also burns the excess fat in the thigh, hips and abdomen.
6. It is helpful in curing nervous weakness and constipation.
7. It rejuvenates the spinal nerves and the brain cells.
8. This asana is a good remedy for piles in the initial stage.
9. It is helpful performing sarvangasana and halasana.

Note:

Raise the legs to progressive hights of 15.25, 35 cm respectively in each round slowly.

2. Leg Rotation

Method: Lie on the back with legs and arms straight, feet to gether. Palms facing the ground and touching the sides of the body. Raise the right leg up to 45° from the ground, keeping the knee straight. Rotate the entire leg Closewise 5 to 10 times in a large circle. The heel should not touch the floor during the rotation. Repeat with the left leg. Bring the leg down and relax.

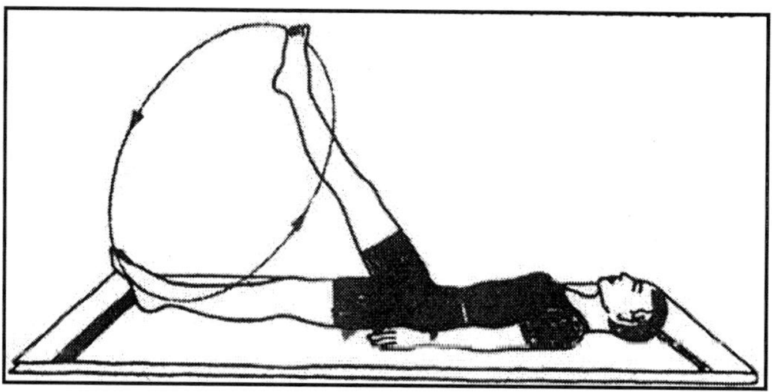

Benefit

1. It is good for obesity, hip joints, toning of abdominal and spine muscles.

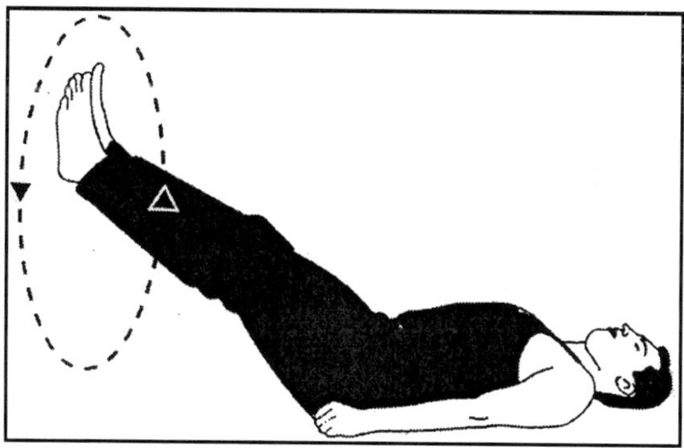

Note:

- You can perform this raising both legs together.
- Rotate both legs clockwise and anti-clockwise 3 to 5 times.
- The circular movement should be as large as possible.
- Concentrate on mental counting, leg rotation and on the effects of the asana on the abdomen and hips.

3. Cycling (Paga Sanchalana)

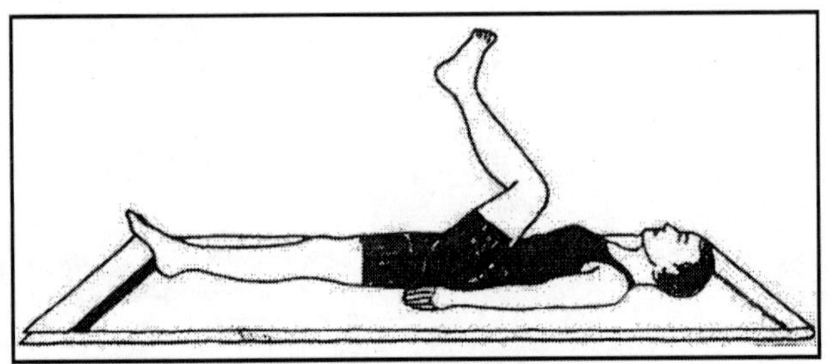

Method: Lie in the basic position. Raise the left leg. Bend the knee and bring to the chest. Raise and straighten the leg. Then lower the straighten leg in a forward movement. Bend the knee and bring it back to the chest in cycling movement. The heel should not touch the floor during the movement. Repeat 10 times in a forward direction and then 10 times in reverse. Repeat with the right leg in cycling movement.

Inhale while straightening the leg. Exhale while bending the knee and bring the knee to the chest.

In stage 2 practise alternate cycling movements as though pedling a bicycle. Practise 10 times forward and then10 times backward. Breathing normally throughout.

In stage 3 Raise both legs and keep them together throughout the practice. Bring the knees to the chest and straighten the legs fully. Slowly lower the legs to gather. Keep the legs above the ground. Bend the knees and bring them back to the chest. Repeat 3 to 5 times forward cycling movements and the same reverse. Don't strain.

Benefits

1. It is good for hip and knee joints.

2. Strengthens abdominal and lower back muscles.
3. It removes constipation and improves appetite.
4. It is also good for removing the back pain.

Note: Take rest when you change the stage or in fatigue.

4. Pawan Muktasana (leg locking)

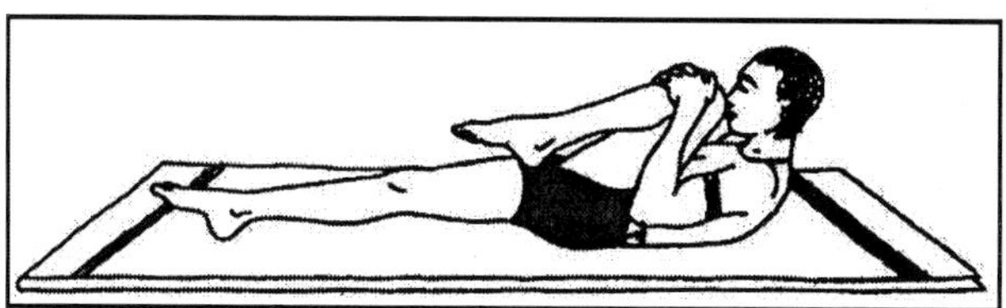

Method: Stage 1: Lie down on the back with the feet close together. Place the palms beside the body. Inhale and raise the left leg and bend it at the knee. Bring the thigh near the abdomen, interlock the fingers, while exhaling and press the thigh against the abdomen and hold the posture for few seconds. Breathe normally, while inhaling, stretch the leg up and while exhaling, bring the leg back on the ground. Repeat the same with the right leg and relax.

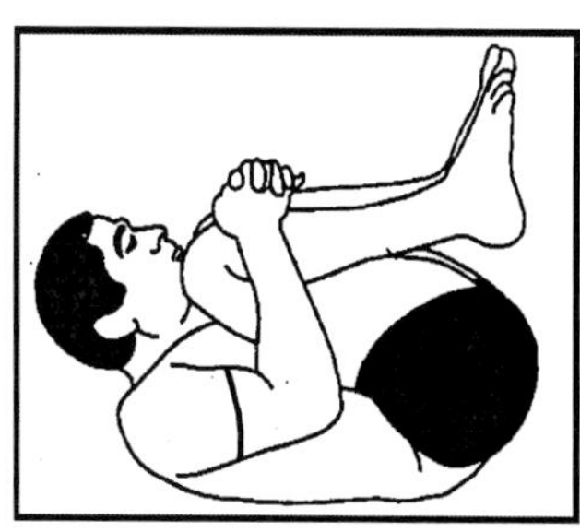

Stage 2: Bend the both legs of the knees. Make a finger lock with the both hands, around them, a little below the knees. While exhaling, bring the thigh close to the chest by contracting the abdominal muscles. Maintain this posture for a few seconds, breathe normally. Then return to the original posture. Repeat the asana twice.

Benefits

1. Pawanmuktasana is very helpful in removing the gases accumulated in the digestive tract.
2. It is good for pains of back, abdomen and buttocks.
3. It smoothens the functions of liver, stomach, kidney and pancreas.
4. Pawanmuktasana strengthens the abdominal muscles and other organs.
5. It is very helpful to remove the constipation, after drinking lukewarm water in the morning.
6. It strengthens the lower back muscles and loosens the spinal vertebrae.
7. It is useful in the treatment of impotence sterility and menstrual problems.
8. Increases the capillary circulation.

Note: Except high blood pressure, heart related problems and cervical spondylosis, one can raise the head and touch the chin to the knees keeping the breath out.

5. Boat Pose

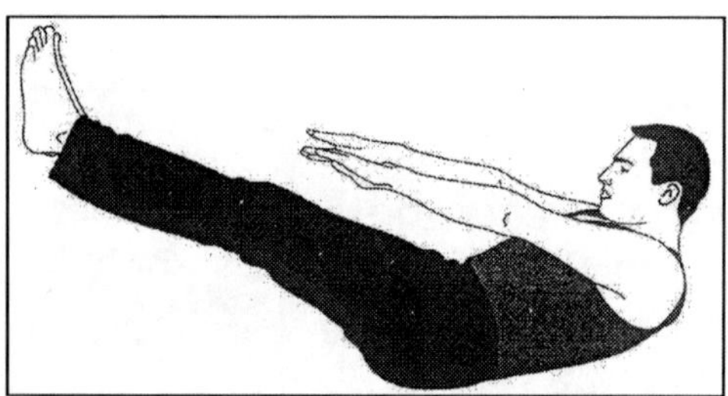

Method: Lie flat on the back with the legs and feet together, palms down, eyes opened, breathe in deeply. Hold the breath and raise the legs, arms, shoulders, head and trunk off the floor. Shoulders and feet should be 15 cm off the floor. Balance the body on the buttocks and keep the spine straight. The arms and toes should be in line. Hands should be opened with the palms down. Concentrate on the toes. Stay for some time in this pose. Breathe out and come back. Relax the whole body. Practise 3 to 5 rounds, relax in shavasana after each round.

Benefits

1. It immediately restores freshness if practised after walking.
2. It is especially useful for eliminating nervous tension.
3. It brings deep relaxation. It may be performed before shavasana.
4. This asana stimulates the muscular, digestive, circulatory, nervous and hormonal systems.
5. It tones up all the organs and removes lethargy.
6. It develops the concentration power and balancing of mind.

Note: Boat pose is called Naukaasana and hastapadasana also.

Energy Developer Yogasanas

This group of asanas is related to improving the energy flow within the body and breaking down neuron-muscular knots. This series is useful for those with reduced vitality and a stiff back. It is especially useful for menstrual problems and tonic the pelvic organs and muscles. It is beneficial for pregnancy before and after. These asanas also eliminate energy blockage in the spine, activate the lungs and heart and improve endocrine function. This group provides good health and fitness.

6. Rope Pullingasana

Method: Sit on the asana with the legs straight and together, eyes opened. Imagine that there is a rope hanging infront of the body. Breathe in while reaching up with the right hand as though to grasp the rope at a higher point. Keep the elbow erect look upward. Pull the right hand down with exhalation, as though pulling the rope downwards. Eye sight should be downward according to hand movement. Repeat with the left hand arm to complete the first round. Repeat 5 to 10 rounds.

Benefits

1. This asana loosens the shoulder joint and stretches the upper back and shoulder muscles.
2. It strengthens the chest and its muscles.
3. It is a good breathing exercise.

7. Kamar Chakrasana

It is called dynamic spinal twist or gatytatmak meru Vaksasana.

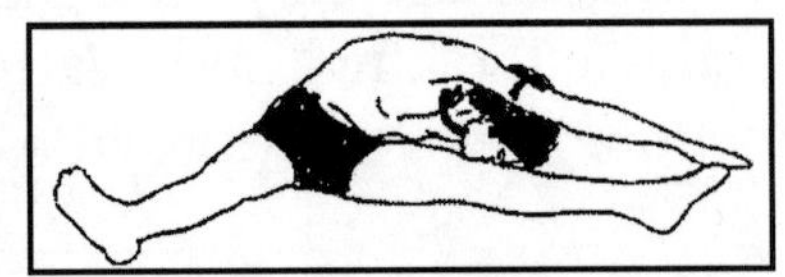

Method: Sit on asana, spread your feet on either side as wide as possible. Hold the left toe with the left hand and the right toe with right hand. First take a long breath. Then exhaling, turn round the trunk towards the left. Now hold the left toe with the right hand. Touch the knee with the forehead. Keep the left hand behind the waist inhaling. Come back to the normal position. Exhaling hold the right toe with the left hand and touch the right knee with the forehead inhaling, Return to the original position. Repeat this process 10 to 20 times.

Benefits

1. It helps us greatly in performing Paschimottanasana and Janushirasana.
2. It also tones up our seminal gland.
3. Sciatica nerve is restored to its natural position.
4. The lower portion of the waist becomes flexible.
5. The muscles of the abdominal region, liver, spleen etc are strengthened and toned up.
6. This asana loosens up the vertebrae and removes stiffness of the back.

Note: People with back pain should avoid this asana.

8. Chakki Chalana

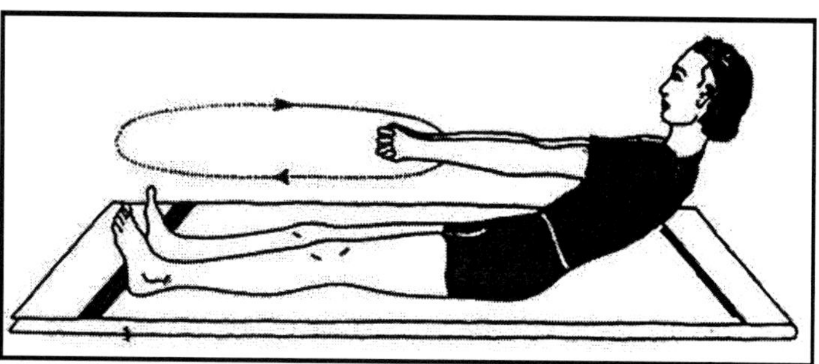

Method: Sit with the stretched legs infront of the body about one foot apart. Interlock the fingers of both hands and keep the arms infront of the chest in straight position throughout. Bend forward as for as possible imagine you are churning a mill (chakki) an old fashioned stone grinder, lean back as for as possible on the backward swing. Move the body from the waist. Repeat the round clockwise and anti-clockwise 5 to 10 times each. Inhale while leaning back. Exhale while moving forward Concentrate on the lumber region.

Benefits

1. It is an excellent exercise for postnatal recovery.
2. It is especially useful for gynaecological disorders.
3. It also removes constipation.
4. This asana has a positive effect on the pelvis and abdomen and eliminates blockages in these areas.
5. It is very useful for regulating the menstrual cycle and may be performed during the first three months of pregnancy.

9. Wood Choppingasana

Method: Sit in the squatting pose with the feet flat on the ground one feet apart. Knees should be fully bent and separated. Clasp the fingers of both the hands together and place them on the ground between the feet. Arms should be straighten throughout during the practice. The elbows should be inside the knees. The eyes should be opened. Imagine, you are chopping the wood. Raise the arms as high as possible above and behind the head, stretching the spine upward. Look up towards the hands. Make a downward stroke with the arms and expelling the breath making the sound 'Ha'! Exhale all the air from the lungs. Bring the hands to the floor in between the feet and the head is facing forward. It is one round. Repeat 5 to 10 rounds. Inhale while raising the hands. Exhale while lowering the hands.

Benefits

1. It has a special effect on the usually inaccessible muscles of the back between the shoulder blades as well as the shoulder joints and upper back muscles.
2. This asana loosens up the pelvic girdle and tones up the pelvic muscles.
3. It is useful for women preparing for child bearing and may be practised during the first three months of pregnancy.

Note: Those people who are unable to sit in a squatting position too difficult should practise in the standing position but you can't get full benefits.

10. Wind Releasingasana

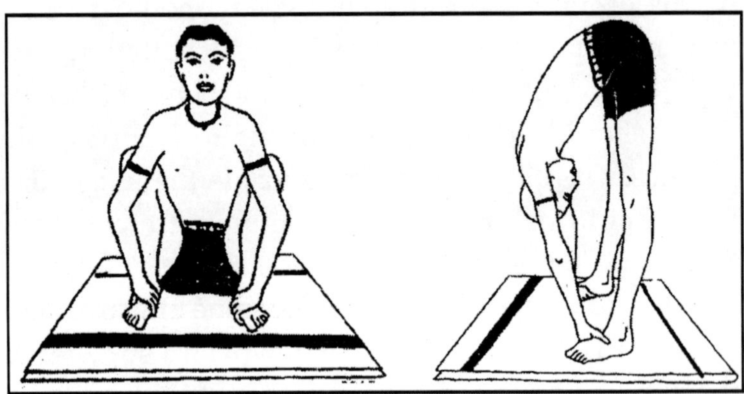

Method: Sit in a squatting pose with two feet apart. Grasp the insteps of the feet, keeping the fingers under the soles with the thumbs above. The upper arms should be pressing against the inside of the knees with the elbows slightly bent. Eyes should be open. Inhale while moving the head back. Direct the gaze upward. This is the starting position. Hold the breath for three seconds, accentuating the backward movement of the head. While exhaling, straighten the knees, raise the buttocks and bring the head forward towards the knees. Retain the breath for three seconds, accentuating the spinal bend. Do not strain. Breathing in return to the starting position. This is one round. Repeat 5 to 7 rounds.

Benefits

1. It is useful for relieving flatulence.
2. It has a beneficial effect on the nerves and muscles of the thighs, knees, shoulders, arms and neck.
3. It gives an equal stretch to the whole spine and both the arms and leg muscles.

4. All the vertebrae and joints are pulled away from each other so that the pressure between them is balanced.
5. Simultaneously, all the spinal nerves and dural sheaths are stretched and toned.

11. Crow Walkingasana

Method: Sit in the squatting position with the feet apart and the hips above the heels. Place the palms on the knees. Walk in small steps in the squatting position. Try to keep the knees flexed so that the hips are not moved away from the heels. Walk either on the toes or the soles of the feet take as many steps as possible, up to 40, and then relax in Shavasana.

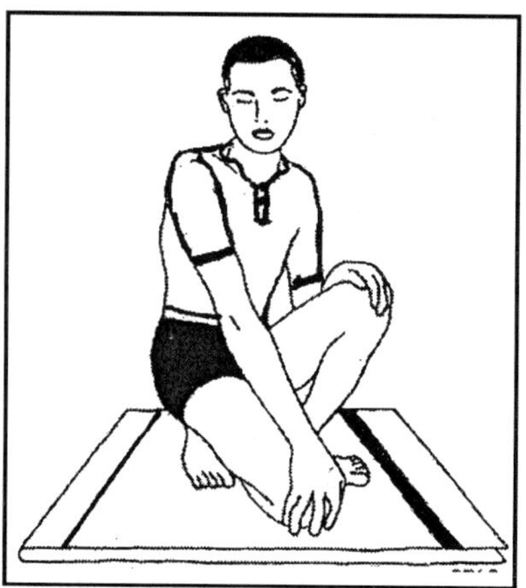

Benefits

1. This asana is helpful to perform the meditative asanas.
2. It helps to remove constipation.
3. It improves blood circulation in the legs.
4. Leg pain is removed.

Note:

- Breathing should be normal during practice.
- Concentrate on the breath, lower back, hips, knees and ankles.
- As you take a step forward bring the opposite knee to the ground.

Relaxational Asanas

Relaxation is necessary after the asana and pranayama. They should be performed before and after the asana session, and at any time when the body becomes tired. These asanas are very simple and effective.

12. Corpse Pose (Shavasana)

This is a simplest and energy blocking asana.

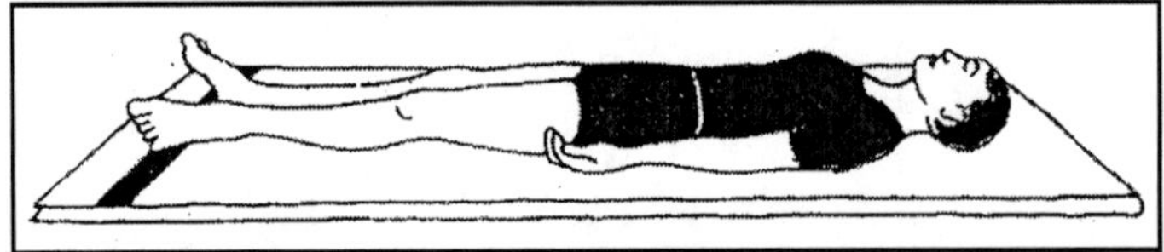

Reversed Corpse Pose

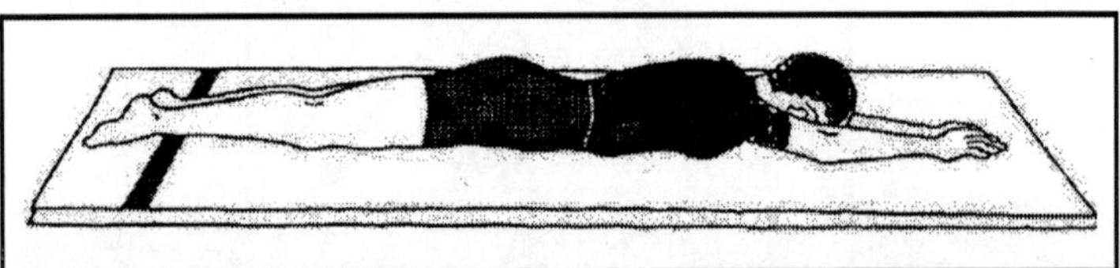

Method: Lie flat on the stomach, stretch both arms above the head with the palms facing downward. The forehead resting on the ground. Relax the whole body and stop all physical movements. Become aware of the natural breath. Begin to count the breaths from number 27 backwards to zero. Repeat mentally "I am breathing in 27', I am breathing out 27. I am breathing in 26. I am breathing out 26, and so on, back to zero. If the next number is forgotten, count again from 27 number. Concentrate on the every part of the whole body and Agya Chakra also.

Benefits

1. It is helpful in slip disc, stiff neck, stooping figure and body relaxation.

Note:

- Mantra may also be chanted mentally with the breath.
- In illness perform it for long period, otherwise a few minutes rest is sufficient.
- Count the breaths consciously.

13. Superior Posture

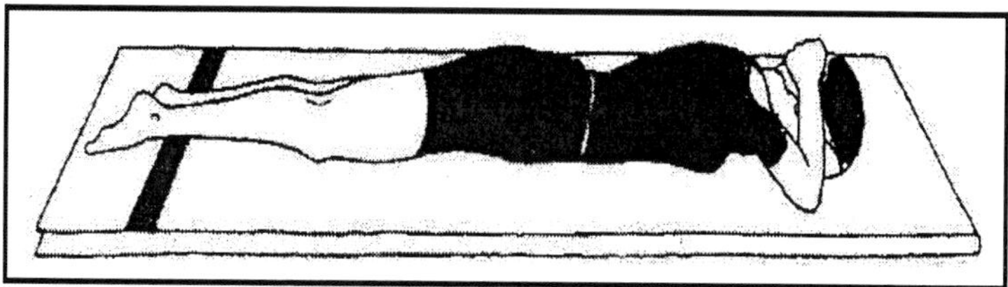

Method: Lie flat on the stomach with the legs straight and the forehead resting on the ground. Interlock the fingers and place the palms on the back of the head or neck. Allow the elbows rest on the ground. Relax the whole body and be aware of the breathing process that should be natural and rhythmical.

Benefits

1. This asana is helpful for all spinal complaints especially cervical spondylitis and stiff neck or upper back.

Note: You can put interlocked fingers under the forehead. Palms facing up.

14. Crocodile Pose

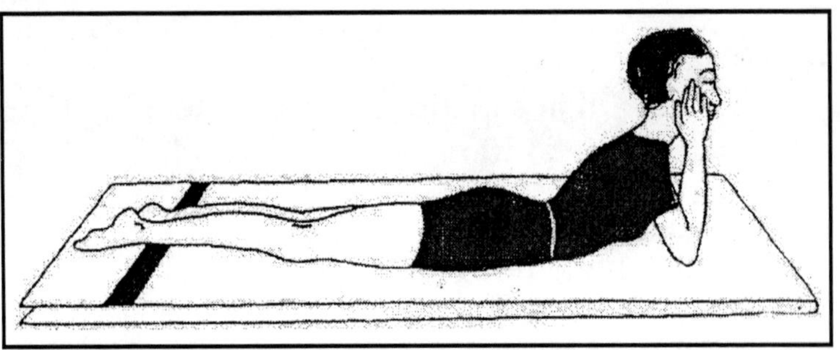

Method: Lie flat on the stomach. Raise the head and shoulders and rest the chin in the palms of the hands with the elbows on the ground, keep the elbows together. Separate the elbows slightly to relieve excess pressure on the neck. Relaxed the body and close the eyes. Practise as long as possible.

Benefits

1. It eradicates the fatigue and gives relaxation to all the parts of the body.
2. This asana is useful to those whose spine or back is injured.
3. This asana is very effective for people, suffering from slipped disc, sciatica, lower back pain or any other spinal disorder.
4. Asthmatics and people who have any other lung ailments practise this asana with breath awareness.

Note:

- Concentrate on spine, from tail bone to neck while inhaling and breathing out, bringing the awareness back down from the neck to the tail bone. Imagine that you are breathing through spine.

15. Shithilasana

Method: Lie flat on the abdominal at full length. Resting the right ear on the ground. Fold the left foot at 90° degrees. Bring the left heel to the right knee. Left hand palm may be placed in front of the face, shoulders are relaxed. Normal breathing with closed eyes be there. Repeat the same process on the other side.

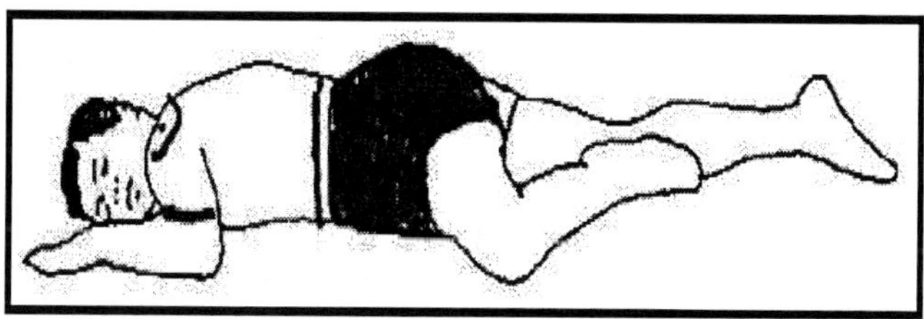

Benefits:

- It gives complete relief from fatigue.
- Helps in sleeping, sets right the B.P., as Shithilasana on right side. Lowers the H.B.P., fever and headache, on the left side.
- Shithalasana increases the body temperature and the cold gets removed.

Meditative Asana

The main aim of the meditative asanas is to sit for long periods of time without moving the body with comfort. For example, in moving water we can't see any thing dropped in the bottom, but in still water we can see clearly the thing.

Swami Shivananda said about the meditative asana, "you must be able to sit in one of the meditative asanas for a full three hours at a stretch without the body shaking. Then only will you gain true **Siddhi,** mastery over the asana, and be able to practise the higher stages of pranayama and dhyana and feal the **atmic ananda,** infinite peace and soulful bliss inside you."

There are some Pre-Meditative asanas which are useful for preparing the body for meditative asanas.

Half butterfly, hip rotation, full butterfly, wind releasing pose, crow walking, abdomen stretch pose and animal relaxation pose. There are some alternative poses which are also useful for meditation. They are:

Vajrasana, ananda madirasana, padadhirasana and bhadrasana; gorakshasana and moolbandhasana.

If you feel discomfort or pain in the legs, slowly unlock the legs and massage them after some time perform again the asana. The leg position should be alternated so that the balance on both sides of the body is maintained. It is more comfortable to place a small cushion under the hips.

16. Sukhasana (easy pose)

It is a easiest pose to sit. It is a relaxing pose.

Method: Sit on the asan (ground) with both legs stretched before you. Now bend one leg and place its foot under the thigh of the opposite leg. Then bend that leg and place it under the other leg. Keep the neck, head and back straight without strain. Close the eyes. Keep hands with gyana mudra/chin mudra on the knees. Relax the body.

Benefits

1. Helps to calm the strained and irritable nervous system.
2. Relieves muscular fatigue of the legs, Knee and thigh joints.
3. It facilitates mental and physical balance.
4. This posture is the easiest and the best
5. It relieves the stiffness of knees and joints..
6. It helps keep the entire body comfortable and straight without any strain.
7. This develops mental and physical potential.

Note:

- It was called "Sitting tailor fashion".
- For those who are extremely stiff, suknasana may be performed sitting cross legged with a belt/cloth tied around the knees and lower back.

17. Kamalasana

It is called half lotus pose

Method: Sit with the legs straight in front of the body. Bend one leg and place the sole of the foot in the inside of the opposite thigh. Bend the other leg and place the foot on top of the opposite thigh. Spine should be straight. Place the hands on the knees in gyana/chin mudra Close the eyes and relax the body.

Benefit

The same as for padmasana, but some less.

Note: Avoid this if you are sciatica or sacral ailments patient.

18. Lotus Pose

It is called Padmasana, it is very effective and important asana for meditation.

Method: Sit with legs extended forward. Bend the right leg at the knee and place the foot on the root of the left thigh. In the same manner fold the left leg and try to keep the left heel as close as possible to the root of the right thigh, so that, both the heels touch each other as near the navel as possible. The head, neck and the spine should be kept straight and knees should touch the ground. Keep your hands in chin/gyana mudra on the knees. You can change the legs after some time. Gradually increase the duration of asana, close the eyes.

Benefit

1. It strengthens and activates the function of the spinal nerves as though in the lower part of the spinal cord and good blood supply.
2. It helps in toning the inguinal parts and brings calmness and freshness to the mind.
3. Padmasana allows the body to be held completely steady for a long period.

4. It holds the trunk and head like a pillar with the legs as the firm foundation.
5. As the body is steadied the mind becomes calm.
6. It directs the flow of prana from mooladhara chakra in the perineum to Sahasrara chakra in the head, heightening the experience of meditation.
7. It gives a relaxing effect on the nervous system.
8. The breath becomes slow, muscles tension is decreased and blood pressure is reduced.
9. It stimulates the digestive process.
10. It increases the psycho-physical energies.

19. Siddhasana

It is called perfect pose

Method: Place the left heel firmly against the perineum, between the anus and genitals. The perineal space is considered very important by the Hatha yogis. It is the centre and source of the vital force.

Then, place the right heel at the root of the generative organ, in such a way that the sole of the right foot touches the left thigh. Let the left toe be inserted between the thigh and the calf muscles on each side. Hands can be placed either in chin mudra or in Brahmanjali, or interlock the hands place them in front of the navel.

Benefits

1. This asana is suitable for the practice of meditation, pranayama, japa and reflection. It was adopted by great sages of India.
2. It has all the advantages of the Padmasana.
3. It purifies the nadis or the astral channels.
4. It helps a yogi to enter into **Samadhi**.
5. This asana develops mental potentiality.
6. It increases the power of concentration.
7. It supplies sufficient blood to the pelvic region.
8. This asana cures syphilis, gonorrhoea, arthritis.
9. It keeps the body in poise and equilibrium.
10. This asana is beneficial for all sports men and women.

Note: Siddhasana should not be practised by those with sciatica or sacral disorders.

20. Siddha Yoni Asana

Method: Sit with the legs straight in front of the body. Bend the right leg and place the sole of the foot flat against the inner left thigh. Place this heel firmly against or inside the labia majora of the vagina. Adjust the body position so that it is comfortable while simultaneously feeling the pressure of the right heel. Bend the left leg and place the left heel directly on top of the right heel so it presses the clitoris, and wedge the left toes down into the space between the calf and thigh so they touch, or almost touch, the ground. Grasp the toes of the right foot and pull them up into the space between the left calf and thigh. Adjust the position so that it is comfortable. Knees should be firmly on the ground. Make the spine fully erect and straight as though it were planted solidly in the earth. Place the hands on the knees is chin/gyana mudra or chin-maya mudra, close the eyes and relax the body.

Benefits As for Siddhasana.

21. Hero's Meditation Pose

Method: Place the left heel under the right buttock. Then place the right leg over the left in such a way that the right foot is near the left hip, and the right knee is above the palms facing downward, place them over the right knee.

Benefits

1. This asana is specially good for the knees.
2. It has all the advantages of other meditative poses.
3. This asana helps in concentration. Mind becomes calm soon.

Vajrasana Group of Asanas

There are many meanings of 'Vajra'. Vajra was the famous weapon of Indra Devata. This weapon was prepared from the bones of Maharishi Dadheechi. 'Vajra' is also a major nadi which is connected to the genitourinary system which regulates the sexual energy in the body. Control of vajra nadi leads to sublimation and control of sexual energy. The vajrasana series is very useful for the digestive organs and reproductive system. It is very easy to perform. For mediation this series can be adopted.

22. Thunder Bolt Pose

It is called vajrasana. Muslims, Zen and Buddhists use this asana for prayer and meditation. Those who are unable to sit in padmasana/siddhasana they may sit in this asana. It is also called pelvic pose.

Method: Sit comfortable, keeping both the legs stretched in front. Bend the right leg at the knee and place the right foot under the right hip. In the same manner fold the left leg and place the foot under left hip. Try to adjust feet so that the toes touch each other and the heels are apart. Keep the knees together and let both the hips fit in between the heals. Place the hands on the knee, palms downward, close the eyes. Keep the spine and neck erect. Breathe normally and fix the attention on the flow of air passing in and out of the nostrils.

Benefit

1. It improves the digestive capacity. It could be done after meals.
2. It eliminates gas trouble.

3. It alleviates the pain of the knees, the legs, the feet and the thighs.
4. It increases the secretion from the glands.
5. It also increases the white blood corpuscles produced in the spleen, the tonsils, the marrow and in other parts of the body.
6. It strengthens the pelvic muscles.
7. It is good for piles and hernia.
8. It is very important meditative pose.
9. It stimulates the vajra nadi, activates prana in sushumna and redirects sexual energy to the brain for spiritual purpose.

23. Bhadrasana

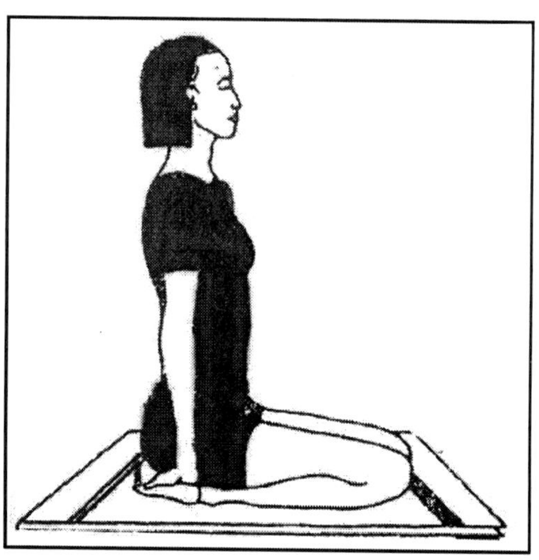

It is called intoxicating bliss pose. This asana is used for meditation pose.

Method: Sit in Vajrasana keep the palms on the heels. Fingers are pointing towards each other keep the spine and head erect. Close the eyes and relax. Concentrate on Agya Chakra and feel that the breathing is coming and going through the eyebrow centre.

Benefits

1. It gives all the benefits of Vajrasana.
2. It is beneficial for awaken Agya Chakra.
3. This asana calms the mind.
4. It relaxes the nervous system.

24. Mukta Bhadrasana

This gracious pose is performed for spiritual development.

Method: Sit in vajrasana place the palms on the knees. Separate the knees as far as possible. Concentrate on the tip of the nose. If the eyes become tired close the eyes for a short time and start again the nose tip gazing. While gazing breathe slowly and rhythmically. If you feel the strain, stop the practice.

Benefits

1. The benefits are the same as for Vajrasana.

2. It develops the Spirituality.
3. It is a nice Meditative pose.
4. It helps in awakening the Mooladhara chakra.

Note: Put a folded blanket under the buttocks.

25. Susumnasana

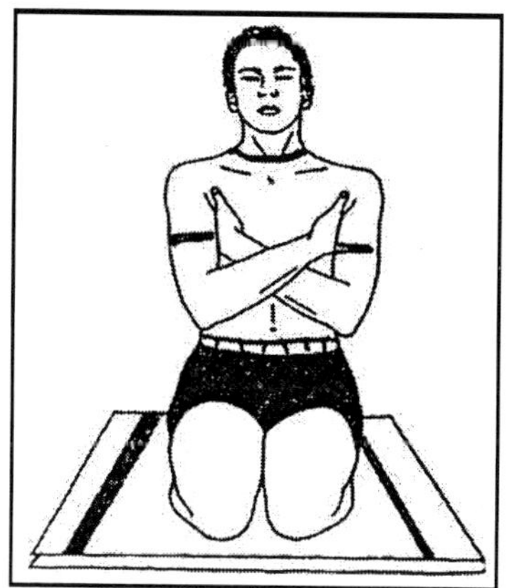

It is a breath balancing pose. It may be used as a preparation for pranayama and meditation. It is like a Kaki mudra.

Method: Sit in Vajrasana. Place the palms under the opposite armpits with the thumbs pointing upward and keeping the thumbs out. For giving pressure you can keep the fists in the armpits. Breathe slowly, deeply and rhythmically. Practise until the flow of breath in both nostrils becomes balanced. Concentrate on breathing process or Agya Chakra.

Benefit

1. It is specially useful when one or both nostrils are blocked.
2. It is useful for flowing the Sushumna nadi.

3. To change the swara place the hand of that side underneath opposite armpit and press it.
4. Sun and moon swara influences the activities of the sympathetic and para sympathetic nervous system respectively.
5. It is useful for preparation of pranayama.

Note:

- To prepare for pranayama practise for 5 to 10 minutes. For meditation extend the periods of times.
- T Shaped Stick (balancing stick/vairagain) may be used as an aid under the armpits.

26. Singhasana

Singha means lion. This asana is like a sitting lion quietly. It is also a meditative pose.

Method: Sit in vajrasana. Keep the knees 40/45 cm apart. The toes are together. Lean forward and place the palms on the floor between the knees, with the fingers pointing towards the toes. Arms should be fully straighten and arch the back. Neck should be erect and backward. Rest the body on the arms. Eyes should be closed. Relax the body and mind meditate on Agya Chakra. The mouth should be closed.

Benefits

1. In this pose body remains static.
2. Alpha waves are generated in the optic system at the back of the head and by closing the eyes.
3. Strong pressure on the palms helps relieving stress and tension.
4. It improves the blood circulation.
5. It tones up the nerves system.
6. It balances the vital energy for meditation.

27. Variation- Roaring Lion Pose

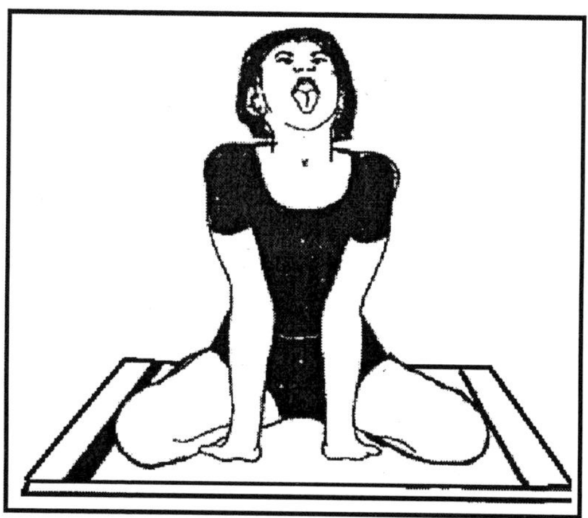

Method: Sit in Singhasana pose, keep the head backward. Open the eyes and perform the Shambhavi mudra (gaze at the eyebrow centre). Relax the body.

Inhale slowly and deeply through the nose. At the end of inhalation, open the mouth and extended the tongue out as far as possible towards the chin. While exhaling slowly produce a clear, steady **'aah'** sound from the throat, keeping the mouth wide open. Completing the exhalation close the mouth and breathe in. It is one round. Repeat 5 to 20 rounds daily. Concentrate on breathing and **aah** sound.

Benefits

1. It removes the diseases of E.N.T. region.
2. It gives the effect on Vishudhi and Agya chakra.
3. It develops a strong and sweet voice.
4. Other benefits are as for Shambhavi mudra.
5. Tension is removed from the chest.

28. Veerasana

It is a hero's pose. When Rama, Laxmana and Seeta were in 'vanavas', Laxmana used to sit in this pose for safety from animal and rakshasas. It is called phylosopher's pose.

Method: Sit in Vajrasana. Raise the right knee and place the right foot flat on the ground near the inside of the left knee. Place the left palm on the left knee and rest the chin on the palm of the right hand. Close the eyes and relax. Keep the body steady and the spine and head erect. Repeat it with the other side. Concentrate on Agya Chakra. Breathing should be slow and deep.

Benefits

1. This is a basic balancing pose which aids in stabilizing the nervous system.
2. This asana balances the mind.
3. It increases the concentration power.
4. It induces physical and mental relaxation very soon.
5. The thinking process becomes very clear and precise.
6. It is beneficial for those who are mentally disturbed.
7. It allows more awareness of the unconscious realms.
8. It is very nice for the kidneys, liver, reproductive and abdominal organs.

   Note: Practise it for a minimum of two minutes each side.

- Be aware of breathing process and erect body.
- If you meditate, concentrate on Agya Chakra.

29. Hare Pose

Shashanka means **moon** and **'hare'**. The moon is the symbol of peace and calm. This pose is called Shashankasana.

Method: Sit in Vajrasana. Relax with closed eyes. Keep the spine and head straight. While inhaling, bring the arms above the head. Keep them erect and shoulder width apart. While exhaling bend the trunk forward from the buttocks. Keep the arms and head straight and in line with the trunk. Moving forward place the hands and forehead should rest on the ground. Bend the arms slightly. Retain the breath for up to 5 seconds in the final position. Inhale and raise the arms and trunk simultaneously to the vertical position. Keep the arms and head in line with the trunk. This is one round. Repeat it 3 to 6 rounds. Hold this position. Increase the duration with normal breathing atleast 3 minutes. Concentrate on Manipura or Swadhisthana Chakra.

Benefits

1. This asana releases pressure of the discs.
2. It regulates the function of the adrenal glands.
3. It tones up the pelvic muscles and the sciatica nerves.
4. It helps to alleviate disorders of both the male and female reproductive organs.
5. It removes the constipation.
6. If practised with ujjayi pranayama in the final position, it helps to eliminate anger and cooling the brain.

Note: Avoid this for the people who are suffering from H.B.P, slipped disc or Vertigo.

Camel Pose

It is known for the name of ustrasana. It has two steps half camel pose and camel pose.

30. First Step (Half Camel Pose):

Method: Sit in vajrasana keeping the knees apart and the ankles at the side of the buttocks. Stand up on the knees with the arms at the sides. Keep the feet flat behind the body. While inhaling stretch the arms sideways and raise them to shoulder level. This is starting position.

While exhaling, twist to the right. Try to hold the left heel or ankle. Side by side stretch the left arm in front of the head so that hand is at eyebrow level. Keep the head slightly back with the eyes gazing at the raised hand. Bring the abdomen forward in the final position and try to keep the thighs vertical. Stay until the breath is controlled and retaining the gaze on the left hand. Inhale and return to the starting position—Repeat on the other side and complete one round holding the right heel with the left hand. Repeat 3 to 5 rounds. Don't strain in any way.

Second Step (Camel pose)

Method: Stand on the knees with the arms at the sides. Lean backward hold the right heel with the right hand and then the left heel with the left hand. Don't strain. Push the abdomen forward, trying to keep the thighs vertical, and bend the head and spine backward as far as possible. Relax the body. Remain in this position for as long as is comfortable. Return to the starting position slowly releasing the hands from the heels one at a time. Keep the breathing normal.

Concentrate on abdomen, throat spine or natural breathing or vishuddhi chakra/swadhisthana chakra. Practise up to 3 times.

Benefits

1. It tones up the abdominal viscera, particularly the liver, pancreas, kidneys and bladder.
2. It expands the chest and strengthens the ribs.
3. It removes the sluggishness of the liver.
4. This asana is beneficial for the digestive and reproductive systems.
5. It alleviates constipation.
6. It removes the backache.
7. It regulates the functions of thyroid gland.

Note: Avoid this asana if you are suffering from lumbago and enlarged thyroid.

- Perform paschimottanasana or Shashankasana after the camel pose.

31. Sleeping Thunder Bolt Pose

It is called supta Vajrasana. It is related to the vajra nadi and energy pathway which connects the sexual force to the brain. There are three methods in practice.

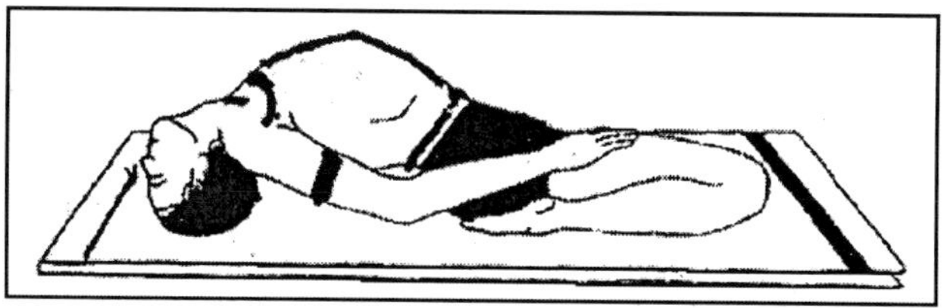

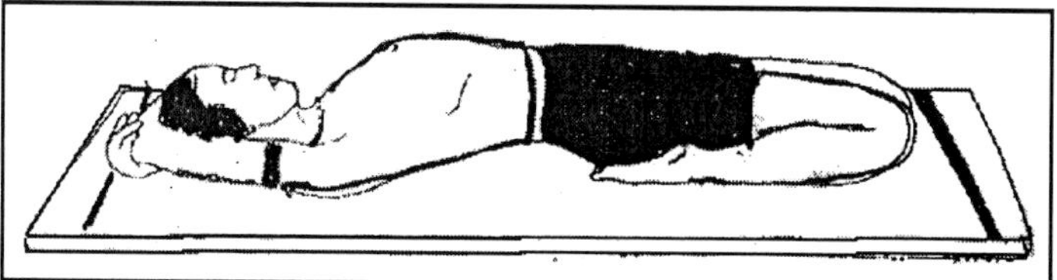

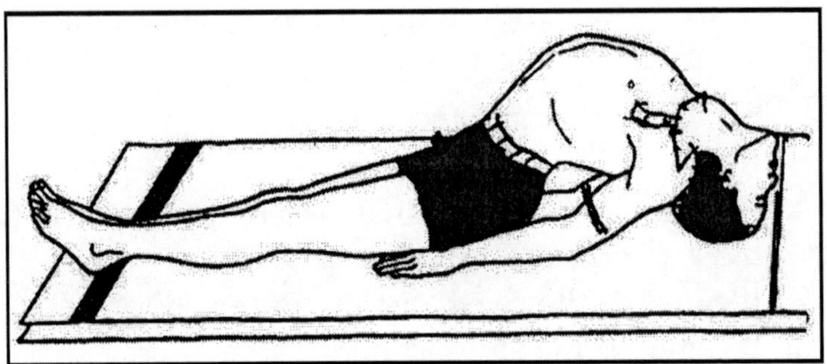

Method: Sit in Vajrasana. Then tilt backwards taking the support of first the right elbow and arm and then the left. Bring the top of the head to the floor, making the arch of the back. Place the hands on the thighs. Touch the knees to the floor in the final position. Breathe deeply and slowly. Beginners should start with only a few seconds to one minutes. Come back in reverse order. Return first in the vajrasana and then straighten the legs.

In the second position join the hands together and place them under the back of the head or fold the arms comfortably above the head. Try to keep the knees on the floor. Close the eyes and relax the Body.

Benefits

1. This is one of the variation of Matsyasana.
2. It is helpful in treating ailments of the neck, back and waist.
3. It makes the spine resilient and stream line the abdomen.
4. This asana massages the abdominal organs.
5. It improves the digestive system and removes the constipation.
6. It tones up the spinal nerves and makes the back flexible.

7. The thyroid gland and the nerves in the neck are influenced.
8. The chest is expanded to full capacity. It bring the more oxygen into the system.
9. It is beneficial for those suffering from asthma, bronchitis and other lung diseases.
10. It is helpful in preparation for sitting in meditation.
11. It develops creativity and intelligence and redirects sexual energy to the brain for spiritual purpose.

Note: Persons suffering from severe pain of knee joints or with slipped disc and lumbago should avoid it.

Standing Asanas

Importance: This series of yogasanas is useful for stretching and strengthening effect on the back, shoulders and the muscles of legs.

- This series is useful for those who are habitual of long sitting or who have stiffness and pain in the spine.
- This series improves posture, balancing and muscular co-ordination.
- They are helpful to keep back straight during meditation or working periods.

32. Palm Tree Pose

It is called tadasana. It is one of the asanas for Shankhaprakshalana.

Method: Stand erect on the ground. Raise your arms above your head. Interlock the fingers and turn the palms upward. Place the hands on top of the head. Inhale and stretch the arms, shoulders and chest upward. Raise the heels onto the toes. Stretch the whole body from top to bottom without moving the body and losing the balance. Hold the breath and position for a few seconds, lower the heels while exhaling and bring the hands to the top of the head. This is one round. Repeat 5 to 10 rounds.

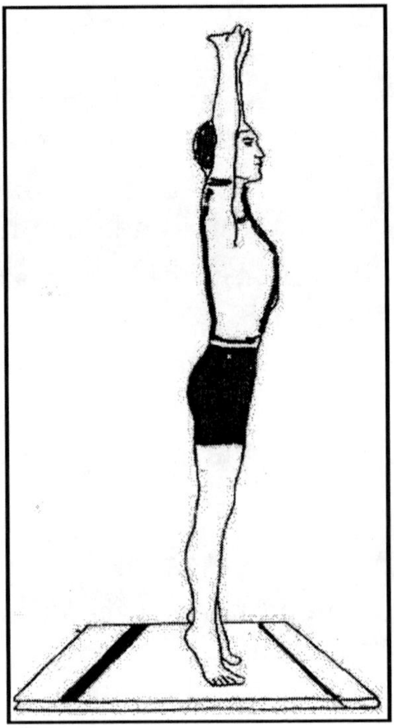

Benefits

1. The stiffness of the body is relieved.
2. It also gives relief in the neck, back and joint pain.
3. This asana makes you slim.
4. It is useful for lengthening the body.
5. It tones up the toes and strengthens the soles of the feet.
6. It improves the blood circulation.
7. It cures the pains and aches in the body.
8. This pose cures nervousness and debility.
9. This asana develops physical and mental balance.
10. It is useful during the first six months of pregnancy.

Note: In the beginning it should be performed with open eyes and afterwards with closed eyes.

33. Tiryakatadasana

This is one of the asanas for Shankhaprakshalana. It is called swaying palm tree pose also.

Method: Hold the position of Tadasana (Palm tree pose) keeping the legs 2′ feet apart. While exhaling bend to the right side from the waist. Perform bahya kumbhaka for a few seconds. Don't move forward or backward or twist the trunk. Breathe in and come slowly to the upright position. Repeat on the left side. Exhale while bringing the arms down to the sides. It is one round. Practise this asana eight times on each side. Concentrate on breathing stretching and balancing or Mooladhara/Manipura Chakra.

Benefits

1. This asana balances the right and left groups of postural muscles.
2. It massages loosens and exercises the sides of waist.
3. Benefits are the same as for tadasana.
4. It removes laziness and tiredness.

Note: It is called Urdhwa Hastottanasana also.

34. Katichakrasana

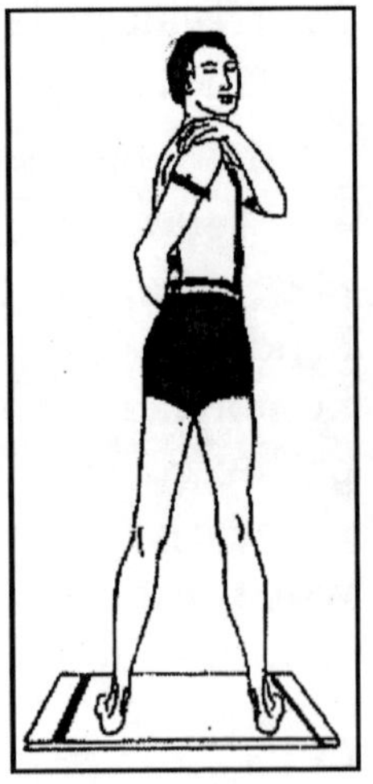

Kati means waist. It is one of the asanas for Shankhaprakshalana. It is performed in a dynamic way.

Method: Stand with the feet about half a metre apart and the arms by the sides. Inhale deeply while raising the arms to shoulder level. Breathe out and twist the body to the right. Keep the left palm to the right shoulder and wrap the right arm around the back. Bring the right hand around the left side of the waist. Look over the right shoulder as far as possible.

Keep the back part of the neck erect. Retain the breath for 3 seconds. Stretch gently the stomach. Breathe in and come back to the starting position. Repeat on the other side and complete the one round. No change in legs position while twisting. Relaxed the body the movement should be natural and relaxed. Concentrate on breathing process, stretching and spinal muscles. Repeat five times on either side and relaxed.

Benefits

1. It is beneficial for correcting back stiffness and defective postural problems.
2. It removes physical and mental tension.
3. This asana tones up the waist, back and hips.
4. It removes constipation.

Note: You can perform Tiryaka Kati Chakrasana (swaying waist rotating pose) after Kati Chakrasana.

35. Dwikonasana

It is a double angle pose.

Method: Stand straight keeping one foot distance between the legs. Bring the arms behind the back and interlock the fingers. This is the basic position. Bend forward from the waist while simultaneously raising arms behind the back as high as possible without any strain. Look forward as for a possible. Keep the face parallel to the ground. Remain in the final position for a short duration and return to upright position. Relax the arms. Repeat it up to 5 times. Concentrate on Anahata Chakra or arms, shoulders and upper back.

Benefits

1. It is especially good for young and growing bodies.
2. This asana strengthens the muscles between the upper spine and the shoulder blades.
3. It develops the chest and neck.

36. Triangle Pose

It is called Trikonasana also because the asana when performed correctly, gives the idea of three angles.

Method: Stand upright with your legs wide apart. Keeping the right hand up and erect, left hand with the left leg. Bend your body (Trunk) to your left side as much as possible without moving your feet. Right hand will be parallel to the ground. Stay in this position as long as you can. Regain your former position and repeat the process by bending in right side after changing the position of hands.

Benefits

1. Trikonasana stretches and strengthens the muscles of calf, waist, thighs, hips, legs, spinal column and adrenal glands.
2. Reduces obesity, cures boils, abscesses, back-ache in the ribs.
3. It increases height.
4. It removes the weakness of lungs and sciatica pain.
5. It tones the entire body within a month.
6. It stimulates the nervous system and alleviates nervous depression.

7. It improves digestion, the appetite and removes the constipation.
8. It also strengthens the pelvic area and tones the reproductive organs.

Note:

- Concentrate on Manipura Chakra.
- This asana should not be performed by those suffering from back conditions.

37. Washerman's Pose

It is also called utthita lolasana

Method: Stand straight with the feet a metre apart. Raise the arms over the head keeping the arms erect. Bend the wrists forward. Bend forward and swing the trunk down from the waist allowing the arms and head to swing through the legs. Be tension free. Raise the trunk so that it is parallel to the ground. On the downward swing the hands as for back as possible behind the feet. After 6 complete swings come back to the upright position with the arms raised, then lower the arms to the sides.

Breathing: Inhale fully through the nose while raising the arms. Exhale forcefully through the mouth on each downward swing with the sound of **'ha'.** This sound should come from the abdomen and not the throat.

Benefits

1. This asana removes tiredness by stimuling the circulation and toning the spinal nerves.
2. It is beneficial for inverted asanas especially on the brain.
3. This is an excellent pre-pranayama practice to clear the lungs.
4. It stretches the hamstrings and back muscles.
5. It loosens the hips and massages the visceral organs.
6. It speeds up lymphatic flow in the major ducts and improves drainage, especially from the abdomen and the base of lungs.

Note:

- Keep the body loose during rhythmic swinging movements.
- Avoid this asana if you suffer from vertigo, high blood pressure or back conditions.

38. Suryanamaskara

'Suryanamaskara' was the familiar tradition in vedic Age. Surya namaskara is a complete sadhana in itself.

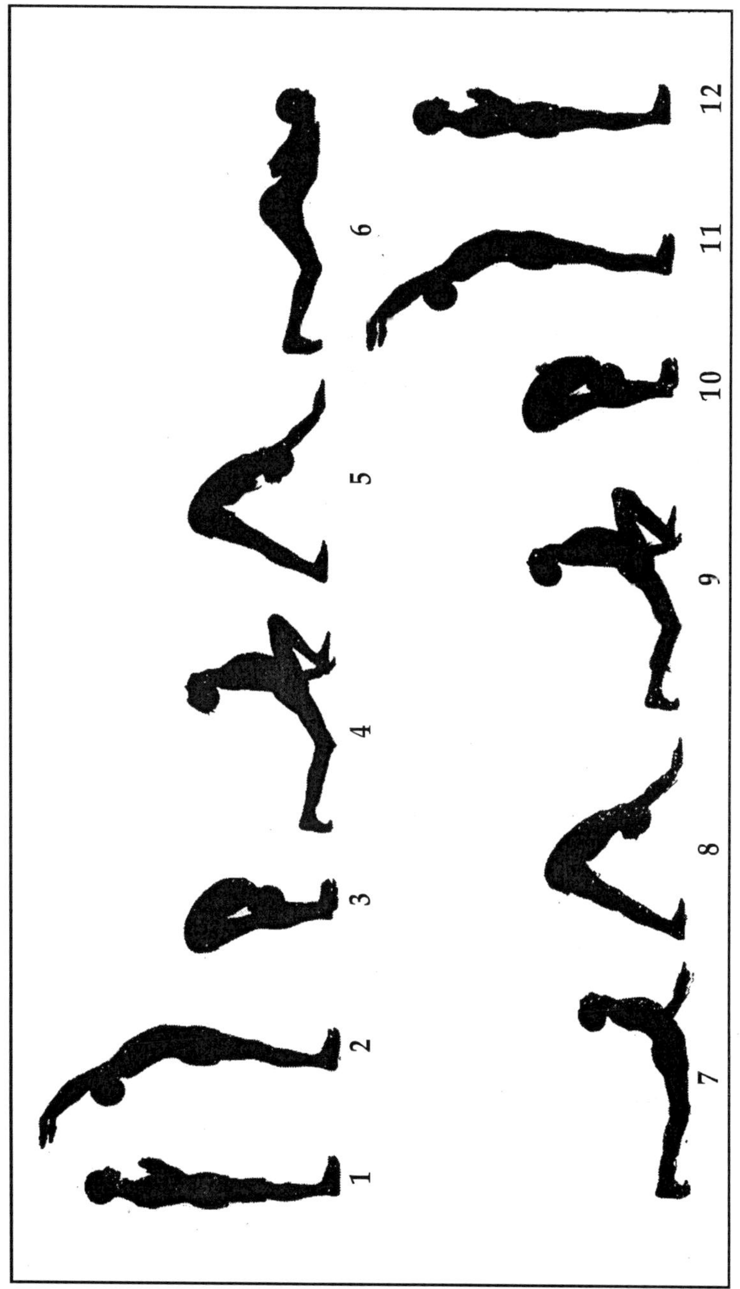
1
2
3
4
5
6
7
8
9
10
11
12

There are four techniques which are included in this group of asanas, as asana, pranayama, mantra and meditation. Surya, the sun is the symbol of spiritual consciousness. In ancient times it was in daily practice. In yoga the sun represented by pingla/surya nadi, the pranic channel which carries the vital force. Spiritual awakening and awareness.

Suryanamaskara is composed of three elements: form, energy and rhythm. The twelve asanas are the base to generate the prana, the subtle energy which activate the psychic body. The ideal time of suryanamaskara is at sunrise the most peaceful time of day. It should be practised in the open air, facing the rising sun. Sun set is also a good time to practise as it stimulates the digestive fire.

Position 1 Prayer pose: Eyes closed, body relaxed, normal breathing, mentally offering homage to the sun. **Mantra-Om Mitraya Namaha** (Salutations to the friend of all). Concentration on–**Anahata Chakra**.

Position 2 Raised arms pose: Eyes closed, raised and stretch both arms above the head, separated arms. Upper trunk backward. Inhale, concentration on Vishuddhi Chakra. Mantra–**Om Ravaye Namaha.**

(Salutations is the shining one)

Position 3 Hand to Foot Pose: Eyes closed, knees erect. Touch the knees with forehead. Bring the palms on the ground on either side of the feet. Exhale, concentrate on swadhisthana Chakra.

Mantra-**Om Suryaya Namaha.**

(Salutations to he who induces activity)

Position 4 Ashwa Sanchalana pose: Eyes closed. Bend the left leg. Bring the right leg back as far as possible. Arms straight. The weight of the body supported on the hands, the left foot, right knee and toes of the right foot, head backward concentrate on Agya Chakra.

Mantra–**Om Bhanave Namaha**.

(Salutations to he who illumines)

Position 5: It is mountain pose. Eyes closed. Both feet back and together. buttocks up. Head between the arms and towards the knees. Legs and arms erect. Heels on the ground. Exhale while the left leg comes back concentrate on Vishuddhi Chakra.

Mantra–**Om Khagaya Namaha.**

(Salutations to he who moves quickly in the sky)

Position 6 It is ashtang Namaskara. Place the toes, knees, palms, chest and chin to the ground. Eyes closed, Normal breathing, Relax. Buttocks, hips and abdomen should be raised.

Mantra–**Om Pushne Namaha**

(Salutations to the giver of strength)

Position 7 Cobra Pose: Lower the buttocks chest up. Head back, inhale, concentrate on Agya chakra. Arms slightly bent.

Mantra–**Om Hiranya Garbhaya Namaha.**

(salutation to the golden cosmic self)

Position 8 Mountain Pose: It is position No. 5. Hands and feet do not move. Raise the buttocks. Lower the heels is the ground. Exhale and concentrate on Vishuddhi Chakra.

Mantra–**Om Marichaye Namaha.**

(Salutations to the lord of the dawn)

Position 9 Ashwa Sanchalanasana: This position is the same as No 4. Palms flat on the ground. Eyes closed. Bend the left leg and bring the left foot forward between the hands. Head backward. Arch the back. Concentrate on Agya Chakra inhale.

Mantra–**Om Adityaya Namaha.**

(Salutations to the sun of Aditi the cosmic mother)

Position 10 Padahastasana: This position is a repeat of 3rd position. Bring the right foot forward near to the left foot. Straighten both knees. Exhale, concentrate on swadhisthana chakra.

Mantra–**Om Savitrye Namaha**

(Salutations to Lord of creation)

Position 11 Hasta Uthanasana: This position is a repeat of position 2. Raise the trunk and bring the arms above the head, keep the arms separated, shoulder width apart. Bend the head, arms and upper trunk backward, inhale while straightening the body. Concentrate on Vishuddhi Chakra.

Mantra–**Om Arkaya Namaha**

(Salutations to he who is fit to be praised)

Position 12 Prayer Pose: This is final and first position. Bring the palms together in front of the chest. Exhale and have normal breathing. Concentrate on Anahata Chakra.

Mantra–**Om Bhaskaraya Namaha**

(Salutations to he who leads to enlightment)

Note: 11 to12 position of suryanamaskara are practised twice to complete one round. In the second half, the positions are repeated with two small changes.

1. In position 16, instead of stretching the right foot backward, stretch the left foot back.
2. In position 21, bend the right leg and bring the right foot between the hands.
3. The beeja mantras are six in number and are repeated in the following order, four times during a compete round of suryanamaskara.

   (*a*) Om Hraam

   (*b*) Om Hreem

   (*c*) Om Hroom

   (*d*) Om Hraim

   (*e*) Om Hraum

   (*f*) Om Hrah.

   When Surya namaskara is practised too fast to repeat the beeja mantras.
4. Beginners should start with one to three rounds and add one more round every month. Practise 12 rounds.

Benefits

1. It stimulates and balances all the systems of the body.
2. It gives combined benefits of Asanas, Pranayama and meditation.
3. It also improves vitality and removes obesity.
4. It is beneficial in cases of bronchial, diabetes, initial stage of arthritis, irregular menstruation and constipation. It also improves the voice and gives peace of mind.
5. It improves the eyesight and cures the diseases of the elimentary canal.

6. The body becomes handsome and radiant.
7. It balances the transition period between childhood and adolescence in growing children.
8. This removes carbon dioxide from the lungs and replaces it with fresh oxygen, increasing mental clarity by bringing fresh oxygenated blood to the brain.
9. It is a very great slimming and trimming lengthening and strengthening exercise.
10. It cures body aches and pains of the spinal cord.
11. Strengthens the neck, arms, back, shoulders, thighs, knees, waist, ankles, heart, lungs, liver, stomach, kidneys, and bowels.
12. Improves and develops the bust in women and relieves of menstrual disorders, renders child bearing less painful and improves the quantity and quality of milk in nursing mothers.

Precautions

- This asana is to be performed at the time of the rising Sun to derive maximum benefits.
- After performing this asana it is necessary to relax by doing Shavasana.

Medium Group Yogasana

Lotus Group of Yogasannas

This series is for them who can sit in the lotus pose without any strain. First of all sukshama vyayama and the meditative yogasanas should be practised. The yogasanas in this series remove physical, emotional, and mental disturbances. They help awaken the energy centres of the body and give tranquility. They develop the capacity to sit in lotus (Padmasana) pose for long periods of time as required for advanced sadhana practices.

39. Yoga Mudrasana

This is called psychic union pose and symbol of yoga. Yoga seal posture.

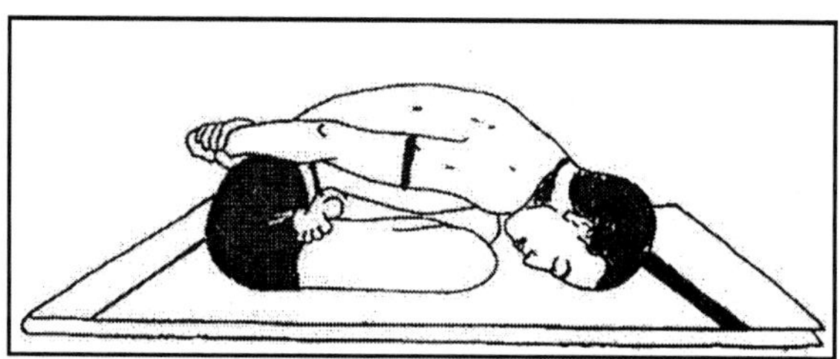

Method: Sit in lotus pose (Padmasana) and close the eyes. Relax, hold one wrist behind the back with the other hand, inhale deeply. Keeping the spine straight bend forward and exhale. Touch the forehead to the ground or as close as possible. Relax the body with normal breathing, inhale slowly and deeply. Return to the starting position. Repeat the pose with the changed legs. Stay for 2 minutes in the final pose if this is not possible repeat the asana a few times. Concentration on Manipura Chakra or breathing process or Bahya Kumbhka.

Benefits

1. This asana is a remedy for constipation.
2. It fortifies the abdominal muscles, and keeps the abdominal organs in their proper place.
3. The entire nervous system, and the sacrolumbar nerves in particular, are toned up.

4. In the case of men, this asana helps prevent sperm deficiency.
5. This is an excellent asana for massaging the abdominal organs.
6. It is used to awaken manipura chakra.
7. It improves blood circulation in the head.
8. It relieves from old age.
9. Reduces belly protuberance, removing fat.

Note:

- It should be followed by a backward bending asana such as ustrasana/matsyasana/bhujangasana.
- People with serious eye, heart or back conditions and those in the early post-operative or post-delivery period should not attempt this asana.

40. Locked Lotus Pose

It is also called Baddha Padmasana. Baddha means caught.

Method: Sit in padmasana. Bring the arms behind the back and cross them. Exhale and catch the big toes, right big toe with right hand and left toe with left hand.

Breathe in deeply, breathe out slowly. This is basic practice and exhale then bend forward, this is advanced form of yogamudrasana. Breathing should be deep and slow, concentrate on breathing or Anahata Chakra. Come back and relax.

Benefits

1. It removes the pain in the shoulders, arms and back.
2. It is used in the process of awakening kundalini.
3. It massages all the internal organs.
4. It is very useful for workers who sit on the chairs.
5. It increases the blood circulation.
6. This asana strengthens the weak persons.

41. Fish Pose

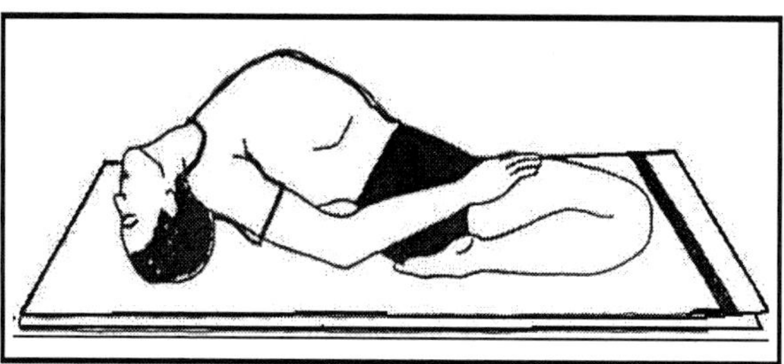

This asana is also called Matsyasana. The shape of this asana is like a fish.

Method: Sit in lotus pose and relax. Bend backward carefully, supporting with the arms and elbows. Lift the chest and take the head back. Lower the crown of head to the ground. Hold the big toes and rest the elbows on the ground. Relax the body, close the eyes and breathe slowly and deeply. Return to the original position, reversing the order of movement. Concentrate on Manipura Chakra or Anahata Chakra.

Variation for beginners

Benefits

1. This asana enlarges the thoracic cage and allows deeper breathing
2. It renders the neck supple and removes aches and stiffness.
3. It regenerates the thyroid and tonsils.
4. This asana also fortifies the muscles in the back.
5. It has a beneficial effect on the spinal column.
6. It removes all abdominal diseases.
7. To remove constipation drink 3 glasses of water and then perform this asana.
8. It also relieves of inflamed and bleeding piles.
9. It is good for asthma and bronchitis.
10. It encourages deep respiration.
11. It removes backache and cervical spondylitis.

Note: Stay in final pose up to 1 to 5 minutes.

42. Garbhasana

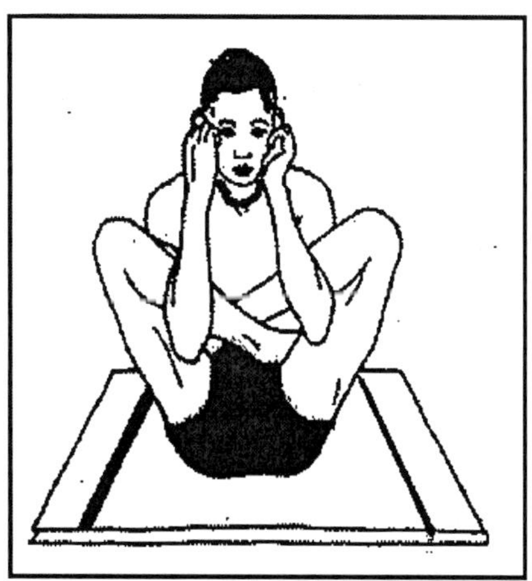

When this asana is performed the pose achieved resemble that of a human foetus in the womb, so this asana is called Garbhasana.

Method: Sit in lotus pose. Insert an arm between the thigh and calf of each leg and bent the elbows under the calves. Fold the arms upward and raise the legs. Hold the ears. Balance the whole body on the coccyx. The eyes may be open or closed. Maintain the final position for as long as is comfortable. Let the hands of the ears lower the legs and slowly release the arms from the legs. Open the padmasana. Change the legs and perform the padmasana. Repeat the garbhasana on the spine. Breathe normally in the final position. It will be shallow breathing. Come back in reverse order.

Benefits

1. This asana helps to cure diseases like colic pain, flatulence, enteritis, chronic fever, constipation.
2. This asana keeps the abdominal organs trim.

3. It cures gas-trouble and increases the digestion power.
4. This asana helps to preserve the semen and the mind begins to have communion with the soul.
5. It has a regulating effect on the adrenal glands and calms an excited mind.
6. It helps alleviate nervous disorders.
7. It helps to control the anger.
8. It also develops the sense of balance.

Note:

- Concentrate on maintaining balance on Manipura Chakra or on the breath.
- It is also called utthankoormasana, the stretching tortoise pose.

43. Kukkutasana

Kukkuta means cock. The shape of this asana is like a cock.

Method: Sit in padmasana. Insert the hands between the calves and thighs, near the knees. Start with the fingers and gradually push the hands up to the elbows. Inhale and raise the body off the floor. Then continue normal breathing. Legs should be raised off the floor up to the level of the elbows. Place the palms of the hands firmly on the ground with the fingers pointing forward. Keeping the head straight and the eyes fixed on a point in front. Raise the body balancing only on the hands. Keep the back erect. Remain in the final position for as long as is comfortable. Come back to the floor slowly. Release the arms, hands and legs. Change the leg position and repeat the pose. Concentrate on breath/maintaining balance or Mooladhara Chakra.

Benefits

1. This asana is beneficial to those who have worms in their intestines.
2. This asana gives invigorates the body and delights the mind.
3. This asana gives the sufficient exercise to the arms. It strengthens the wrists, the elbows and the shoulders.
4. This asana is very useful to women as it cures uneasiness, pain in the hips and heaviness caused by menstruation.
5. All the benefits derived from Utthita Padmasana.
6. It develops a sense of balance and stability.
7. It is used in the process of kundalini awakening due to the stimulation of mooladhara chakra:

There are two more asanas used in this series as—Lolasana and tolangulasana.

Backward Bending Yogasanas

Backward bending yogasnas are very useful in stimulating and extroverting. They expand the chest and encourage inhalation. They are associated with the attitude of embracing life. They need strength and energy to perform. Backward bending yogasanas stretch the abdominal muscles and tone and strengthen the muscles controlling the spine, helping prevent slipped disc and other back conditions.

The practice of backward bending yogasanas can correct postural defects and neuromuscular imbalance of the vertebral column. These asanas help to circulate purify and enrich the blood in the region. Backward bending yogasana create a negative pressure in the abdomen and pelvic, helping neuro circulatory toning of all the related organs. They all massages the abdomen and pelvic organs by stretching the muscles in this area, especially the rectus abdomini.

43. Narsinghi Pose

It is called sphinx asana also.

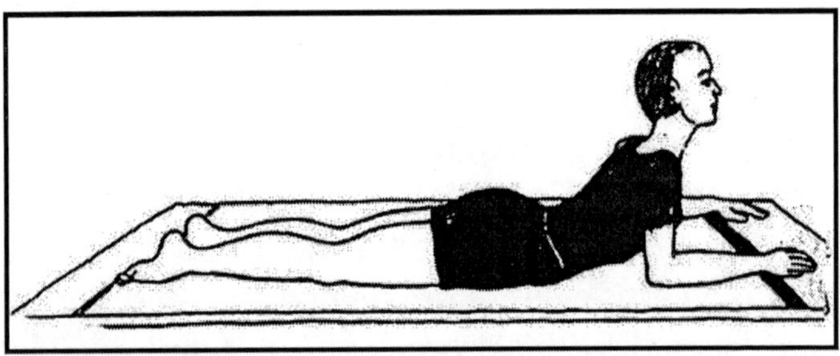

Method: Lie flat on the stomach with the forehead resting on the ground. The legs straight and feet together, the soles of the feet should be uppermost. Bend the arms and place the forearms on the ground with the palms downward on the each side of the head. The forearms and elbows are close to the body. Relax the body.

Raise the head and shoulders with inhalation upper arms should be vertical position. The palms for arms elbows will remain on the ground. Relax then come down. This is one round. Hold this position 3-4 minutes or 5 minutes. Concentrate on Swadhisthana Chakra or breath/relaxing the back.

Benefits

1. It is a good preparatory pose for bhujangasana, follow with a forward bending asana.
2. It is especially good for stiff back and those with a cute back pain or slipped disc may relax in it, for as long as they are comfortable.
3. The benefits of this asana are the same as for bhujangasna but at a reduced level.

Note:

- It is a good preparatory pose or cobra pose follow with a forward bending.

44. Cobra Pose

It is a famous asana called bhujangasana.

Method: Lie flat on the stomach with the legs straight, feet together and the soles of the feet uppermost. Place the palms of the hands flat on the ground, below and slightly to the side of the shoulders. The fingers should be together and pointing forward. Rest the forehead on the ground, close the eyes. Relax the body especially the lower back. Slowly raise the head, neck and shoulders. Straightening the elbows, raise the trunk as possible Gently move the head backward. The navel is raised 3 cm above only. Hold the final position. To return back bring the head forward. Bring the arms lower bending the elbows come down slowly. Put the forehead on the ground. Relax the lower back. This is one round. Practise 5 rounds. Gradually increase the length of time in the final pose. Concentrate on swadhisthana chakra.

Full Cobra Pose

Benefits

1. In diseases like cervical spondylosis, bronchitis, asthma and consinophilia. It has a therapeutic value.
2. It removes weakness of the abdomen and tones up the reproductive system in women.

3. Cobra pose gives good exercise to the back muscles and vertebrae.
4. It removes backache and keeps the spine supple and healthy.
5. It promotes better communication between the brain and the body.
6. This asana tones up the ovaries and uterus and helps alleviate menstrual and other gynacological disorders.
7. It stimulates the appetite, alleviates constipation, cures liver and kidneys disorders.
8. The secretion of cortisone is maintained and the thyroid gland is regulated.
9. Cobra pose has a strong effect on all the organs relating these chakras—Swadhisthana, Manipura, anahata and Vishuddhi.

Note:

- People suffering from peptic ulcer, hernia, intestinal T.B. or hyperthyroidism should not practise this asana without expert guidance.
- It may be performed in conjunction with shalbhasana and dhanurasana for effective general health of the back and spine.

45. Twisting Cobra Pose

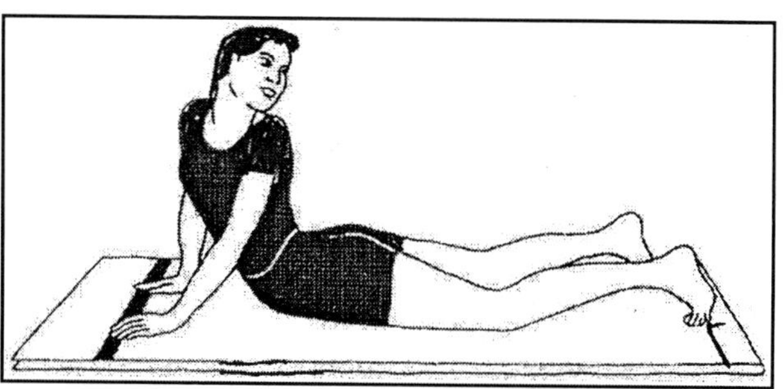

Method: Lie flat on the stomach with the legs separated about half a metre. The toes should be tucked under and the heels raised so that the foot rests on the ball of the foot. Place the palms of the hands flat on the floor, below and slightly to the side of the shoulders. The fingers should be together and pointing forward. The arms should be positioned so that the elbows point backward and are close to the sides of the body. Rest the forehead on the floor and close the eyes.

Relax the whole body, especially the lower back.

Slowly raise the head, neck and shoulders. Straightening the elbows, raise the trunk as high as comfortable. Use the back muscles more than the arm muscles. The head should be facing forward, instead of bending backward as in bhujangasana. Twist the head and upper portion of the trunk, and look over the left shoulder. Gaze at the heel of the right foot. In the final position, the arms remain straight or slightly bent as the shoulders and trunk are twisted. Relax the back and keep the navel close to the floor. Stay in the final position for a few seconds. Face forward again and repeat the twist on the other side without lowering the trunk. Return to the centre and lower the body to the floor. This is one round. Practise 3 to 5 rounds.

Inhale while raising the torso. Exhale while twisting to the side, inhale to centre, exhale to the other side and again inhale to centre. Exhale while lowering the torso to the floor.

Concentrate on the stretch of the muscles of the back and intestines, and the diagonal stretch of the abdomen or on Swadhisthana chakra.

Benefits: As for bhujangasana, with increased influence on the arms and the intestines.

Note: This asana is performed as a part of the shankhaprakshalana series.

46. Half Locust Pose

It is called Ardha Shalbhasana, because it is performed by one leg. There are two methods.

Method: Lie flat on the stomach with the hands under the thighs, palms downwards/hand clenched. Place both the legs straight throughout the practice. Place the chin on the ground. Give a bit stretch forward (neck). Using the back muscles raise the left/right leg as high as possible keeping the other leg straight relaxed and keep in contact with the ground. Hold this position for as long as is possible without stress lower the leg to the ground. Repeat the same method with the other leg. This is one round. Repeat 5 rounds, concentrate on Swadhistana Chakra.

Benefits

1. It increases the cardiac output by strengthening the cardiac muscles and valves.
2. It strengthens the entire spine cord, increases its flexibility, inducing perennial youth.
3. It massages the abdominal organs and torso with blood circulation with pull of gravity.
4. It alleviates constipation. It removes sciatica pain and slipped disc disorders.
5. It is beneficial with weak and stiff back.
6. It activates the brain cells.

Note:

- Inhale while raising leg. Stay in final position and exhale while lowering the leg.
- Avoid this in case of high blood pressure, ulcer, stiffness of shoulders, pregnancy and menstruation.

47. Dhanurasana

Method: Lie face down, arms stretched in front. Bend the legs at knees and catch the ankles with corresponding hands. Lift the knees and thighs of the ground. Simultaneously, inhale and raise the head and chest until you are poised on abdomen, slowly come back, put legs and chest on the ground, take rest and relax the body.

Full Dhanurasana

Benefits

- It corrects ailments of spinal column, neck, lumber, hands, legs, abdomen and chest.
- It cures gastro intestinal ailments, dysentery.
- It improves digestion system.
- It removes obesity and diabetes.
- 'Dharan' sets in its original position.

48. Shoulder Pose

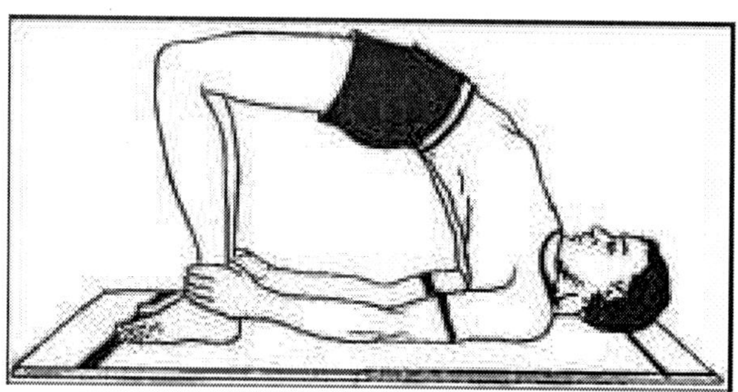

It is also called Setubandhasana or kandharasana. It is very useful for spine disorders.

Method: Lie flat on the back. Bend the knees. Place the soles of the feet flat on the ground with the heels touching the hips. The feet and knees be hip width apart. Hold the ankles with the hands. This is basic position. Raise the buttocks and arch the back upward. Raise the chest and navel as high as possible. Chin should be near the chest. Hold the pose for as long as is comfortable and lower the body to the basic position. Release the ankle and relax the body in Shavasana.

Inhale deeply while raising and holding the breath in final pose. Breath slowly and deeply in final pose. Exhale while lowering the basic posture. Concentrate on Anahata/vishuddhi chakra. Repeat 5 to 10 rounds.

Benefits

1. This asana relieves foul gas accumulated in the stomach.
2. It makes the vertebral column elastic and flexible.
3. It stimulates blood circulation in the muscles and the nerves of the arms and the hands. It strengthens and enlarges the rib box.
4. It cures the swelling in the thigh and strengthens the loins. It brings melody to the voice. It improves the eye sight. It is good for menstrual disorders.
5. It cures the diseases such as constipation dysentery, asthma, T.B., diabetes and advanced stage of pregnancy.
6. It is useful for women who have tendency to miscarry.

49. Konasana

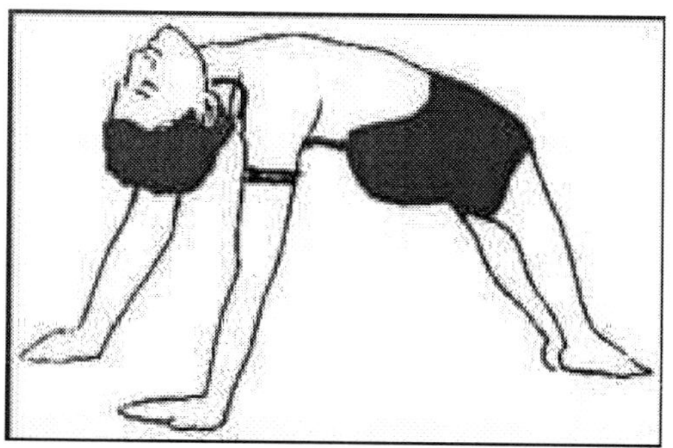

Konasana is also called setuasana because its shape is like a bridge or triangle.

Method: Sit with the legs stretched forward. Place the palms on the ground on either side of the body. about 30 cm behind the hips. The elbows should be straight, fingers pointing back and the trunk slightly reclined. This is basic/starting position. Raise the hips and lift the body upward. Let the head hang back and down. Try to place the soles of the feet flat on the ground. Keep the legs and arms straight. Hold this position as you can lower the hips to the ground. This is one round. Repeat up to 10 times. Concentrate on Manipura chakra.

Benefits

1. It is a basic practice of Chakrasana.
2. It tones up the lumbsr region of the spine.
3. It is beneficial for cervical spondylosis.
4. It is good for Achilles tendons.
5. It activates the nervous system, endocrine glands, and massages the kidney, pancreas, liver and bladder.

6. It increases the supply of blood to brain and cervical region.
7. It tones up the thighs and arms muscles.
8. It activates the Udana Prana.

Note: In case of Blood pressure, heart diseases, stomach ulcer or weak write avoid this asana.

50. Wheel Pose

This asana also is called Chakrasana. In practicing this asana, the spine is twisted in such a way that the body forms a semicular shape, hence this asana is called chakrasana or wheel pose.

Method: Lie flat on the back. Draw the legs until the heels are closed to the hips and the soles touch the ground. The gap between the legs should be of 4″-6". Bend the arms at the elbows and place them on the ground on either side of the head.

Raise the body from the waist to the back part of the head. Breathe in the normal way. Tilt the head backward as far as possible, keep the hands straight. Keep the body steady. Don't shift either the arms or the legs from their position. Get final position for about a minute. Then inhale and lower the body to the ground and bring it to the original position. Then breathe normally. Relax the body.

Benefits

1. This asana gives all the benefits of Dhanurasana, Shalbhasana and Bhujangasana.
2. It removes shoulder pain due to long period of Sarvangasana.
3. It is beneficial to the nervous, digestive, respiratory, cardiovascular and glandular systems. It influences all the hormonal secretions and relieves various gynaecological disorders.

Note: In case if illness, weak wrists, pregnancy and in tiredness this asana should not be practised.

51. Gomukhasana

'Go' (गो) means a cow. 'mukha' (मुख) means face. When this asana is performed the performer's posture resembles a cowhead. So it is called Gomukhasana. This is one of the main 84 asanas.

Method: Place the left heel on the right side of the anus. Bend the right leg in such a way that the right knee rests on the left knee and the sole of the right foot touches the lower part of the left thigh. Take the left arm round the back, bend it at the elbow and bring it upward. Now raise the right arm, bend it at the elbow and take it to the back. Raise the first and the second fingers of the left hand. Lower the first and the second fingers of the right hand. Try to close the fingers of both hands behind the back. The spine and head should be erect. Change the hand and leg. Repeat it up to 5 to 15 minutes in total. Concentrate on 'Manipura Chakra'.

Benefits

1. This asana strengthens the chest, the lungs and the heart. Joints become flexible and strong.
2. Moolbandha stops automatically in this asana. It is useful for pranayama and long time meditation.
3. It cures constipation, dyspepsia, loss of appetite, backache and arm-sprain. It cures rheumatic arthritis.
4. It is an excellent asana for inducing relaxation.
5. It cures tension, anxiety kidneys and diabetes ailments.
6. It alleviates cramp in the legs, makes the leg muscles supple.

Forward Bending Yogasanas

Forward bending yogasanas loosen up the back maintaining good health and increasing vitality. During a forward bending asana each of the vertebra is separated, stimulating the nerves, improving the circulation around the spine and nourishing the spinal cord. It has a positive effect on the organs of the body and mind. This group of asanas is very important for making the back muscles supple and strong. They involve in compressing and massaging the abdominal organs such as the liver, kidneys pancreas and intestines and bring in stretching the leg muscles and tendons.

Forward bending is a passive process in which force of gravity is utilized to stretch the muscles. Forward bending asanas use gravity to help release tension and pain. Forward bending associated with chest compression and exhalation, induces relaxation, sense of bowing and humility. It removes rigidity and eliminates fear.

When practising forward bending asanas from a sitting position particularly those in which the legs are separated, it is helpful to sit with the perinium on the ground rather than on the coccyx.

52. Back Stretching Pose

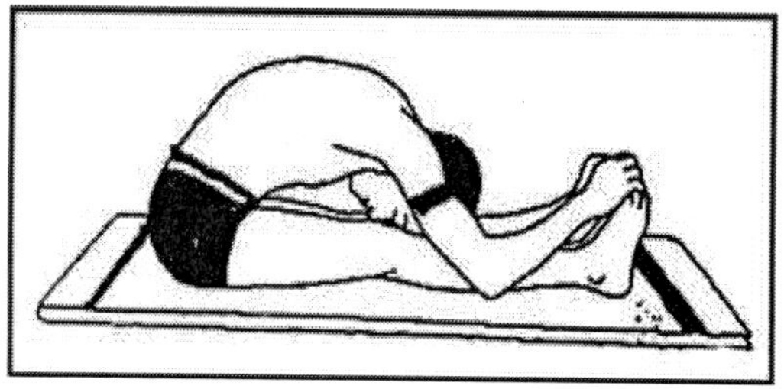

Its other famous name is Paschimottanasana. This asana is also known as ugrasana, Lord Shiva is believed to be the god of annihilation. This asana is difficult to practise. In other words Paschim means back. Tana means streteching. Stretching the lower back is called paschimottanasana.

Method: Sit on the ground with the legs outstretched, feet together and hands on the knees. It is the basic pose. Bring the hands over the head in stretching position. Exhale and bend forward slowly from the hips and try to grasp the big toes with the fingers and thumbs. Move slowly without forcing. Relax the back and elbows should touch the ground. Try to touch the knees with forehead. Don't strain. This is final position. Hold this position as long as is comfortable and relax. Return slowly to the basic position. This is one round. Perform 5 rounds.

Inhale in the basic position. Exhale slowly while bending forward, breath slowly in the final position. Concentrate on the abdomen relaxation of the back muscles or the Swadhisthana Chakra.

Benefits

1. Its effects are that the life force flows through the Sushumna nadi and it kindles gastic fire.
2. The excessive fat around the abdomen is reduced.
3. It tones up the kidneys, the stomach, the liver and other abdominal organs.
4. It tones up the intestines and improves digestion.
5. This asana cures constipation, indigestion, liver diseases and loss of appetite.
6. This asana helps the joints to regain elasticity.
7. It rejuvenates the entire spine.
8. It makes the body handsome and shapely.
9. It strengthens the pelvic muscles.

10. It cures hicough, prolapse, menstrual disorders, diabetes, colitis, kidney complaints, bronchitis and eosinophilia.
11. It stimulates circulation to the nerves and muscles of the spine.
12. It removes excess weight in this area and helps alleviate disorders of the uro genital system.

53. Spinal Bending Pose

It is also called merudandakarshanaasana.

Method: Lie on the right side with the left leg on the right leg. Bend the right elbow and place that on the ground. Raise the head and torso, rest the head in the right palm. The upper and fore arms should be in a vertical shape. Put the left hand on the left leg. This is the basic pose. Raise the left leg as high as possible, catch the left toe by left hand. Keep the legs straight Hold this final position. Lower the raised leg and arm to the basic position and repeat 5 times. Repeat on other side.

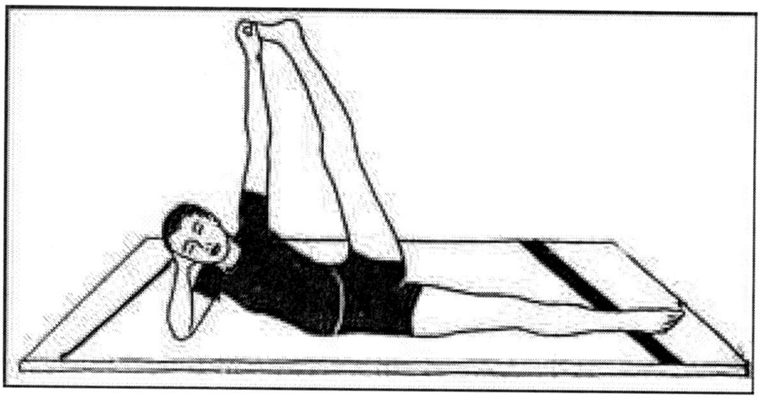

Inhale while raising the leg and arm. Retain the breath as long as you can hold the final pose. Exhale while lowering the leg and arm. Concentrate on the Swadhisthana chakra or breathing process.

Benefits

1. This asana relaxes the nerves under the knee, inner thigh and abdominal muscles.
2. This asana stretches the muscles of the sides of the body and makes them strong and flexible.
3. It reduces weight on the hips and thighs.
4. It is a preparation for forward bending asanas.

Note:

People suffering from slipped disc, sciatica or cervical spondylitis should avoid this practice.

54. Padahastasana

This asana is forward bending pose. It can be performed in a dynamic forward bending style.

Forward Bending Pose   Dynamics Forward Bending Pose

Method: Stand upright on the mat. Keep the legs close together, straight and erect the knee. Don't allow the knees to bend under any circumstances. Keep the hands on the respective thigh. Inhale. Exhale while bending downward. Keep the palms under the feet or hold the ankles with the palms. Keep the forehead on the knees. Suspending the breath, maintain this position for a few seconds. Inhaling return to upright position. Repeat 6 to 8 times. Follow the ratio of 2:4:2.

Benefits

1. It makes the waist-line and hips symmetrical.
2. It reduces the fat from various parts of the body.
3. It relieves the back pain and prevents auto-intoxication.
4. This asana massages and tones the digestive organs.
5. It alleviates flatulence, constipation and indigestion.
6. All the spinal nerves are stimulated and toned.
7. Inverting the trunk increases the blood flow to the brain and improves circulation to the pituitary and thyroid glands.
8. The dynamic form of Padahastasana also helps to remove excess weight.
9. It removes nasal and throat diseases.
10. It increases concentration and vitality.

Note: This asana should not be practised by the people suffering from serious back pain, sciatica, heart disease, high blood pressure and abdominal hernia.

Twisting Yogasanas

The spine is the most important part of the human body. The aim of these asanas is to purify the nervous system and make the spine stronger and more efficient by twisting the spine in various ways. It also has strong influence on the abdominal muscles, alternately stretching and compressing them as the body twists from one direction to the other. The samanaprana region is related to Manipura Chakra a plexus of main nadis/ pranic channels, supplying the whole body. These asanas have a strong effect on total health and vitality.

55. Vakrasana

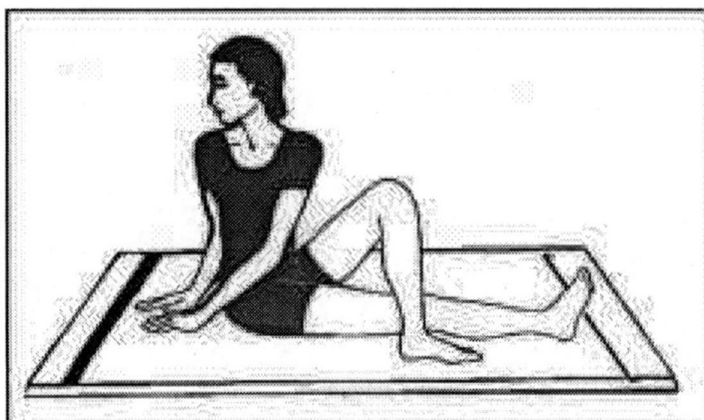

'Vakra' means curved/slanting/oblique/twist. from vakra the pose is called vakrasana.

Method: Sit with the legs stretched in front. Turn the trunk slightly to the right and place the right hand behind the body, close to the left hip with the fingers pointing backward. Bring the left palm near the right hip as close as possible to the right hand. Bend the left knee and place the foot out side the right knee. Twist the trunk and head as far to the right as is comfortable. Keep the spine erect and upright. The hips should remain on the ground (mat). The right elbow may bend a little. This is the final pose. Relax the lumber region. Look over the right shoulder as far as possible. Bring the trunk in front, rest and twist again. Repeat 5 times. Practise on the other side.

Inhale before twisting. Retain the breath while twisting. Exhale while comes the trunk in front Concentrate on Manipura chakra.

Benefits

1. It is a very good practice to make the spine flexible.
2. It is helpful in treating enlarged and congested liver and inactive kidneys.
3. It brings relief to hypertension, constipation and diabetic patients.
4. It improves the function of the abdominal organs.
5. It removes backache, neck pain, lumbago and mild form of sciatica.
6. It is helpful for beginners preparing for the more difficult spinal asanas such as ardhamatsyendrasana.

Note:

- It should be practised after forward and backward bending asnas and inverted asanas.
- People who are suffering from severe back conditions, ulcers, hernia should not perform this asana.

56. Half Spinal Twist Pose

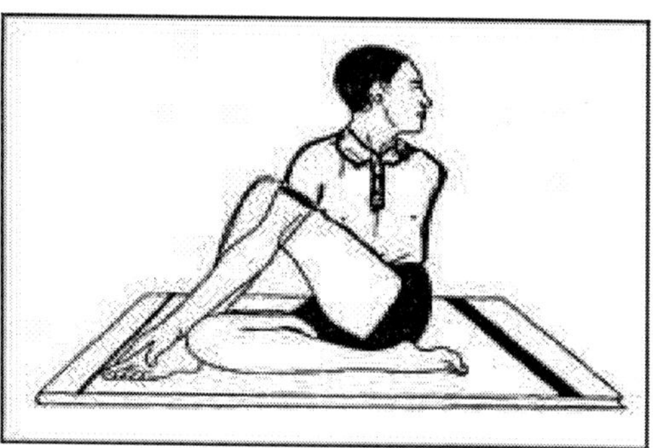

It is a 'spinal twist' and a 'trunk twist. This is named after the great yogi Matsyendranath. So it is also called Ardha Matsyendrasana. Actually this asana is an advanced stage of vakrasana.

Method: Sit on the mat stretching both the legs forward. Bend the right leg and place the right heel near the left hip, bend the left leg, place the left foot on the outer side of the right thigh. Turn the trunk to the left cross the right arm over the left knee and catch hold of the left big toe with the right hand. Now turn the trunk a little more to the left with the chin over the left shoulder. Take the left hand over the back and get a firm hold of the right thigh. Now twist the spine, but steadily, keeping the chest erect and forward. Maintain the pose as long as you comfortably can for about five seconds to begin with.

Return stage by stage. Repeat this procedure on the other side. Inhale in the forward position. Exhale while twisting the trunk. Breathe deeply and slowly without strain in the final position. Inhale while returning to the basic position. Concentrate on Agya chakra/spine/ the movement of the abdominal created by the breathe in the final position.

Benefits

1. This asana exercises the spine and ensures the free movement.
2. It also massages the liver, spleen, bladder, pancreas, intestine and other abdominal organs.
3. This asana stretches and strengthens the spinal nerves. It makes the back muscles supple.
4. It is highly recommended for treatment of obesity, dyspepsia, diabetes and urinary disorders.

5. It is useful for mild cases of slipped disc.
6. It alleviates digestive ailments.
7. It regulates the secretion of adrenaline and bile.
8. It is used for sinusitis, hay fever, bronchitis, constipation, colitis, menstrual disorders, cervical spondylitis.

Note:

- Women more than two or three months pregnant should avoid this asana.
- People suffering from peptic ulcer, hernia, hyper thyroidism should perform under the guidance of a qualified Yoga teacher.

Reversed Yogasanas

Reversed yogasanas invert the action of gravity on the body. Generally these yogasanas improve health, reduce anxiety and stress, and increase self-confidence. They also increase mental power, concentration, and capacity to sustain large work loads without strain. They ensure rich supply of blood to flow to the brain. The enriched blood flow also allows the pituitary gland to operate more efficiently, tuning the entire endocrine system. This has a positive effect on the metabolic processes and on ways of thinking. In these yogasanas the breath becomes slow and deep encouraging correct respiration. The abdominal organs receive a powerful massage, helping them to perform their functions more efficiently. Reversed yogasanas are used to sublimate and transform sexual energy into spiritual energy. They stimulate the chakras, open Susumna nadi and help to awakening kundalini. These postures improve the quality of meditation and concentration.

Reversed yogasanas should be practised at least three hours after taking food. Always practise these yogasanas on a folded blanket thick enough to protect the vertebra of the neck and back of the head. Beginners should only remain in the final pose for a few seconds. Duration may be increased gradually. Rest in Shavasana after these yogasanas are performed. People suffering from high blood pressure, slipped disc should not practise these yogasanas. Perform these yogasanas with their counterposes slowly and gently. Never combine Mayurasana with reversed yogasanas.

In this series Bhumipadmastakasana, Moordhasana, Vipareetakarani asana, Sarvangasana, Padmasarvangasana. Poorwa halasana, Halasana, Druta halasana, Sheersasana, Salamba Sheersasana, Oordha padmasana etc are included.

57. Plough Pose

The word 'Hala' in Sanskrit means 'plough' and when the body is supine and backward stretched it takes the shape of a plough or 'hala' and hence the phrase Halasana (Plough pose).

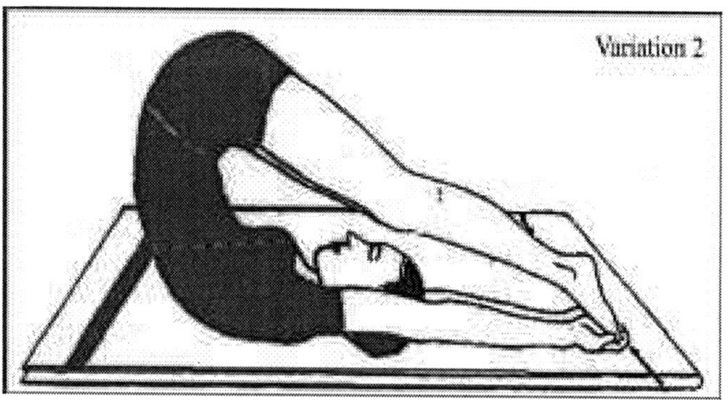

Method: Lie flat on the spine and with your palms on the ground/mat. Raise both legs in a steady movement up to a 30° angle and maintain the pose for a few seconds. Next raise them to 60° and then up to 90° or the vertical position and pause. Bring the legs towards the head without bending the legs and then slowly raise the hips and the lower part of the back. Bring down the legs until the toes touch the ground beyond the head. Push the legs further from your head and maintain this stage for a few seconds. You can keep your palms on lumber region folding the elbows or catch hold the toes with the palms. Return back slowly. Rest in Shavasana and normalize the breathing.

58. Head Stand Pose

'Sheershasana', 'Kapali-asana', 'Vrukshasana' and head stand pose and vipreetakarani pose are the well known asanas related to head postures. This asana is the king of yogasanas and highly beneficial for general health. There are three stages to perform this asana.

Method: Sit in vajrasana. Relax the body bend forward and keep the fore arms on a four fold blanket, and inter-lock the fingers and elbows should be 30 cms apart from the knees. Place the centre of the head on the ground taking the support of the fingerlock.

Raise the knees from the ground and straighten them. Bring the feet closer to the body. With your weight on the elbows, raise the feet off the ground. Keep the knees bent, but straighten the thighs. Straighten the knees and maintain the whole body in a vertical position for 30 seconds, gradually adding about 1 minute per week and practise up to 3 to 5 minutes, not more than 30 minutes with closed eyes.

Now the return journey begins. Bend at the knees. Lower the thighs, bringing the knees close to the chest. Touch your feet to the ground. Slide your feet away from the body and straighten the knees. Bring your knees to the ground lift the fingerlock and loosen your fingers to return to the starting pose.

Breathe normally in the final pose. Concentrate on sahasrara chakra/balancing/the brain centre. It should be followed by tadasana, and then shavasana.

Benefits

1. Full blood supply to the brain, the nervous system, the sensory organs, the endocrine glands, the digestive organs.
2. It is a good practice that strengthens the vertebral column and slimming.
3. In this pose, gravity helps the venous blood to return to the heart a positive help in the case of varicose veins.
4. This asana makes the body beautiful, healthy and active.
5. The adjustment of the cranial bones is facilitated.
6. People suffering from haemorrhoids, fistula and prolapses, will notice great improvement.
7. It develops will power, concentration, strength, agility, patience and intelligence, confidence and feeling of staying longer in this pose.
8. This asana is very powerful for awakening Sahasrara chakra.
9. It relieves anxiety and other psychological disturbances.
10. It is recommended for the prevention of asthma, hay fever, diabetes and menopausal imbalance.
11. This asana helps an aspirant to observe celibacy. It is a nectar indeed.
12. It cures the diseases of the eyes, the nose, the head and the throat.

Note: Head stand asana should not be done by those who have weak eyes, ear or throat infections, insomnia, constipation, high blood pressure, heart disease, thrombosis, chronic catarrh, kidney problems, impure blood, pregnancy or menstruation.

Balancing Yogasanas

Balancing asanas group develops a balanced mind and a more mature outlook of life. This group develops the cerebellum and concentration. It balances at the emotional, mental and psychic levels. These yogasanas are especially noted for balancing the nervous system and removing anxiety and stress. Balancing asanas may be difficult to perform at first but practice makes it perfect.

59. Eagle Pose

When Garudasana is performed, the pose of the body appears to be that of an eagle bird, so this asana is called Garudasana/eagle pose.

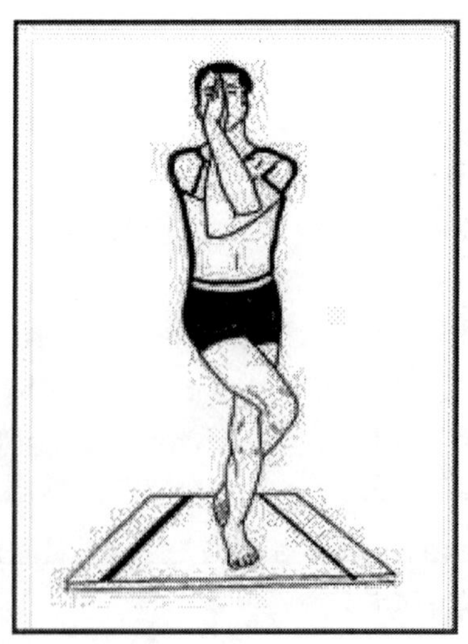

Method: Stand erect, keep the left leg straight on the ground and bring the right leg over the left thigh above the left knee. The right leg should be entwined around the left leg in the same way as creeper encircles the trunk of a tree, and stick to it. The right thigh should be entwined around the left thigh. Interlock the arms in the same manner. The palms should touch each other. Arrange the fingers in such a way that they look like the beak of an eagle, keep the arms in front of the face, breathe in the normal way. Hold this position 10-15 seconds. Change the hands and legs alternately.

Benefits

1. This asana is helpful for restraining the mind.
2. It alleviates pain in the thighs and calf muscles.
3. It cures rheumatism of the arms and legs, swelling of cells of the testicles. It relieves Sciatca and hydrocele.
4. It strengthens the legs and blood vessels and loosens the joints.

60. Lordshivas Pose

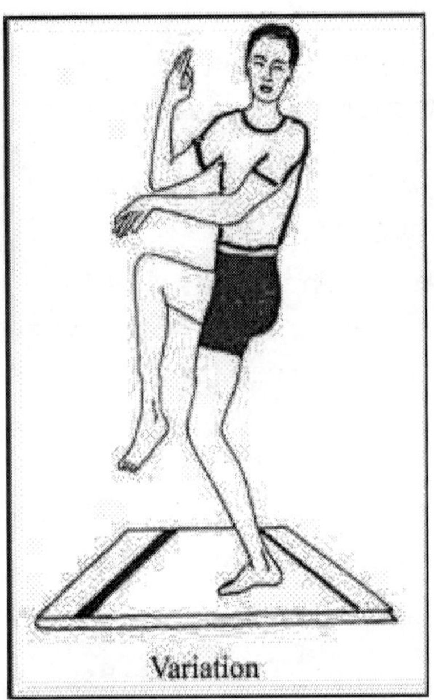
Variation

This posture of the body while practising this asana resembles Natraja/lord Shiva's dance pose. So this asanas is called Nataraj-asana. This pose inspires one to go ahead, and work.

Method: Stand erect with both the legs straight. Fix the eyes on a fixed point at eye level. Bend the left knee and grasp the ankle or big toe with the left hand behind the body. Slowly raise and stretch the left leg backwards as high as possible bringing right hand up in straight and gyana mudra position. This is final pose. Hold this position as long as possible. Lower the right arm to the side. Lower the left leg. Bringing the knees together. Release the left ankle and lower the foot to the ground. Lower the left arm to the side. Relax, then repeat with the right leg. Breathe normally throughout the practice. Repeat upto three times on each side. Concentrate on maintaining balance or Agya chakra.

Benefit

1. It gives sufficient exercise to the shoulders, the hips, the knees, the ankles, the palms and the spine.
2. It relieves the pain in the waist and makes the waist flexible. It exercises all the joints of the body.
3. It controls the nerves and helps to develop the concentration and makes the legs supple.

61. Padangusthasana

It is also called tiptoe pose. In ancient times, the persons who lived in Gurukulas and observed celibacy used to practise this asana regularly.

Method: Keeping the legs apart, squat on the toes. Balance the body weight on the left leg. Carefully lift the right leg with both hands, twit it and place the upturned right foot high on the left thigh. Remain firm and erect on the left toes. Join the palms together in front to the chest as in prayer and fix the gaze ahead at eye level. Breathe naturally and stay steady and relaxed in the pose.

Using the hands carefully and smartly bring the right leg down and resume the squat pose. Lower the heels and buttocks to the ground. Straighten the legs and relax. After a short time repeat on the other side. Repeat 2-3 times on each side.

Benefits

1. This asana stimulates veerya nadi.
2. It cures physical disorders like wet-dreams, impotence and diabetes.
3. If this asana is practised along with Sheersasana sarvangasana and bhujangasana. It helps one in observing celibacy.
4. The semen is sublimated by practising this and it changes into vital energy.
5. It regulates the reproductive system.
6. It also remedies flat feet and strengthens the toes and ankles.
7. This relieves stiffness in the back and weakness in the abdominal organs.

62. Bakasana

'Baka' means a stork (bagula). Bakasana is one among the best of the asanas. Baka is famous for its concentration.

Method: Squat on the mat with the feet apart. Balance on the toes and place the hands flat on the mat in front of the feet, with the fingers pointing forward. The elbows should be slightly bent. Lean forward and adjust the knees so that the inside of the knees touch the outside of the upper arms as near as possible to the arm pits.

Lean forward further, lifting the feet off the mat. Balance on the hands with the knees resting firmly on the upper arms. Bring the feet together. Focus the gaze at the nose tip. Stay in this pose as long as possible. Slowly come back. Retain the breath in side in the final position. If stay for a short time breathe normally. Stay in this pose for 2 or 3 minutes.

Benefits

1. This asana strenghtens the organs of the abdomen and chest. The spine also achieves strength, flexibility and vitality.
2. The prana gets sublimated in this asana. It bestows mental peace.
3. It stimulates the digestive, the respiratory and the nervous system.
4. Kapalabhati performed during this asana bestows many benefits.
5. It develops the sense of physical balance.

Note: People suffering from high blood pressure, heart diseases or cerebral, thrombosis should not try this asana.

Advanced Yogasana

Without flexible body the series of advanced yogasanas should not be practised. Have mastery over the all category of asanas first then try the advanced yogasanas without strain.

63. Tortoise Pose

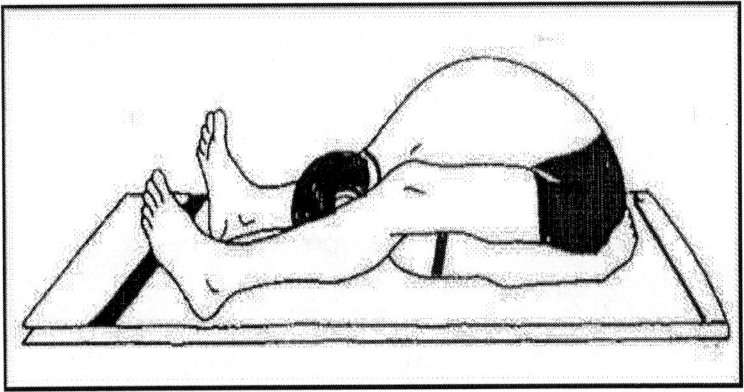

This asana resembles to the tortoise (koorma), the incarnation of lord Vishnu. Tortoise can withdraw its limbs inside from external danger. It is a symbol of Pratyahara.

Method: Sit on the mat with the legs out stretched. Separate the legs as wide apart as you can. Bend the knees slightly keeping the head in contact with the mat. Lean forward from the hips and place the shoulders under the knees, palms touching the hips move the body forward until the forehead or chin touches the mat between the legs. Don't strain in any way. This is the final position. Relax the body closing the eyes. Breathe slowly and deeply. Stay in this position as long as you can. Return to the basic pose. Perform a counter pose and relax in shavasana.

Exhale while bending and breathe normally in the final pose. Hold this pose for up to 3 minutes concentrate on Manipura Chakra/relaxing the spine/breathing.

• *Variation*

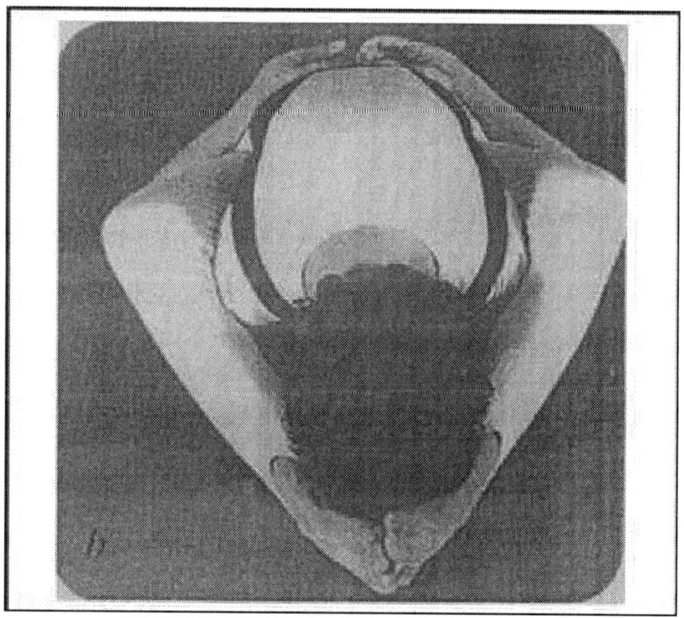

Benefits

1. This asana develops concentration, quietness, steadiness, wisdom, determination, patience and perseverance.
2. It tones up all the abdominal organs. It treats diabetes flatulence, constipation. It increases circulation in the spine, soothing the nerves and relieving head and neck ache.
3. It provides introversion, mental relaxation, sense of inner security and surrender. It removes fear and anger.

64. Archer's Pose

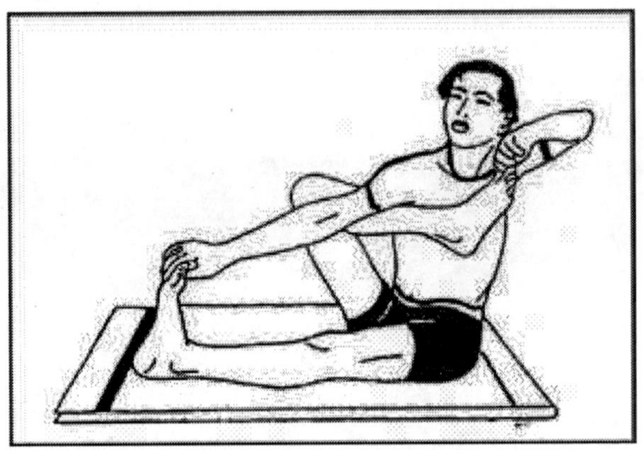

It is also called Akarasana dhanurasana. It is a action like a archer discharging arrows from the bow. This asana is very graceful.

Method: Sit with the out stretched legs, cross the arms in straight position. Catch hold the big toe of the right leg with the left hand, wrapping the first two fingers around the big toe to form a loop. Grasp the left big toe with the right hand. Pull the right foot up under the right arm. Put the right foot on the left thigh. Keep the right arm, spine and head erect. Pull the right big toe towards the left ear. The right knee will touch the right elbow. This is the final pose. Inhale and stay as long as you can, come back, exhaling the breathe, lower the right foot to the left thigh stretch the leg forward and release the hands. Repeat on the other side. Repeat 2 times one each side. Concentrate on Swadhisthana chakra/breathing/stretching.

Benefits

1. It tones up the chest and abdominal organs.

2. This asana alleviates women's complaints of irregular menstruation, the disorders of ovary and pain in the lower part of the abdomen.
3. This asana cures the pain in loins tonsillitis, indigestion, constipation, the tumors in the armpit, gout, pain in the legs etc.
4. This asana gives full exercise to the joints of the hands and the legs, the joints and the muscles of the neck and the spine. It revitalizes them.
5. This is an excellent asana for loosening the hip joints and making the legs supple. It relieves the tension in the back and neck.

Note: Those who suffer from asthma, T.B., cough get relief from this asana.

65. Mayurasana

'Mayura' means peacock. When this asana is performed the body assumes the posture. Which resembles a peacock, so it is called it Mayurasana. It has the capacity to digest the poison.

Method: Kneel on the mat with the knees slightly apart. Place the feet together. Lean forward and place both palms between the knees on the mat with the fingers pointing towards the feet. Bring the elbows and fore arms together. Lean further forward and rest the abdomen on the elbows and the chest on the upper arms. Stretch the legs backward so they are straight and together. Stretch the legs. Raise the heels and hold the legs parrallel to the ground. Hold this pose for 5 to 20 seconds. Hold the breath at the time of raising the body. Exhale while come back. Gradually increase the stay or perform 3 rounds. Concentrate on Manipura chakra/ balancing.

- *Variation*

Padma Moyurasana

Benefits

1. It is great energizing exercise.
2. It amazingly increases the power of digestion.
3. It cures the diseases caused by the excess 'Vata, Pitta and kafa' (wind, bile and phlegm).
4. It stops the bleeding caused by piles. It also prevents diabetes. It prevents obesity in the body.

5. This asana stimulates the circulation of the blood in the body. The body becomes bright and radiant.

Note: The people who are suffering from high blood pressure, heart diseases, hernia, ulcer, weakness, and pregnant women avoid this asana.

66. Gorakshasana

Guru Gorakhnath preferred this meditative asana. So that this asana is also called gorakshasana. It also is called moolbandhasana.

Method: Sit with the legs out stretched infornt of the body. Bend the knees and bring the soles of the feet together. Draw the heels towards that body. The outside of the feet should remain on the mat. Keeping the hands behind the buttocks with the fingers. Raise the buttocks on to the heel, so that the heel press the perineum. The knees remain on the mat. Don't strain the ankles. Keep the hands on the knees in chin/gyana mudra. Practise nasikagra drishti. Stay as you can then release the legs and stretch them forward. Concentrate on the pressure of the heels at the perineum.

Benefits

1. This asana induces Moolbandha automatically. It is used for awakening the Mooladhara chakra.
2. It is an important asana for the conservation of sexual energy.
3. It strengthens the reproductive and eliminatory organs.
4. It also makes the legs and feet supple.
5. This asana reverses the flow of apana directing it upward to the higher centres for use in meditative states.

Note:

- Breathe normally throughout the practice.
- Concentrate on Mooladhara chakra.

◆ ◆ ◆

4

Controlling the Life Force

What is Pranayama?

Pranayama is generally defined as breath control. The word Pranayama is comprised of two roots Prana+Ayama. Prana means 'Vital energy'/'Life Force'. This energy is present in all the gross matter and living creatures. It is more subtle than air which flows in the nadis or energy body. The word ayama means control or 'extension of Prana' or various modes of Prana. Pranayama thus means control of the prana.

What is Prana?

Prana is much more than mere breath. Prana is the power behind and within breath. It is cosmic energy that pervades the whole nature/universe. Prana is force, magnetism and electricity. It is due to prana that digestion, excretion and secretion take place. By regular practice of pranayama, 'Prana' like electricity is stored up. Pranayama is like a big store house that radiates energy, vigour and vitality. By controlling Prana one can control all the forces of the universe like mangnetism, electricity, gravitation, cohesion, nerve

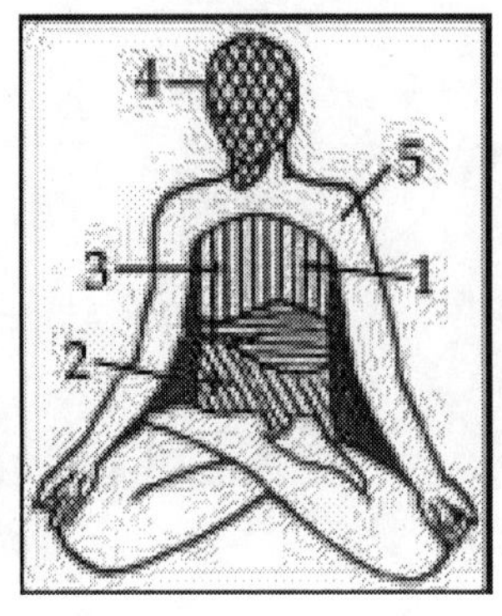

currents and thought vibrations. It is owing to vibration of prana that five organs of action and five organs of knowledge perform their respective functions. Just as gold smith removes the impurities of gold heating it in the furnance and blowing the blow pipe vigorously so the impurities of body and mind can be removed by the practise of Pranayama.

The Prana with different names performs different functions in the human body. Each of these has a specific name and aim:

1. **Prana:** It circulates in the area around the heart and controls breathing.
2. **Apana:** It circulates in the lower region of the abdomen and controls excretory functions (urine and stool).
3. **Samana:** It stimulates the gastric juices and aids digestion.
4. **Udana:** It remains in the thorecic cage and controls the absorption of air and food.
5. **Vyana:** It spreads throughout the body and distributes the energy from food and breath.

These are main prana. There are five sub-pranas as: Naga, Kurma, Krikara, Devadatta and Dhananjaya. Naga does eructation and hiccup. Kurma performs the function of opening the eyes. Krikara induces hunger and thirst. Devadatta does yawning. Dhananjaya causes decomposition of the body after death.

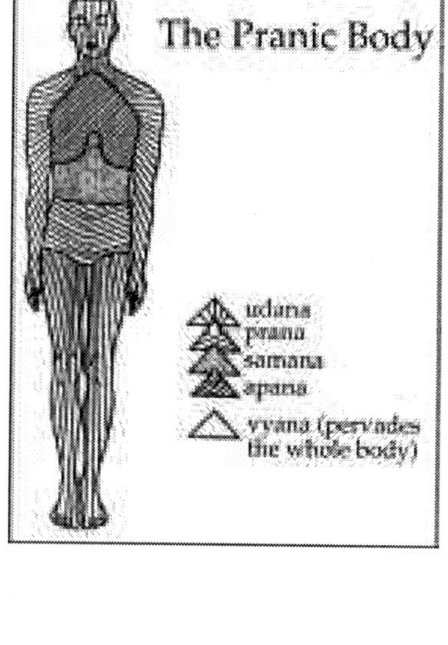

In our pramic body there are five sheaths known as

1. Annamaya Kosha — material body
2. Manomaya kosha — mental body
3. Pranamaya kosha — vital energy body
4. Vigyanamaya kosha — psychic body
5. Anandmaya kosha — bliss body.

These five sheaths function together to form an integral whole. The practises of Pranayama work mainly with pranamaya kosha. The pranayama kosha is made up of five major pranas. Which are collectively known as the 'Pancha Prana'.

Chakras

The subtle body has thousands of chakras, but there are seven main chakras or life energy centres that are apligned along the spine, starting from base and rising to the crown to head. Chakras are like swirling vortexes of energy that process store and distribute pure energy

around the body and are associated with particular characteristics and elements.

Awakening of Yogic Prana

Prana is a set of energy that keeps us alive and it flows in our body through circuits known as Nadis.

1. **Physical Prana:** When physical prana is awakened a person develops a certain level of immunity from infections, processes high stamina and can easily digest food. The recommended asanas for awakening physical Prana are:
   - Paschimottanasana
   - Janushirasana
   - Ustrasana
   - Bhujangasana.

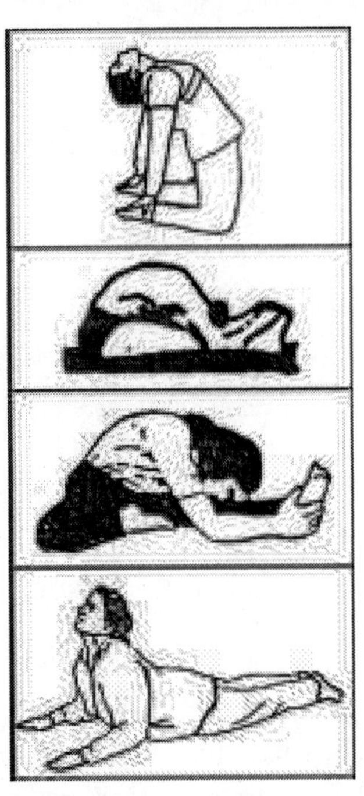

2. **Pranic Prana:** There are five main pranic prana: Mahaprana, Apana-prana, Samana prana, Udana prana and Vyana prana.

A. **Mahaprana:** 'It is connected to the Anahata chakra and flows in an upward direction rising like fire. On the physical plane, it controls the function of the heart, lungs and the respiratory system and regulates blood circulation. It maintains the emotional balance within the body. On the mental plane, it develops logical abilities and clarity. At the psychic level it produces the healing energies.

Activation Process

(i) Put your right hand at the middle of your chest, and left hand in gyana mudra on left knee. Inhale, hold breath, and then exhale gradually through the nostrils.

(ii) Visualize an expanding flame in the heart. Chant Om and practise Ustrasana.

(iii) Sit in Sukhasana keep the hands up like W shape eyes closed. Breathe normal keeping palms upwards.

B. Apana Prana: It is situated in the hip area and is connected to the Mooladhara and Swadhisthana

Chakras. It flows down towards the earth. On the physical plane, it governs the release of toxins (sweat, faeces and urine). If a person is weak, detoxification will not be successful. At the emotional level it creates excitement.

Apana prana

Activation Process

(i) Sit in vajrasasna, inhale through nostrils, while moving out stretched arms upwards then exhale through the mouth while moving out stretched arms downwards.

(ii) Stand on knees and exhale sharply through the mouth while bouncing your firsts up and down.

C. **Samana Prana:** It is situated in the stomach and is connected to the Manipura chakra. It flows in a circular direction. It controls the digestive system and governs the storage, production and distribution of energy from food.

Activation Process

Bhastrika Pranayama: Sit in vajrasana in the chin lock posture. Inhale and exhale forcefully through the nostrils with your hands on the stomach.

Note: This pranayama must be done on an empty stomach as this can induce vomiting because of the energy created.

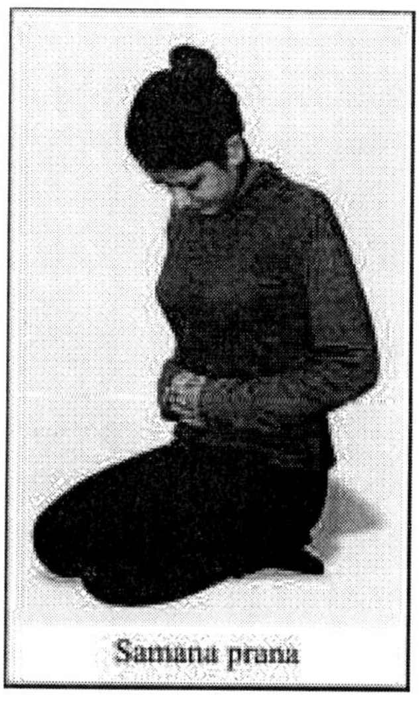

Samana prana

D. Udana Prana: It is located in the neck and head. It is connected to the Vishudhi, Agya and Sahasrara Chakras. It flows in an upward direction. It controls also the five senses and the actions of the limbs. All forms of higher consciousness experiences (Samadhi, kundalini etc.) are only possible with its activation.

Udana prana, Bhramari Pranayama

Activation Process

(i) **Ujjayi Pranayama:** Tones up your neck muscles and breathe slowly in and out of the nostrils.

(ii) **Bhramari Pranayama:** Sit or in padmasana crossleged and place your index fingers on your ear lobes, close your mouth and make a humming, sound like a bee in different tones. Chant hum and focus on the throat area.

E. **Vyana Prana:** It works through the nervous system. It is the energy network that links all the chakras. Any benefit from powerful exercises or kriyas are useless if Vyana Prana is weak, as the energy created does not get disturbed to the others bodies.

Vyana Prana

Activation Process

Nadi Shodhana Pranayama: Place your right thumb on your right nostril. Now use it as control opening and closing of the right nostril. Inhale through the first nostril and exhale through the second nostril and vice versa. Repeat this way of alternate breathing for at least five rounds starting with the opening of the nostril. This pranayama helps to balance the Sun (Pingla) and Moon (Ida) energies.

F. **Mental Prana:** It is the prana of the mental body and creates the mental energy field—the stronger it is the greater is the mental ability to express and convince others.

Activation Process: I (Trataka)

(i) Concentrate on a black spot, placed at your nose level and at a distances of four feet away from your self, for at least five minutes. People suffering from headache will be benefited by this practice. Do it before going to bed. It also strengthens the mental energy field and the power of concentration.

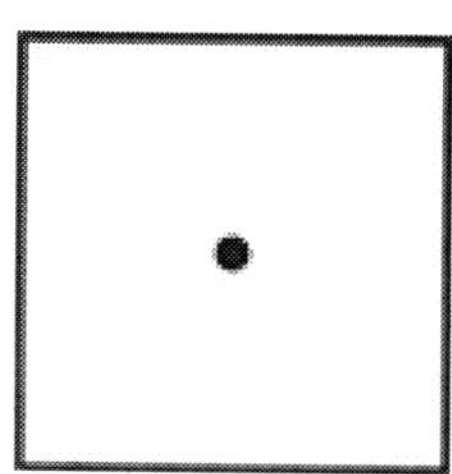

(ii) Chant the Ram Mantra and concentrate on the navel area sitting in meditative pose.

G. **Psychic Prana:** It is the prana of the psychic body. It creates the psychic energy field which when strong makes one feel emotionally balanced. It induces a feeling of selflessness and unconditional love, If psychic prana is weak, one becomes extremely emotional, swinging back and forth from very happy to sad moods, seek; attachments outside the self; and feel unfulfilled.

Psychic Prana

Activation Process

(i) Yogic chant — Om Yam Ma

(ii) Vedic chant — Om Vaiyu Namaha.

Aspects of Pranayama

There are five main aspects of breathing these are:

(i) Inhalation (Pooraka)

(ii) Exhalation (Rechaka)

(iii) Internal breath retention (Antar Kumbhaka)

(iv) External breath retention (Bahir Kumbhaka)

(v) Spontaneous breath retention (Kevala Kumbhaka)

Actual aim of pranayama is to increase Kumbhaka. There must be a gradual development of control over the function of respiration. The practice of inhalation, exhalation and Kumbhaka influence the flow of prana in the nadies purifying regulating and activating them, there by inducing physical and mental stability.

A Process of Pranayama: / Balancing Energy

Pranayama is a technique of breathing by which the brain is influenced. You should know that the brain has two hemispheres. These two hemispheres of the brain are connected with two nostrils. The breath which you inhale through the left nostril influences the right hemisphere. Similarly when you breathe through the right nostril, it influences the left hemisphere. The two breathing systems are related to the sympathetic and parasympathetic nervous systems. When you practise pranayama, then you are creating an influence, an impression, on the two hemispheres of the brain, thereby you are creating balance between the sympathetic and parasympathetic nervous systems. When there is harmony in the nervous system and brain, the mind separates itself from the senses.

Bandhas: Increasing the Voltage or Energy Level

When you retain the breath then you have to do something more. You have to create a pressure at three points in the body. At the time when you are holding the breath, you must contract your throat, the anus and abdominal muscles, and these three contraction should be practised when you are holding the breath. This effects the main three nadis: you must have noticed that sometimes the right one flows, sometimes the left one flows. That is due to sympathetic and parasympathetic nervous systems which are controlled by the solar and lunar cycles. It is the right time for meditation.

Effects of Pranayama

I. Physiological effects

The practice of pranayma helps in the efficient functioning of different systems of the body.

1. By inspiration, expiration and retention in pranayama there is a rise and fall of diaphragm and contraction and relaxation of the abdominal muscles which get accentuated and their constant movement and massage to the bowels and the kidney help in removing congestion if there is any. The nerves and muscles of the bowels and the kidneys get toned up. The function of elimination is carried on more effectively.
2. Healthy respiration depends on strong respiratory muscles and good elasticity of the lungs. Through pranayama the chest is expanded to its fullest extent, several times putting the lungs on the utmost stretch.
3. The organs of digestion and absorption like the stomach the pancreas and the liver, are all exercised in pranayama. This is done by gentle massage given to them by the diaphragm and the abdominal muscles. Congestion of liver is removed and unhealthy pancreas are corrected in their functioning. Gastric disorders are removed.
4. Yogic seers have looked upon pranayama as the one exercise that could make every life process

healthy. Some of them were to enthusiastic in their optimism about the efficacy of pranayama that they ruled out other exercises for securing the health. Pranayama not only controls different physiological functions but in the control of life processes it vitalizes the whole human organism.

5. There is a gentle massage to the heart during pranayama and it helps circulatory system work satisfactorily.
6. During pranayama the diaphragm and lower abdominal muscles pull up the lower part of the spine as a whole.
7. During pranayama the veins, blood from the brain is drained very thoroughly and fresh arterial blood is supplied to the brain on a larger scale. Uddiyanabandha enables to get the largest supply of rich arterial blood.

II. Scientific Effects

8. Heart rate reduces significantly during antrika Kumbhaka.
9. Kumbhaka performed immediately after Kapalbhati brings effect on PQ interval upto 300 ms (Dostalek and Lepicoveka 1983)
10. EEG changes were found more pronounced during Bhastrika than during Kapalbhati. Development of chirhythm was observed during Kumbhaka.
11. In pranayama Voluntary Kumbhaka and extended expiration better utilizes oxygen under lower ventilation and a specific effect of carbon dioxide is possible. During expanded expiration the level of the excitability of the organism is lower.

(Roitbak, 1960, Tejskal, 1968, Dostalek,1976). Therefore relaxation is more intensive and full shavasana is possible during and after expiration.

12. **Suryabhedi pranayama** provoked long trains of chi-waves in the left prerolandic and both rolandic area and a 26Hz. Sinusoidal wave pattern in the right post rolandic area. Occasionally at the height of chi-wave activation in a 1-2 episode of waves in the theta band occurs in the pre-rolandic derivation attaining amplitudes of 1200uv. When trains of bi-phasik paroxysmal sharp waves (11 to 16Hz) occur in the parieto occipital derivation, post-rolandic apha and pre-rolandic beta may be recorded at the same time. (Dostalek Roldan, Lepecoveka, 1980).

    The excitatory effect rests upon influence of respiratory centre (Dostalek, 1974,1975) and upon rhythmical stimulation of viscera. During Bhastrika its component Kapalbhati stimulates rhymatically abdominal viscera and vegitative plexuses. It has been proved that rhythmic introceptive stimulation acts very significantly upon the functional tone of the central nervous system (Verbonova, Nicolov, 1982).

    Apart from the stimulation of heart in particular exercise in yoga by mechanical pressure directly, most effects should be realized indirectly via central nervous system.

13. CO^2 percentage in expired air was found to have significant relationship with the duration of one round in various ratios for puraka-rechaka and puraka-kumbhaka-rechaka.

III. Psychological Benefits

Pranayama is a technique for regulating one's all emotional and mental states and even the way in which one behaves. Changes in the respiration induce changes in the rest of the autonomic nervous system. Pranayama controls autonomic nervous system and this system regulates the secretion of adrenaline thyroxin and other hormones of the body. The breath forms a bridge between the conscious and the unconscious. Emotions such as anger, depression and fear all have their characteristic patterns of irregular breathing.

Through pranayama one learns to consciously alter his breathing and thus his emotional state. One can attain a calm or an alert state through smooth and even diaphragmatic breathing.

IV. Curatives Effects

Gheranda Samhita, Hathayogapradipika and other texts describe the curative benefits of different techniques of pranayama. Suryabhedi pranayama cleanses the frontal sinuses, destroys the disorders of vata and diseases caused by worms.

Ujjayi removes diseases from throat (H.P. 11-50) caused by phlegm and increases gastric fire (H.P:11:52-53). It removes disorders like phlegm, flatulence, indigestion, rheumatism, consumption, cough, fever and enlarged spleen. (gh. S:V.66-67).

Sitkari overcomes hunger, thirst, sleep and removes sloth or idleness. (H.P:11:55-56).

Shitali destroys diseases like glandular enlargements and disorders of the spleen and toxin. (H.P:11,58). It removes indigestion and disorders of bile and phlegm. (Gh.S.V.69).

Bhastrika cures all the diseases of three humours and increases gastric fire. (H.P.11, 65 66)

Bhramari brings peace and tranquility (H.P. 11,68).

V. Spiritual Benefits

Pranayama induces altered states of consciousness. The practice of pranayama introduces high pressures, both in the central canal of the spinal cord and the ventricles of the brain. These pressures centrally stimulate the whole nervous system which helps the human consciousness to be internalized and super-consciousness perceptions possible. Gheranda samhita (V-57) sums up the results of pranayama as follows:

"By the practice of pranayama one gets the power of levitation and feeling of lightness. Diseases are cured Kundalini is awakened and the state of 'unamani' (undisturbed state of consciousness) supervenes and finally the mind is filled with Bliss. A person who practices pranayama becomes happy."

Bandhas in Pranayama

Bandha means 'lock'. In advanced pranayama practices relating organ functions are consciously locked to accumulate the prana energy and to properly direct its flow to a particular place for awakening the sleeping Kundalini. There are three kinds of bandhas, Jalandhara Bandha, Moolabandha and Uddiyana Bandha. Jalandhara Bandha in combination with Moola Bandha unites prana with Apana in our inner being. Bandhas are necessary for Kumbhka.

Mudra and Pranayama

To control the prana mudras are used. Generally

Mudra means forming. Mudras as a collective concept cover many operative aspects in Hathayoga and pranayama. Mudras are symbolical gasture and actions of hands, fingers, eyes to achieve spiritual rituals. When mudras are properly performed they gather cosmic energies closing a circuit of nerves currents in the body and lead us to gain consciousness for mystical experiences.

There are four mudras that used in pranayama like

1. Pranava mudra/pranayama mudra

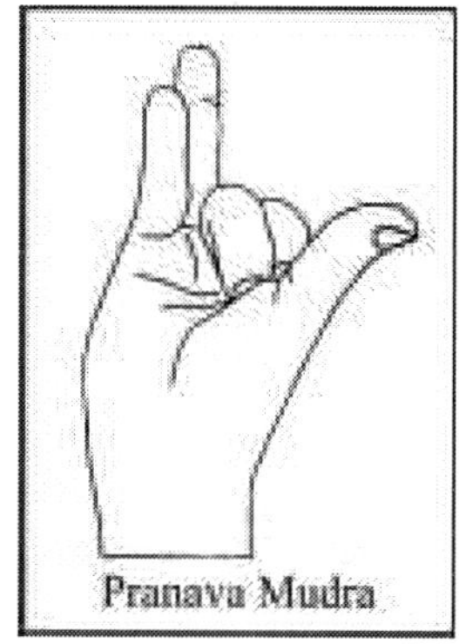

Pranava Mudra

2. Shanmukhi Mudra/yaoni mudra

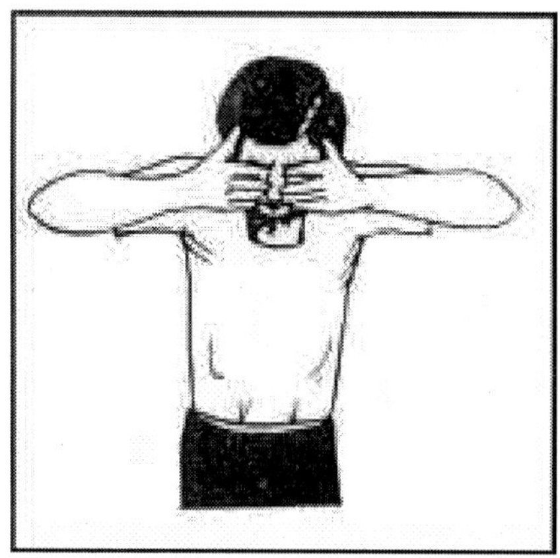

3. Khechari mudra/Tongue Bandha

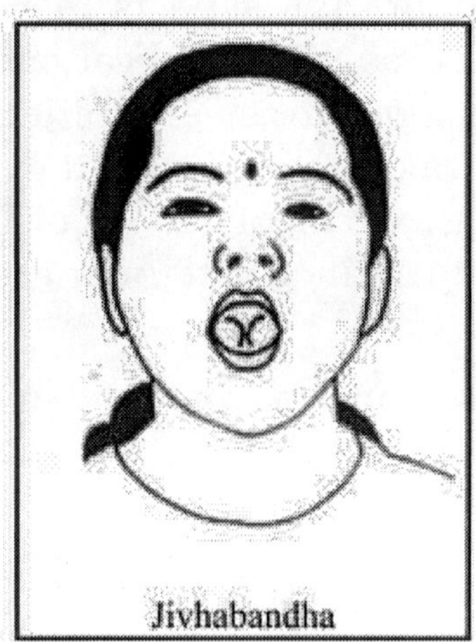

Jivhabandha

4. Dhyana Mudra/Gyana Mudra

Dhyana Mudra

Asanas in Pranayama

All the meditative postures are generally used in pranayama as follows:

Sukhasana, padmasana, swastikasana, siddhasana and vajrasana.

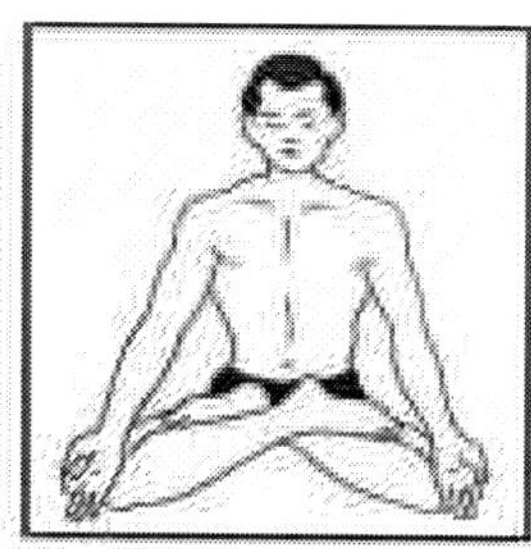

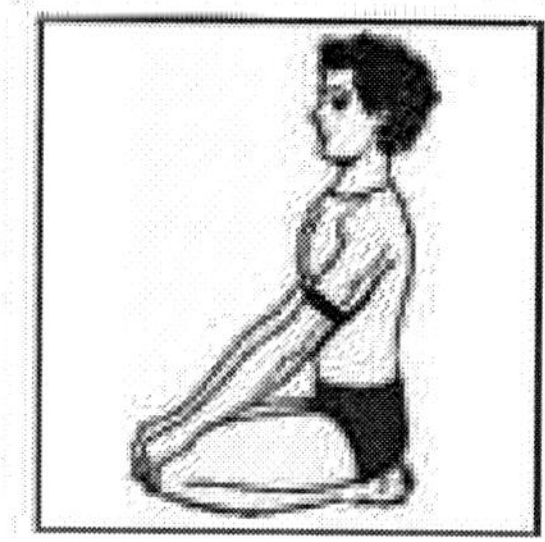

Shatkarmas before Pranayama

To clear the nostril passage and stomach Shatkarmas play an important role. Neti-(sutra and Jala). Dhauti, Basti, Nauli, Kunjala etc) are helpful in the practice of pranayama. Kapalbhati works as a cleansing process and is also a pranayama. If there is any blockage in the body the good result will not come out. So that we should remove the impurity of the body first.

General rules for practice

There are some preliminary instructions for practice of the pranayama.

1. **Place:** The ideal place for pranayama is a secluded spot on the bank of a river or on the beach. The room where pranayama is practised should be well ventilated, quiet, clean and pleasant. Avoid practice direct in sunlight because the body will become over-heated. Practising in a wind, air conditioning

or under a fan may disturb the body temperature and cause cold.

2. **Asana:** Don't sit on a bare place. Put blanket under your hips covered with white sheet. Sit straight keeping the spine and neck erect in any meditative pose.

3. **Time:** An empty stomach is mandatory. Therefore the best time for practice is before break fast early in the morning, if practised in the evening, Keep a gap of at least five hours after consuming solid food. Practising before sunrise or after sunset are the ideal times.

4. **Posture:** Pranayama is best done in a meditative pose.

5. **Clothes:** Loose, comfortable clothing made of natural fibres should be worn during the practice. The body may be covered with sheet or blanket in winter.

6. **Bathing:** Take a bath before commencing the practice at least or wash the hands, face and feet. Don't take a bath for at least half an hour after the practice.

7. **Sequence:** Pranayama should be performed after asanas and before meditation. After the long practices sadhaka may take rest in shavasana for a few minutes.

8. **Diet:** A balanced and sattvic diet is recommended. Take a combination of grains, pulses, fresh fruits and vegetables with a little milk product, if necessary. In advanced practice take milk, almonds and ghee.

9. **Be tension free:** Don't have feelings of strain at all. Don't try your capacity too fast. Practise with ratio. Breath retention should be comfortable.
10. **Precautions:**
    - Children below 12 should not attempt advanced pranayama. However, they may be inspired to breath in and out slowly and rhythmically.
    - Advanced sadhana of pranayama should be practised under a qualified yoga instructor.
    - Use Bandhas and Mudras while practising pranayama.
    - Smoke spoils the spiritual atmosphere. So avoid smoke and intake of tobacco.
    - Pranayama should not be practised during illness. Simple techniques such as deep breathing. Breath awareness and abdominal breathing in Shavasana may be performed.
    - If you feel constipation and less quantity of urine, dry motion then stop consuming salt and spices, and drink plenty of water. In the case of loose motion, stop the practice for a few days and take a diet of rice and curd or yoghurt.
11. It is not necessary to practise all kinds of pranayama daily. Their practice should be gradually increased day by day.
12. Ten minutes regular practice is sufficient for maintaining good health.
13. Decide what pranayama one should practise.
14. Sweat coming out of the body during pranayama should be rubbed into the body itself.

15. Practise three or four pranayamas regularly every day you will yourself realize and appreciate their beneficial effects.

1. Sahaja Pranayama

Sahaja means spontaneous or natural. It is also called Sukhapoorvak pranayama.

Method: Sit in comfortably in any meditative posture or lie in shavasana. Relax the body and close the eyes. Concentrate on your breathe, observe your breathing process. Observe and feel the breathe flowing in and out around the nose. Don't control the breath. Don't change the rhythm of breathing. Feel the coolness of the breath, when it enters the nostrils and warmth when it flows out. Observe the breath with a Sakshi Bhava, a detached witness. Feel the breath flowing through the back of mouth, throat, chest trachea, bronchial tubes and in lungs. The lungs are expanding and relaxing. Observe and feel that rib cage is expanding and relaxing. Feel and observe the abdominal movements. Feel the abdomen moving out slightly inhaling on and while exhaling let it go in. Keep the chest immobile. While doing this feel that with every inhalation you are drawing in cosmic energy, vital and bliss, power and peace and with every, exhalation you are throwing out tension, disease and all impurities. Have a clear mind and don't entertain any other extra thought in the mind. Become aware of the whole breathing process. Repeat this 15 to 30 times.

Benefits

1. Sahaja (sukh poorvak/natural breathing) provides deep relaxation to the mind and the body.

2. It improves concentration and strengthens the nervous and the respiratory systems.
3. It is useful in relieving depression, anxiety, hypertension, lack of concentration and cardiac problems.
4. It is extremely beneficial to the people suffering from cough, cold and respiratory ailments.
5. It also removes congestion in the nostrils during sleep.

2. Diaphragmatic Breathing

It is called abdominal breathing also. The diaphragm is a membrane which separates the lungs and thoracic cavity from the abdominal organs. When one inhales deeply, the diaphragm expands (Lowers down) and helps to absorb the maximum quantity of oxygen. While exhaling, the diaphragm relaxes and rises forcing the lungs to expel carbon dioxide.

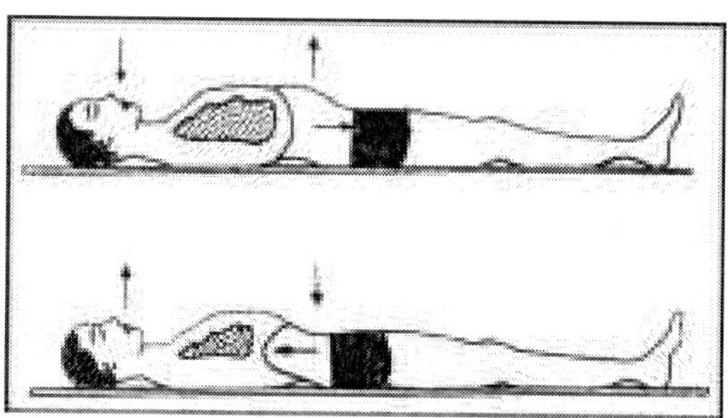

Method: To perform diaphragmatic/abdominal breathing lie flat on the back, keeping the legs together and arms at the sides. Relax the entire body. Inhale slowly and deeply, simultaneously making the abdominal muscles move outwards to the maximum extent. Hold the breath for a while. Then exhale slowly and deeply, allowing the abdominal muscles to move inwards to the maximum extent. Concentrate on abdominal movements only. Without moving the chest.

Benefits

1. This respiration improves the functioning of Civer, Pancreas, Spleem, Kidneys, Stomach and intestines.
2. It corrects diaphragmatic breathing gives effective movement to the abdominal organs and does a natural massage to the cardiac muscles.
3. The lower lobes of the lungs are being utilized.
4. It improves lymphatic drainage from basal part of the lungs.
5. It improves oxygenation of the blood and circulation.
6. It provides a great improvement in the state of physical and mental well being.

Note: You can place your right hand on the abdomen just above the navel and the left hand over the centre of the chest.

3. Chest Breathing

In this breathing middle lobes of the lungs are utilized. It is called thoracic breathing also. Lungs are situated under the chest, which are protected by the ribs. During the respiration, the ribs and the upper position of the chest move, particularly during the inhalation. The chest cavity and the lungs expand bringing in more of oxygen.

Method: Sit in meditative pose or stand comfortably or lie down flat on the back keeping the legs together

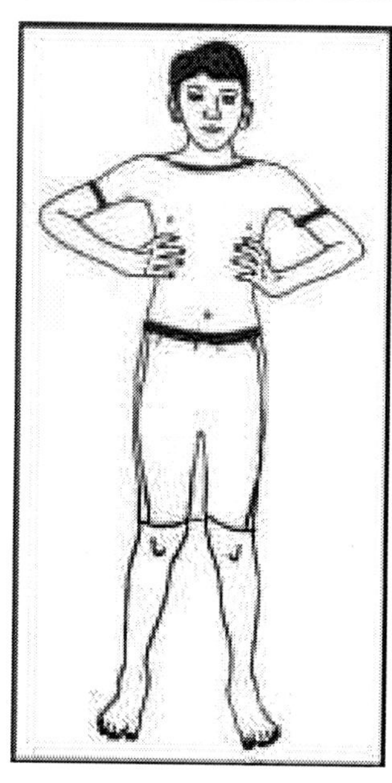

and arms on the sides, close the eyes. Focus on the chest cavity take 2-3 deep, long, slow and silent breaths. As you breathe in feel the expansion of chest cavity stretch in rib cage and full expansion of lungs. Feel the overall expansion in the chest cavity opening up the middle lungs. As you breathe out feel the relaxation in rib cage of chest cavity and contraction of the lungs. Breathe in and breath out to the maximum of your capacity. Imagine your chest cavity to open up and close like an umbrella for some time. Don't use the diaphragm repeat several times.

Benefits

1. This exercise will strengthen the trachea, thoracic region and air-sacs.
2. It expends more energy than abdominal breathing.
3. It purifies the blood, improves circulation and calms the heart.

Note: Many people continue this type of breathing long after the tense situation has passed, creating bad breathing habits and continued tension.

4. Upper Chest Breathing

It is called clavicular breathing and it is the final stage of total rib cage expansion. It occurs after the middle lobes breathing. This requires maximum expansion on inhalation and only the upper lobes of the lungs are ventilated.

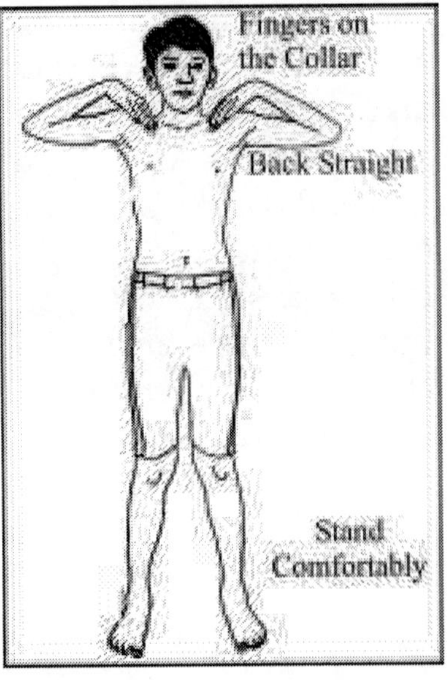

Method: Stand/sit in meditative pose/lying on one's back. Close the eyes. Relax the body, perform the chest breathing for a few minutes. Inhale fully expanding the rib cage. As you breathe in feel the stretch in the collarbone, and the rounding off the shoulders. As you breathe out feel the relaxation in the collarbone and shoulders. Allow the breath to open up the blockage of the upper lungs as you breath in and breath out to your capacity. Exhale slowly first releasing the lower neck and upper chest, than relax the rest of the rib cage back to its starting position.

Benefits

1. Upper chest breathing is only used under condition of extreme physical exertion and when experiencing obstructive air-way diseases such as asthma.
2. It thoroughly cleans and fortifies the upper chest.

Complete Breathing

It is the yogic breathing Combining the three techniques as explained before. It is based on maximum inhalation and exhalation. The aim of this process is to control of the breath, correct poor breathing, practise and increase oxygen intake.

Method: Sit in a comfortable meditative pose. Keep the hands on the knees with mudra. Palms should be facing up. Keep the focus on the chest cavity. Breathe in, start filling up the lungs feeling the expansion in the lower abdomen. Then feel the chest cavity expanding and finally the stretch in collar bone and rounding of the shoulders. Feel the whole body expanding like a balloon. As you breathe out feel the relaxation first in the collar bone and shoulders then in the chest cavity falling and then finally the contraction of the abdomen.

As all these movements happen feel the breath filling the body from bottom to the top and emptying from top to the bottom. Visualize the breath level rising and falling in the body with inhalation and exhalation like the water level in bucket or mercury level in the thermometer. Make sure there are no jerks as you breathe in and breathe out. Let the breathe be very smooth, co-ordinated. Full, complete, silent and prolonged, continuous and steady. The order is extremely important to gain maximum benefit. Hold the breath for a few seconds after exhalation it is one round. Perform 5-10 rounds and slowly increase to 10 minutes daily.

Benefits

1. It is especially useful in situation of high stress or anger for calming the nerves.
2. It is useful in cold, bronchial diseases and other general weakness and heart trouble.

3. It allows the lungs to remain active and helps in resisting the germs that invade the lungs tissues.
4. The oxygenated blood nourishes the entire system.
5. Complete yogic breathing is a gift of nature.
6. It is very helpful in maintaining a perfect health.
7. We are filled with a feeling of mental and physical peace.
8. Heart beats become regular.

5. Nadi Shodhana Pranayama

Method 1: Basic practise of purification

Sit in any meditative pose. Keep the neck and spine erect. Relax the body and close the eyes. Practise yogic breathing for some time. Adopt pranva/pranayama mudra with the right hand and place the left hand on the knee in gyana mudra. Close the right nostril with the right thumb. Inhale and exhale through the left nostril 6 times. Concentrate on your normal breathing. Then release the pressure through right nostril. Press the left nostril with the ring finger. Inhale and exhale through the right nostril 6 times normally. Bring the right hand on the right knee. Breathe 6 times through susumna (both the nostrils). This is one round. Practise 5 rounds or do it for a duration of 3 to 5 minutes with out any noise. Practise this method for 15 days then shift to method at number two.

Method 2: Alternative Breathing

This kind of breathing is called Anuloma and Viloma. In this method the duration of respiration is controlled. There is no retention only pooraka and rechaka are included in this practice.

Close the right nostril with the thumb and breathe

in through the left nostril, simultaneously count 1-4 or OM four times. Close the left nostril with the last two fingers. Release the pressure of the thumb on the right nostril count 1-4 or OM four times. Pooraka and rechacka should be equal. Again inhale through the right nostril along with the counting as done before and exhale through the left nostril, counting as before. This is one round practise 6 to 10 rounds.

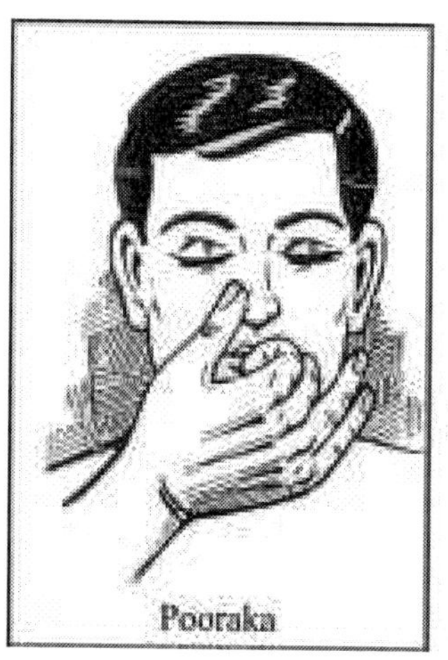

Pooraka

Rechaka

After some days practice, increase the length of pooraka and rechaka counting 20:20, if you feel discomfort reduce the count. Adopt the 1:2 ratio for example, if you inhale in 5 counts you have to exhale in 10 countings. Increase the count to ratio 12:24. After perfection achieving move on to method No 3. do 10 to 20 rounds.

Benefits

1. This pranayama provides a peace of mind.
2. It helps to clear both the nostrils.
3. It removes the stress related ailments.

4. It helps in the treatment of cardio vascular and nervous system disorders.
5. It relaxes the body and various body systems.
6. It maintains the temperature balance in the body.
7. It keeps the body warm in winter and cool in the summer.
8. It helps in purification of blood and cleansing of the nerves channels in body.
9. It increases the concentration power magically.

Method 3: Antrik Kumbhaka Sahita

In this process pooraka-kumbhaka-rechaka are included. This is very useful pranayama. Kumbhaka is real pranayama. It is an advance practice.

Sit in any meditative posture. Keep the left hand in gyana mudra on left knee, close the eyes, close the right nostril and breathe in slowly and deeply through the left nostril for a count of 6 and close both the nostrils with pranayama mudra (Pranava mudra) and hold the prana in the lungs for a count of 6 or for the duration of vacating Gayatri mantra or Savita mantra. Open the right nostril and exhale slowly for a count 6. Breathe in from the right nostril for a count of 6. Hold the breath for the count of 6.Then breathe out through the left nostril for a count of 6. It is one round practise 10 rounds.

After mastering the ratio of 1:1:1 increase the ratio to 1:1:2 or 6:6:12 seconds. After some weeks of practice after perfecting the ratio, increase the ratio to 1:2:2 or 6:12:12 seconds. Increase one unit like 7:14:14. gradually increase the count over a period of one or two ratio to 1:3:2 and 1:4:2. This is the last ratio. Perform 20 rounds daily maximum according to your capacity.

After mastering this method move to the method No 4.

Method 4: Antrika Kumbhak and Bahya kumbhaka.

	Pooraka Inhalation	Kumbhaka Retention inner	Rachaka Exhalation	Retention (Kumbhaka) outer
Ratio	1	4	2	2
	6 sec	24 sec	12 sec	12 sec
	7 sec	28 sec	14 sec	14 sec

Benefits

1. It maintains flexibility of the arteries, veins and capillaries and prevents heart disease and improves general stamina and vitality of the body.
2. It increases the will power and endurance.
3. Helps the Kundalini Shakti rise up by piercing the six major Chakras.
4. Relieves anxiety and depression.
5. Regulates the body clock.
6. Relaxes and soothes the nervous systems making it efficient and alert.
7. Balancing Ida and Pingla nerves (cold and hot temperature currents).
8. Helps in purification of blood, maintaining blood pressure, reducing and relieving of obesity, tension headache, migraine, insomnia anxiety etc.
9. It also induces tranquility, clarity of thought and concentration.
10. The whole body gets nourished by an extra supply of oxygen.

11. Carbon di-oxide is efficiently expelled and the blood is purified of all toxins.

Note:

1. Nadi shodhana pranayama may be practised in conjunction with bandhas for retention of breathe.
2. It may be necessary to adjust the ratio of the breathe to suit to the individual capacity.
3. The flow of breathe must be pretty, smooth, with no pressure and jerks.
4. Perform jala neti or breath balancing exercises before commencing.
5. Be aware of wandering tendency of the mind.
6. Concentrate on Agya Chakra.
7. Nadi shodhana should be practised after asanas and heating or cooling pranayamas, and before bhramari and ujjayi pranayamas.
8. The best time to practise is early in the morning.
9. Each method should be practised for a minimum of 6 months but method No. 1 which may be practised for 2-4 weeks.

6. Surya Bhedi Pranayama

Surya bhedi means to pierce or purify Pingla Nadi. Pingla is associated with the right nostril and so it carries the warm stream where as Ida is associated with the left nostril and carries the cold breath stream. There are three types of surya bhedi pranayama.

Method 1: Sit in any meditative pose. Close the eyes and relax the body. Close the left nostril with the ring finger and inhale slowly and deeply through the right nostril. Then close both nostrils, retain the breath and perform Jalandhara and Moolabandhas. Hold for just a few seconds. Release both bandhas. Exhale slowly through the right nostril by keeping the left nostril closed with the last two fingers. This is one round. 10 round are sufficient in the beginning. Gradually increase the length of kumbhaka after some months. The ratio should be 1:1:1 1:2:2 and letter to 1:4:2.

Method 2: Right in, left out Breathing

Keep the left nostril closed using prana/Pranayama mudra and inhale at a steady flow for 8 to 10 seconds or as long as your ability through the right nostril. Then close the right nostril and release slightly the finger pressure from the left nostril. Exhale deeply at steady flow for a period of about 10 to 20 seconds. This is one round. Perform 10 rounds in the beginning. Inhale through right nostril and exhale through left nostril again and again. Take normal breathing after 2 or 3 rounds.

Method 3:

Inhale	Retention	Exhale	Rounds
through right nostril 8 to 10 secs	with bandhas Jalandhara Moolbandha 30 seconds	through left noistreil 16-20 secs	10 per day

- Relax and take normal breathing after 2 or 3 rounds.

NB: Method No 3 differs from Method No 2: The sense is that after inhaling through right nostil the breath is retained along with the application of bandhas (locks) to make it all the more effective.

Benefits

1. This practise creates heat in the body.
2. It removes the **Vata Dosha** or wind element.
3. It stimulates and awakens the pranic energy by activating pingla nadi.
4. It enables physical activities to be peformed more efficiently.
5. It helps to alleviate depression.
6. It is especially recommended for those who are dull and lethargic.
7. It is very useful in the treatment of low blood pressure, infertility, worms, cough, cold and asthma.
8. It makes the mind more alert and perceptive.

Note:

1. It may be harmful if you practise more than 30 minutes.
2. Never practise Surya bhedi pranayama after intake of food.

7. Chandra Bhedi Pranayama

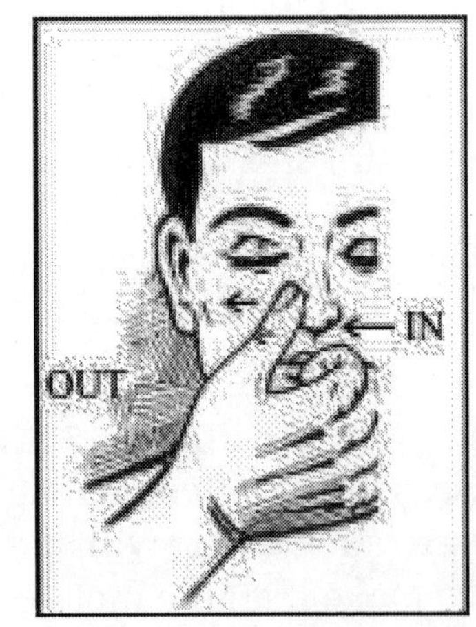

In Chandra Bhedi pranayama the left nostril is used for inhaling and right nostril for exhaling. The whole process is the same as in Suryabhedi pranayama, but only one difference is that the inhalation is implemented through left

Simhasana

Jalaneti

Nati

Chakra

Right Nauli

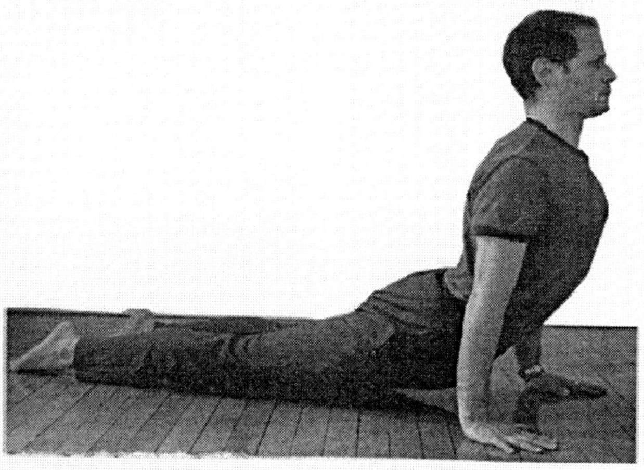

Urdhva Mukha Svanasana

Sidhasana

Valakhilyasana

Sheershasana

Eka Pada Rajakapotasana

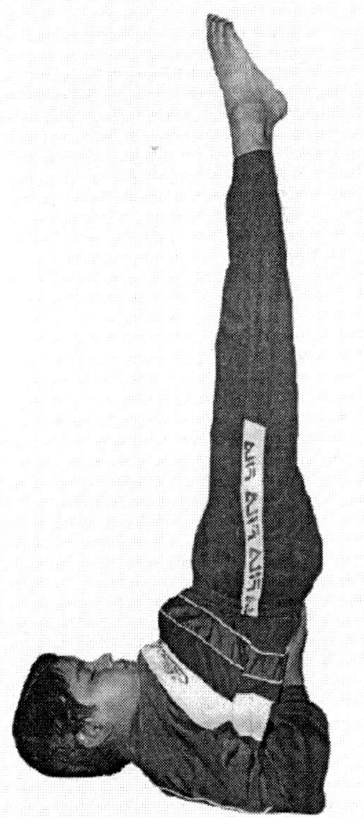

Sarvangasana

Garbhasana

Tiryak Ashava Sanchalanasana

Gorakshasana

Padangusthasana

TRATAKA

nostril and the exhalation is done through right nostril. Repeat it 20 times for four times a day.

Benefits

1. Chandrabhedi pranayama helps in increasing anabolic activity to increase the weight if done on empty stomach.
2. It helps in maintaining the peace within and to lower down the high blood pressure.
3. It also promotes coldness in body.
4. It removes the fatigue and excess of heat in the body.
5. It helps to keep the mind calm.
6. Many diseases caused by the excess bile in the body are cured.

8. Hissing Breath

It is also called the cooling breath or sheetali pranayama. It is a unique among the breathing practises. As the inhalation is through the mouth rather than the nose.

Hissing Breathe

Method: Sit in any meditative pose with the hands on the knees in gyana mudra or chin mudra. Close the eyes and relax the body. Take 2-3 deep long breaths Roll your tongue in between the lips like a pipe. Breathe in through the pipe of tongue as long as you can with a sound. Take the tongue in and gulp down the breath. Hold the breath as long as you can. Exhale through both the nostrils. You may feel cooling wave on the tongue and the upper palate.

Perform it for 5 to 10 minutes, 2-3 times a day in summer season and once in afternoon of winter.

Benefits

1. This pranayama cools the body, mind and brain centres.
2. It cools and reduces mental and emotional excitation.
3. It encourages the easy flow of prana throughout the body.
4. It provides muscular relaxation.
5. It controls over hunger and thirst.
6. Helps in curing skin diseases, tumor, enlargement of spleen, liver, indigestion and constipation. It reduces high blood pressure and acidity in stomach.
7. It lowers down the body temperature in high fever.
8. It is helpful in insomnia performing before going to bed.

Note:

1. This pranayama may also be practised along with Jalandhara bandha.
2. People suffering form cold, asthma, low blood pressure must avoid this practice.

9. Seetkari Pranayama

'Seet' means cool 'kari' means action. This pranayama is also ment for prectising summer season or in hot atmospheres.

Method: Sit erect in any meditative pose. Close the eyes and observe the breath. Swallow and dry out the mouth. Breath out through the mouth completely. Keep the mouth slightly open. Push forward the lower jaw. Press the tip of the tongue to the back of the teeth. Hold the teeth lightly together. The tongue may be kept flat or folded against the soft palate in khechari mudra. Expand the lips and breathe slowly and deeply through the teeth. Close the mouth. Keep the tongue flat. A smooth hissing sound is made and a sweet coolness is felt. Concentrate on the hissing sound and cool air. Hold the breath. Exhale consciously and steadily through the nose in a controlled manner. Relax and let in the normal breathing. Practise for 5-7 minutes or 10 rounds.

Benefits

1. It keeps the teeth and gums healthy.
2. This pranayama will prepare for concentration and meditation.
3. It helps H.B.P. fever irritable and hot tempered, maladaptive behaviour, fasting, skin infections, tumors, enlargement of liver and spleen, indigestion, constipation etc.

10. Humming Bee Breathing

Due to the sound like a Bhramari (bee) it is given the name Bhramari pranayama also. In this practice inhalation and exhalation are performed through the both nostrils. It is very effective pranayma for all.

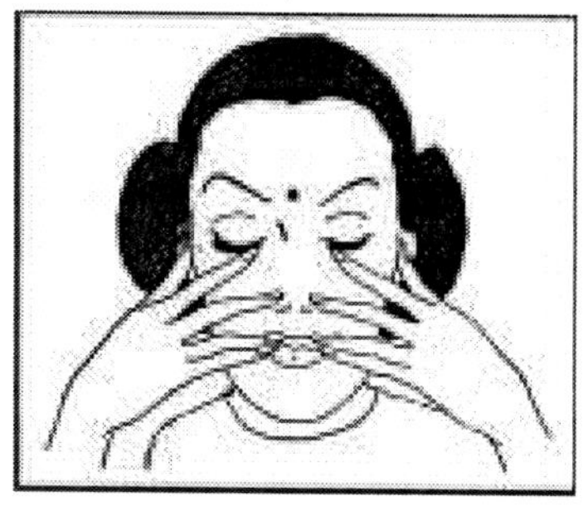

Method: Sit erect in any comfortable meditative pose. Relax the body and close the eyes. Plug the ears with the corresponding thumbs. Put the index finger gently on the eyelids and middle fingers on the nostrils flaps and thereby the last two fingers come to rest on upper and under the lips. Lift the elbows in a horizontal line. Inhale deeply and hold the breath pressing the fingers as long as possible. Breathe out from nose creating a resonating sound of humming bee and feel the vibration at the bridge of nose jaw and vocal cord. The humming sound should be smooth, even and continuous for the whole duration of exhalation. The sound should be soft and sweet making the front of the skull reverberate. This is one round. Concentrate on the sound and Agya chakra. In the beginning 5 to 10 rounds are sufficient. Then slowly increase from 10 to 15 minutes. In case of extreme mental tension, anxiety practise for upto 30 minutes. Practising in the midnight is very effective for sadhana. You can do it 2-3 times a day.

Benefits

1. This pranayama promotes a sweet, clear voice and is highly recommended for singers.
2. It is also useful in preventing insomnia, tension, depression, hypertension and nervous disorders.
3. It is very beneficial for women during pregnancy in preparation of labour.
4. It makes an impact on the mind producing peace and joy. It is useful for Samadhi/meditation.
5. During this pranayama blood circulation increases in the brain hence memory increases.

6. It reduces blood pressure. It speeds up the healing phenomenon of body tissues.
7. It helps to release the pains and tension.
8. It calms down anger and agitation.

Notes:

- People suffering from severe ear infection should not practise this prayanayama.
- Those with a heart disease must practise this with out doing kumbhaka (breath retention).
- In advance stage use Jalandhara and Moolabandha in kumbhaka. Don't strain while performing kumbhaka.
- Try to increase the time period of exhalation.
- You may also practise this pranayama with the chanting of OM by laying more stress on the chanting "M" and vibrating it for as long as possible.

11. Energy-Renewing Pranayama

This pranayama is also known as the psychic breath, Ujjayi. It may be performed in any position standing sitting or lying. It is also called sobbing breath. It can be done without Jalandhara bandha or even while walking. This is the only pranayama which can be done at all times of the day and night.

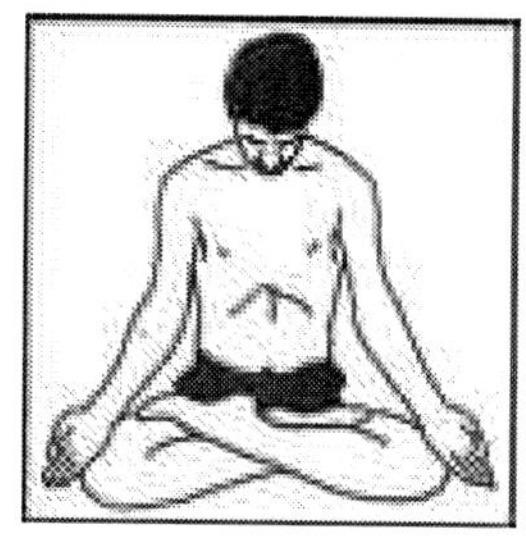

Method: Sit in any comfortable meditative pose like Padmasana, Siddhasana or Virasana. Perform Jalandhara

Bandha. Hands should be in gyana mudra on the knees. Close the eyes and look inwards. Exhale completely. Take a slow, deep, steady breath through both nostrils. Produce a sobbing sound due to the vibration in the vocal cord feeling the grinding touch of the inhaled breath in the throat. Hold the breath. Exhale from both the nostrils or with the left nostril closing the right nostril. Practise for 5 to 20 minutes. Twice a day or 15-20 rounds at a go. Remove Jalandhara bandha and relax.

Benefits

1. Reduces the heat of the head and kindles gastic fire.
2. Activates the digestive, respiratory and nervous systems.
3. It clears the nasal passages and removes phlegm from the throat.
4. It is excellent for neutralizing high blood pressure.
5. It soothes the nerves and tones up the entire body.
6. It counteracts many diseases of the ear, nose and throat.
7. It helps in relieving allergic cold, swelling of tonsils hypertension and insomnia.
8. It improves the oxygen supply.
9. It calms the mind and helps in maintaining good health.
10. Ujjayi alleviates fluid retention. It removes disorders of the dhatu which are seven in number.

Note:

- Those suffering from heart disease should not combine bandhas or breathe retention with Ujjayi.

- Inhalation and exhalation must be equal.
- When this breathing has been mastered, fold the tongue back into khechari mudra. If the tongue becomes tired release it, again fold it.
- Concentrate on the throat.

12. Forehead Shining Pranayama

It is called kapalbhati pranayama. Kapal means **Skull** and Bhati means **Shining**. It is one of the Shat- Karmas. It is a cleansing pranayama. It is the gate way to meditation.

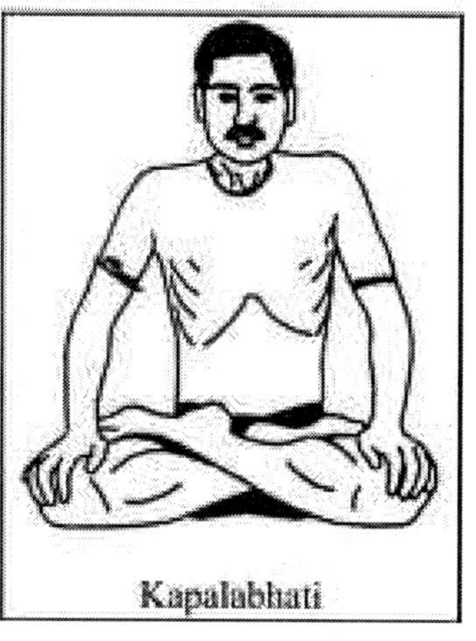
Kapalabhati

Method: Sit in any meditative pose with the head and spine erect and the hands resting on the knees in gyana mudra, close the eyes. Inhale deeply through the nose, expanding the abdomen. Exhale with a forceful contraction of the abdominal muscles. The next inhalation must take place passively and spontaneously, involving no effort. perform 10 respiration in beginning. Inhale and exhale deeply. This is one round. Practise 3 to 5 round. Take from 10 to 20 breaths. Concentrate on Agya chakra.

Benefits

1. It helps in the elimination of gases from the lungs and purifies the frontal portion of the brain.
2. It aids in combating chronic bronchitis, asthma, cerebral thrombosis, diabetes and nervous

disorders, caused by excessive wind, bile and phlegm.

3. It relaxes and revitalizes the mind by improving concentration.
4. It removes sleepiness and prepares the mind for meditation.
5. It can be useful for women during childbirth.
6. It balances and strengthens the nervous system and tones up the digestive organs.
7. Helps to clean the sinus and respiratory system.
8. Brings heat to the body when it is cold.
9. Eliminates the cough accumulated in wind pipe.
10. It develops the capacity of lungs.

Note:

- Let every exhalation be strong, aggressive, audible and prolonged.
- Don't change the facial expression by squeezing the nose, cheeks forehead and eyes.
- Don't tighten the jaws.
- Let there be no movement in shoulder.
- Whenever practising the pranayama session should be performed as the first pranayama.
- Don't do it during pregnancy, high blood pressure, menstruation, diahorrea, fever, abdominal ulcer cough and asthmatic attacks.

13. Bellows Breath

It is called Bhastrika pranayama also. Bhastrika means bellows. It consists of forceful and quick inhalation and exhalation. The sound produced due to this resembles that of the bellows of a black smith.

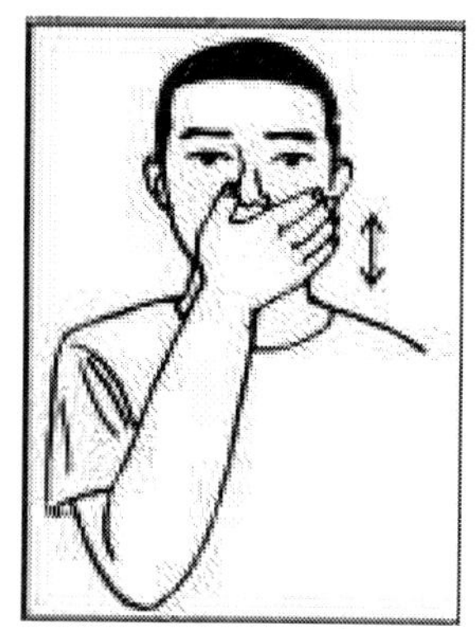

Method: Sit straight in any comfortable meditative posture left hand should be kept on the left knee in gyana mudra.

Left nostril: Put the right thumb on right nostril and press slightly. Exhale through the left nostril. Breath in and out forcefully, without straining, through the left nostril 10 times, count each breath mentally. The abdomen should expand and contract rhythmically with the breath. There should be a snuffing sound in the nose. After 10 respirations breathe in deeply through the left nostril keeping the right nostril closed. Fill the lungs as much as possible, expanding both the chest and abdomen force. Hold the breath inside for a few seconds. Exhale through the left nostril.

Right nostril: Close the left nostril and breath in and out forcefully 10 times through the right nostril. Inhale slowly and deeply through the right nostril. Close both the nostrils and hold the breath in for a few seconds. Breathe out slowly through the right nostril.

Both nostrils: Open both nostrils. Put the right hand on the right knee. Breath in and out forcefully through the both nestrils10 times counting mentally. Inhale slowly and deeply through both nostrils. Close both nostrils and hold the breath for a few seconds. Breathe out slowly through both nostrils together. This is one round.

There are three breath rates.

Slow	One breath every two seconds.
Medium	One breath every second.
Fast.	Two breathes per second.

The number of respirations may be increased by 5 per month from the initial count of 10 to a maximum count of 40 to 50 respirations through the left, right and both nostrils. Slowly increase rounds upto 5 and retention up to 30 seconds. Concentration should be on the breathing process or on the Manipura chakra.

Benefits

1. It reduces the swelling in the throat.
2. It kindles the gastric fire and gives temporary heat to the body.
3. It cures chest ailments and T.B.
4. It clears the respiratory passage from the accumulation of phlegm.
5. The spinal region and brain, the roots of the nerves receive large quantity of fresh blood supply.
6. It helps in mobility of fat particularly around the abdomen. It makes the body light.

7. It helps in preparing the mind and body for deep meditation.
8. It helps in increasing the capacity to hold the breath.
9. It is most effective to raise the kundalini by opening up the blockage of the Susumna chennel.
10. It helps improve the functions of the digestive organs, the sinus, stops a running nose and gives relief to bronchitis and asthma patients.

Note:

- Avoid it in case of high blood pressure, by pass surgery, menstruation, pregnancy and palpitation.
- Relax after every 10-10 pumping to calm down the heart beat and blood circulation.
- Don't change the facial expression during the practice.
- Don't tense the jaw, shoulders and arms.
- This pranayama is for winter season.
- It removes diseases of vata, pitta and kapha.
- In advance stage apply three bandhas also.

◆ ◆ ◆

5

Role of Bandhas

'Bandha' literally means a 'lock'. In yoga Bandhas are a type of postures in which certain organs or parts of the body are contracted and controlled in order to influence the vascular nervous and glandular systems. The Bandhas aim to lock the pranas in particular areas and redirect the flow into susumna nadi for the purpose of spiritual uplift and awakening of latent power.

Bandhas are used independently or with mudra and pranayama practices. These Bandhas stimulate Mooladhara, Swadhisthana, Manipura. Anahta, Vishuddhi, Agya chakras. These chakras are situated in the spinal chord and get involved fully during the practice of Pranayama.

They play a role in maintaining the pranic energy in particular area by holding, pressing, lifting and pulling, while performing a physical action.

Bandhas also give a massage to the endocrine and nervous systems, improving the activity of Ida. Pingla and Susumna nadis. The three main nadis are mainly responsible for maintaining oxygen balance in the body and are the treasure of mystic powers.

Bandhas possess remarkable curative value in many physical ailments concerning organic and functional disorders. Their psycho-physiological utility is remarkable.

Bandhas and Granthis

There are four 'Bandhas' – Jalandhara, Moolbandha Uddiyana and Mahabandha. The last being a combination of the first three.

There three Bandhas are related to three granthis/ psychic knots.

1. Moolbandha is associated with **Brahma** Granthi.
2. Uddiyana Bandha is associated with **Vishnu** Granthi.
3. Jalandhara Bandha is associated with **Rudra** Granthi.

These Granthis prevent the free flow of prana along susumna nadi and are helpful in awakening the chakras and rising of kundalini shakti.

1. Brahma Granthi

Brahma Granthi

Brahma Granthi is associated with

A. Mooladhara Chakra and

B. Swadhisthana Chakra

Brahma Granthi is linked with

- Servical instinct.
- Instinctive Knowledge.
- Awareness
- Desire.

When Brahma Granthi is opend/Transcended, the Kundalini Shakti is able to rise beyond Mooladhara and Swadhisthana Chakras.

2. Vishnu Granthi

This granthi is associated with

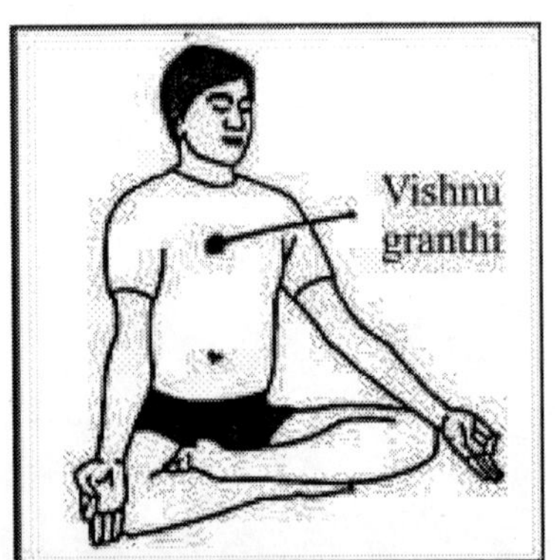

C. Maipura Chakra

D. Anahata Chakra.

These both Chakras are linked with—

- The Sustenance of physical aspect
- Emotional aspect

- Mental aspect of human existence.

Manipura Chakra sustains Annamaya Kosha or physical body. It governs the

1. Digestive systems and
2. Metabolism of food in the human body.

Anahata Chakra sustains Manomaya Kosha and Pranamaya Kosha, the energy body.

When Vishnu Granthi is opened/transcended, energy is drawn from the universe and not from the localised centres within the human being.

3. Rudra Granthi

This granthi is associated with

E. Vishudhi Chakra and

F. Agya (Ajna) Chakra

Vishuddhi Chakra and Agya (Anja) chakra sustain vigyanamaya kosha/ the intuitive/ higher mental body, and represent the transformation of an existing form/ idea/concept into its universal aspect.

When Rudra Granthi is pierced individuality, is dropped, the old age awareness is left behind. The

Kundalini Shakti crosses the Agya (Ajna) chakra and reaches at Sahasrara Chakra to merge in Shiva.

Jalandhara Bandha (Chin Lock)

Introduction

Jalandhara Bandha is the lock which controls the network of nadis in the neck. This bandha is generally performed along with the pranayama. This may be done in any meditative pose. It is performed in Sarvangasana and Kumbhaka pranayama. There is no need of Jalandhara Bandha for short time Kumbhka.

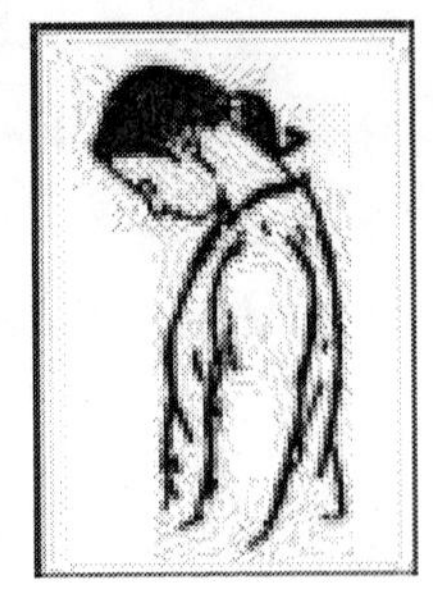

Method: Sit in any meditative pose with palms on the knees. The neck and the spine should be straight. Relax the whole body. Inhale slowly and deeply through the nose. Retain the breath inside bending the head forward. Contract the throat, stretch the neck and press the chin tightly against the chest particularly the sternum. The position may be held as long as the breath is retained in side then release the lock and the neck while exhaling.

Before starting the next round, take a few normal breaths. During the performance of Jalandhara Bandha the air is completely sealed in the thoracic region and the effect comes on the lungs.

Benefits

1. Jalandhara Bandha controls the function of the thyroid and parathyroid glands.
2. This Bandha has considerable curative value in the disorders of the throat.

3. Jalandhara Bandha compresses the carotid arteries.
4. Jalandhara Bandha helps to regulate the circulatory and respiratory systems.
5. This practice produces mental relaxation. It relieves stress, anxiety and anger.
6. It develops meditative introversion and one pointedness.
7. It regulates the metabolism.
8. The thyroid and parathyroid glands are massaged.

Remarkable Indications

- The practice may also be performed with external breathe retention.
- If practised on its own, it should be performed after asana and pranayama and before meditation.
- Concentrate on the throat pit or Vishuddhi chakra.
- When the throat is contracted the two vocal cords also get contracted.
- When the breath is retained without this Bandha. The pressure will be felt immediately on the heart and the practitioner may feel dizzy.
- Don't inhale or exhale until the chin lock and arm lock have been released and the head is fully upright.
- If any sensation of suffocation is felt, immediately stop the practice and take rest.
- This practice may be repeated up to 5 times.

2. Moola Bandha (Root Lock)

Introduction: Contraction and release of the anal region and the perineum is Moola Bandha. This is very important Bandha. The Moola Bandha is practised in standing position as well as in any of the meditative poses like Padmasana or Siddhasana or Sukhasana or Vajrasana. The physical and tantric significance of this Bandha is tremendous. The Moola Bandha is usually applied on the kumbhaka. It is directly related and linked to pranayama.

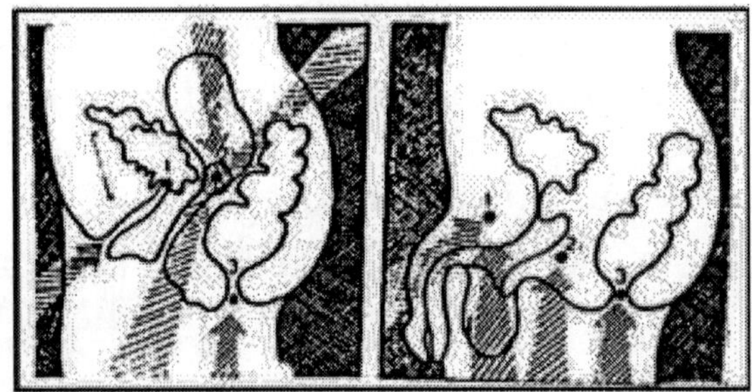

Method:

Step-1: Sit in Siddhasana/siddha yoniasana (for women). Close the eyes. Relax the whole body. Take the natural breathing for a short time. Then focus on the perineal/vaginal region. Contract this region by pulling up on the muscles of the pelvic floor and then relaxing them. Continue to briefly contract and relax the perineal/vaginal region as rhythmically and evenly as possible.

Step-2: Contract this region slowly and hold the contraction. Continue to breathe normally; don't hold the breath. Be aware of the physical sensation. Contract a little tighter, but keep the body relaxed. Contract only the muscles of the Mooladhara region. In the beginning the anal and urinary sphincters also contract, but as the awareness and controls are developed, this will be minimized and eventually will cease. The practitioner will feel one point of movement against the heel. Relax the muscles slowly and evenly. Adjust the tension in the spine to help focus on the point of concentration. Repeat 10 times with maximum contraction and complete relaxation.

Benefits

- Moola Bandha strengthens the sphincter muscles.
- It cures maladies like piles, fistula, disorders of the urinary tract.
- It removes the constipation and tones up the colon and prevents digestive disorders.
- The correct performance of this Bandha increases sexual retentive power of the practitioner.
- It generates vitality and helps to awaken the Kundalini Shakti.
- The intestinal peristalsis is stimulated.
- Moola Bandha stimulates the mooladhara chakra.
- It keeps the balance between prana and Apna Vayu.
- It improves the working efficiency of the sympathetic nerves.
- The practice of Moola Bandha along with the

Jalandhara Bandha in pranayama, controls the flow of prana and maintains the energy of the body.

- It relieves gas and painful menstruation. It strengthens the adrenal glands intestines and the reproductive organs.
- It is also effective in the treatment of psychosomatic and some degenerative illness.
- Its effects spread throughout the body via the brain and endocrine system.
- It is very beneficial in cases of asthma.
- It is used in Mahabandha also.

Uddiyana Bandha

Introduction: Literally 'Uddiyana' means to fly. Allow the abdominal muscles to fly in the cavity of the chest is called Uddiyana Bandha. It is also called-Abdominal Retraction lock, Raising the Diaphragm or diaphragm lock. Uddiyana Bandha is normally applied on the exhale and forcefully applied on the inhale. In other words we can say uddiyana Bandha is restraint of the flying up impulse of abdominal contraction.

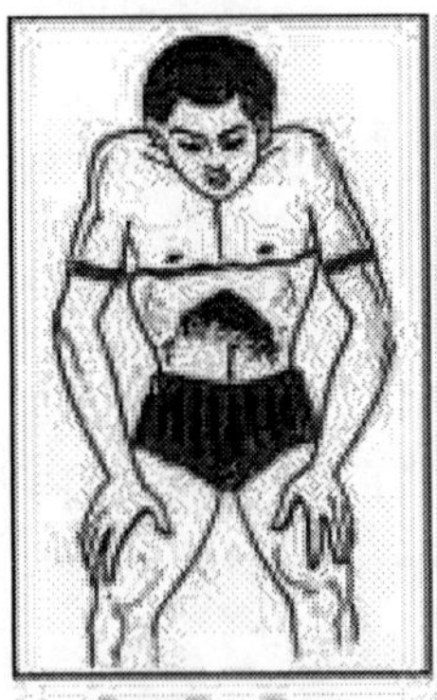
Standing Pose

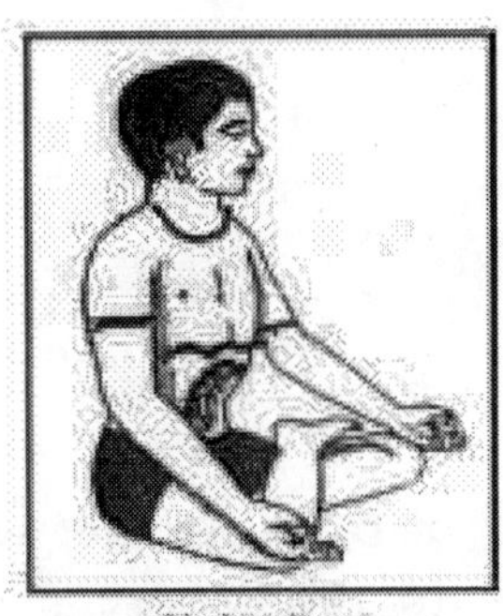
Sitting Pose

Method in Sitting Position

Sit in Siddhasana/Padmasana/siddha yoni asna (for women). Knees should be touched on the floor and the back and head remaining straight and erect. Press the hands on the knees. Exhale fully drop the head forward like Jalandhara Bandha. Contract and draw the stomach muscles in and take them upward above the navel portion. Retain the abdominal lock and the breath out side as long as you can without straining. Then release the Uddiyana Bandha, bend the elbows and lower the shoulders. Raise he head and then inhale slowly. Remain in the position until the respiration returns to normal, then begin the next round.

Benefits

1. Uddiyana Bandha removes constipation and stimulates the digestive fire, removes intestinal disorders and the worms.
2. It activates the liver and the kidneys.
3. It regulates the function of the Adrenal glands and hypogastric plexus.
4. It gives a gentle massage to the intestines and the heart muscles.
5. It allows the pranic force to transformation through the central nerves channel of the spine up into the neck region.
6. It stimulates the sense of compassion and can give a new youthfulness to the entire body, the spine should be straight.
7. This Bandha cures all the abdominal and stomach problems. Diabetes is controlled by this bandha.

8. Lethargic tendencies are driven away and over active person becomes tranquil.
9. It cures dyspepsia and liver trouble.
10. It is helpful to perform the Nauli.
11. Uddiyana Bandha stimulates the Manipura Chakra.

Remarkable Indications

- Uddiyana Bandha must always be practised on an empty stomach and the bowels should also be empty.
- Agnisar Kriya is an excellent preparatory practice.
- Practise first in standing position.
- Persons suffering form heat troubles and peptic ulcers should not perform this Bandha.
- It is also prohibited for pregnant women.
- It should not be practised by middle age persons suffering from excessive wind.
- Begin it first with three turns maintaining Uddiyana Bandha for five seconds. Increase duration gradually to fifteen seconds. The maximum number of rounds should not exceed eight.

Jivha Bandha (The Tongue Lock)

There is a useful tongue exercise known as Jivha-Bandha or the tongue lock.

Method: Take a hand-mirror to put the tongue lock correctly. Open the mouth wide and place the tip of the tongue close behind the front teeth. When this contact is made draw up the lower jaw a light so that an upward pressure on the tongue can be exerted to let it fill all the space of the hard palate and that position of the soft palate that can be reached by it.

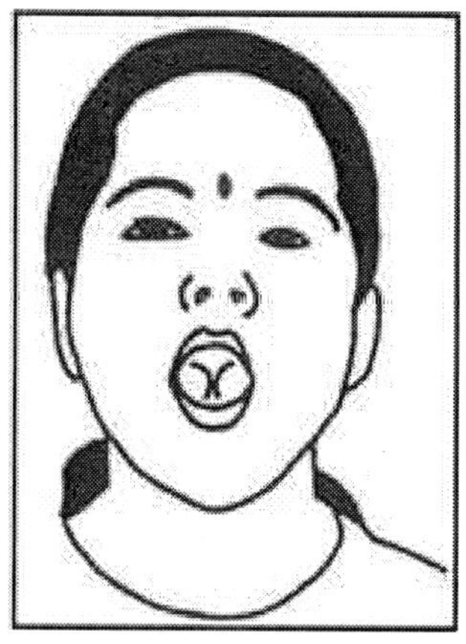

Note:

1. The tongue lock can be practised independently as a single exercise as well as a part of vipreeta-karani. It is also practised with Simhasana. If combined with Vipreetakarani. Jivha-Bandha should be done with the mouth shut.
2. The movement is to be done ten times a minute three minutes will be sufficient.

Benefits

1. The muscles of the neck are exercised and the blood circulation therein is improved.
2. The cervical nerves and the ganglia rendered healthier.
3. The pharynx and the larynx are exercised and their health promoted.
4. The thyroid is rendered healthier.
5. The auditory apparatus is made more efficient.

6. The salivary glands function more satisfactorily.
7. Jivha-Bandha removes congestion of the pharynx.
8. It has been found very useful in treating tonsillitis.
9. It cues deafness due to thickening of the eardrum.

Maha Bandha (Tri Bandha)

Method: Sit in any meditative pose with the hands on the knees. The spine and head should be erect. Close the eyes and relax the whole body. Breathe in slowly and deeply through the nose. Exhale forcefully and completely through the mouth. Hold the breath outside. Perform Jalandhara, uddiayna and moolabandhas in this order as long as you want without tension. Relase moola, uddiyana and Jalandhara in this order. Inhale slowly when the head is upright. This is one round. Keep the eyes closed, relax the body and let the breath return to normal before practising another round.

Benefits

1. Maha Bandhha gives the benefits of all the three bandhas.

2. It affects the hormonal secretions of the pineal gland. It regulates the entire endocrine system.
3. Every cell of the body is rejuvenated by this bandha.
4. It soothes anger and introverts the mind prior to meditation.
5. It can fully awaken prana in the main chakras.
6. It leads to the merger of prana, apana and samana in agni mandala, which is the culmination of all pranayamas.

Remarkable Indications

- Remain aware of each chakra for nine seconds and then proceed to the next.
- Get perfection in three bandhas first. This bandha should be practised in the last.
- Maha Bandha can also be performed from utthan Padmasana.
- People suffering from high or low blood pressure, heart illness, stroke, hernia, stomach or intestinal ulcer, and those recovering from any visceral ailment should avoid this practice.
- Pregnant women should also not attempt this practice.

◆ ◆ ◆

6

Know About Mudras

What is Mudra?

Mudra menas gesture recorded as stimulate. They tone up the control on the nervous system. They also control the Pranic energy and involuntary physiological function by giving a smooth pressure on a particular point.

Mudras are the precursors to pratyahara, in which the sadhaka could secure perfect control over the indriyas (senses).'Mudras' and 'Bandhas' are fundamentally related to each other and they play a crucial role together during the performance of Pranayama and Asanas. They help in concentrating one's and on a single point like the pratyahara.

Mudras form the techniques of activating the glandular functioning and the dormant power centres. Mudras help to approach nearer to the inner conscious energy. Yogis can never progress unless they have mastered the mudras. It is found by experience that the mudras are very very effective and beneficial.

All the mudras bestow power and health on the

regular practitioner. All of them are very important and effective. The benefits of mudras are undoubted. They are scientific, and aim at correcting the organic disorders of the body. Functional disorders are thus automatically cured.

Mudras can be described as psychic, emotional devotional and aesthetic gestures or attitudes. A Mudra is also defined as a 'seal' short cut or circuit by-pass. A Mudra may involve the whole body in a combination of asana, pranayama, bandha and visualisation techniques or it may be a simple hand position.

Prana and Mudras

In Tantric literature it is said that prana is arrested through the practice of Mudra the mind becomes introvert inducing states of Pratyahara or sense withdrawl and Dharna, concentration. Mudras are important techniques for awakening the Kundalini.

Groups of Mudras

There are five groups of mudras as follow:

1. **Hand Mudras:** In meditation some hand mudras are used like Gyana mudra, Chin mudra, Bhairava mudra, Apanvayu mudra, and Yoni mudra.
2. **Head Mudras:** In this category some mudras are related to kundalini yoga and many of them are related to meditation. Eyes, ears, nose, tongue and lips are used in this groups Shambhavi mudra, Kaki mudra, Akashi mudra, Shanamukhi mudra, Nasikagra dristi, Khechari mudra, Bhujangini mudra, Bhoochari mudra and unmani mudra.
3. **Postural Mudras:** In this group physical postures combined with breathing and concentration

techniques are used as Yoga mudra, Vipreeta Karani mudra, Prana mudra Manduki mudra, Tadagi mudra, Pashini mudra.

4. **Lock Mudras:** Bandhas and Mudras are used in this group for awakening the kundalini as—Maha vedha mudra, Maha bheda mudra and Maha mudra.
5. **Perinial Mudras:** These mudras redirect the prana from Root chakra to the brain. These mudras are related to sublimating sexual energy are in this group as Ashwini mudra and Vajroli/sahajali mudra.

There are 25 mudras described in Gheranda Samhita. Here some of the main mudras are being explained.

1. Chin Mudra

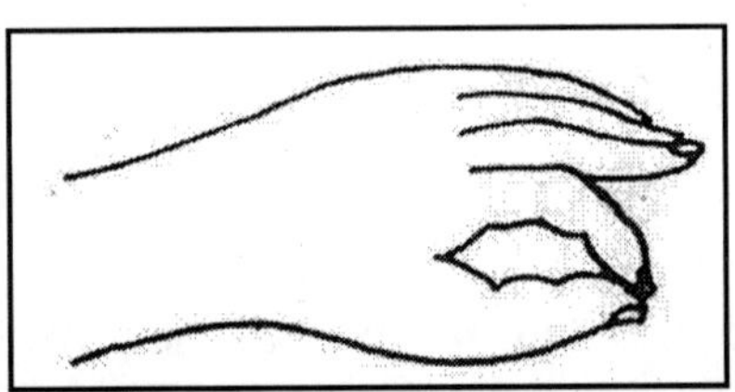

Method: Sit in any meditative pose fold the index fingers so that they touch the thumbs tips. Straighten the other three fingers of each hand so that they are relaxed and slightly apart. Place the hands on the knees with the palms facing down. Relax the hands and arms.

2. Gyana Mudra

Method: Sit in any meditative pose. Perform Chin Mudra and put on the knees. Palms of both the hands face should be upwards.

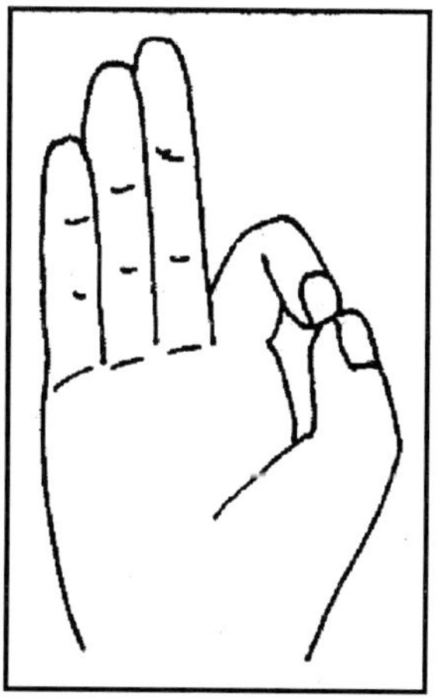

Both mudras should be performed while practising meditation or pranayama.

Benefits

- Chin mudra and Gyana mudra are simple but important psycho-neural finger locks which make meditation and pranayama more powerful.
- The chest area is opened up when the palms face upward in gyana mudra. Sadhaka feels lightness and receptivity.
- When the finger touches the thumb, a circuit is produced which allows the energy that would normally dissipate into the environment to come back in to the body and upto the brain.
- Placing the hands on the knees stimulates a hidden nadi which provides energy at mooladhara chakra.
- Gyana mudra and chin mudra create another pranic circuit which maintains and redirects prana within the body.
- The practice of these mudras is beneficial for alleviating the disorders of the brain.
- These mudras are practised to reduce the instability of the mind and faster our spiritual development.
- This is suitable for meditation.
- This mudra is good for elimination of stress and strains.

3. Veetraga Mudra

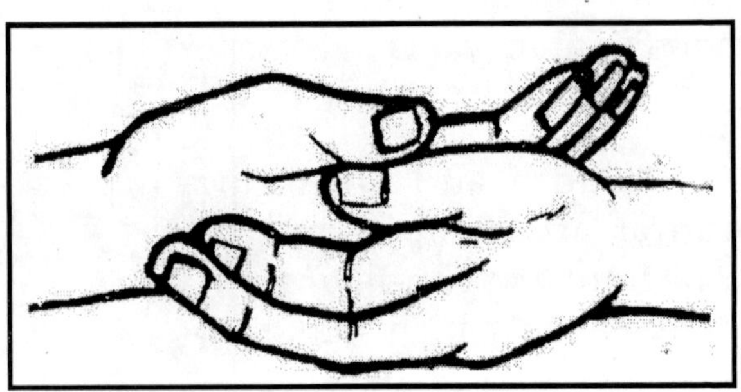

It is called Dhyana mudra, Bhairava mudra, Brahamanjali mudra. This is the purest form of enlightenment and used in meditation.

Method: Sit in any meditative pose like padmasana, sukhasana and vajrasana. Put the left palm near the navel. Right palm will be kept over it. Thumbs will remain on each other touched. Close the eyes and relax the whole body. Sit in a motionless state.

When the left hand is placed on top of the right palm, this practise is called Bhairavi mudra. Bhairavi is the female counter part of Bhairava (force of Shiva).

Note:

- The two hands represent Ida and Pingla and the union of the both palms is the aim of joining with Supreme consciousness.

Benefits

1. It develops feelings of vairagya dispassionate.
2. It balances energy and develops stability.
3. It leads to equation among elements a state of perfect balance.
4. It is helpful in meditation.

4. Sanjeevani Mudra

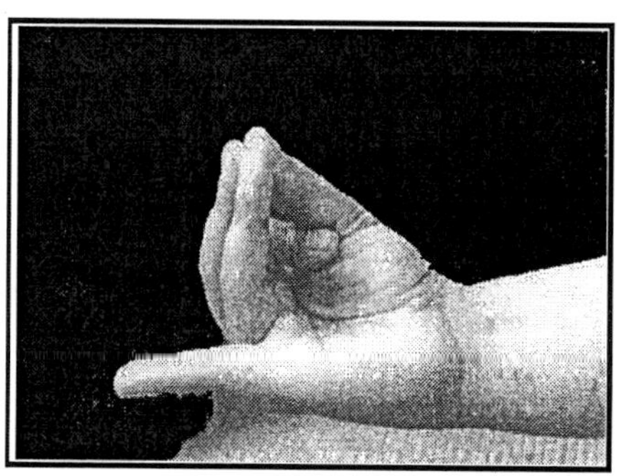

This mudra is called Apanvayu mudra or Hridaya mudra also. It is a combination of two mudras—Vayu mudra and the Apana mudra. The duration of time should be 30 minutes. Concentrate on the breath in the chest area or Anahata Chakra.

Method: Sit in any meditative asana with the head and spine erect. Place the tips of the index fingers at the roots of the thumbs and of the tips of the middle and ring fingers to the tips of the thumbs so that they are all placed together. The little fingers remain straight. Place the hands on the knees with the palms facing upward. Close the eyes and relax the whole body. Keeping it motionless.

Benefits

1. It removes gas, acidity, teeth pain and wind diseases.
2. Heart becomes strong. Heart pain, and engina, low rhythm of heart and broken heart beat get cured.
3. This mudra diverts the flow of prana from the hands to the heart area.
4. It improves the Vitality of the physical heart.

5. This mudra helps to release pent-up emotion and unburden the heart. It may be practised during emotional conflict and crisis.
6. Body and nerves are purified.
7. Constipation and piles get alleviated.
8. Blockage of urinary track and disorders of kidneys are removed.

5. Yonimudra

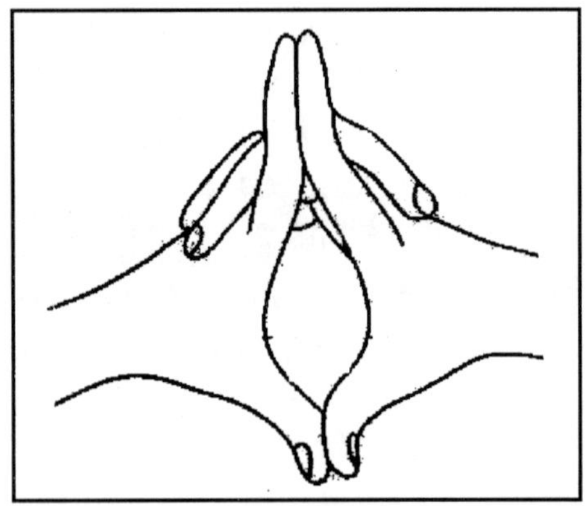

Method: Sit in a meditative pose keeping the head and spine straight. Keep the palms of the hands together with the fingers and thumbs straight and pointing away from the body. Keeping the pads of the index fingers together, turn the little, ring and middle fingers inwards so that the backs of the fingers are touched. Interlock the three last fingers (little, ring and middle). Bring the thumbs towards the body and join the pads of the fingers together to form the base of a yoni shape.

Benefits

1. Placing the tips of the index fingers and thumbs together further intensifies the flow of prana.

2. This mudra makes the body and mind more stable in meditation and develops greater concentration, awareness and internal physical relaxation.
3. It helps balancing the energies in the body.
4. It helps balance the activities of the right and left hemispheres of the brain.
5. It redirects prana back into the body which would otherwise be dispersed.

Note: I like this mudra very much.

6. Shambhavi Mudra

This is the practice of eye brow centre gazing. It is called Bhrumadhya Dristi also. Shambhavi means Parvati Shambhu means lord Shiva. It is an integral part of kriya yoga. It is a powerful method of awakening Agya (Ajna) Chakra. It should be performed under the guidance of a guru. I learnt it under the guidance of Swami Bhaskarananda Paramhansa of Sawai Madhopur (Rajasthan). I used to practised the same for 45 minutes in Padmasana. It can be practise in Simhasana the lion pose.

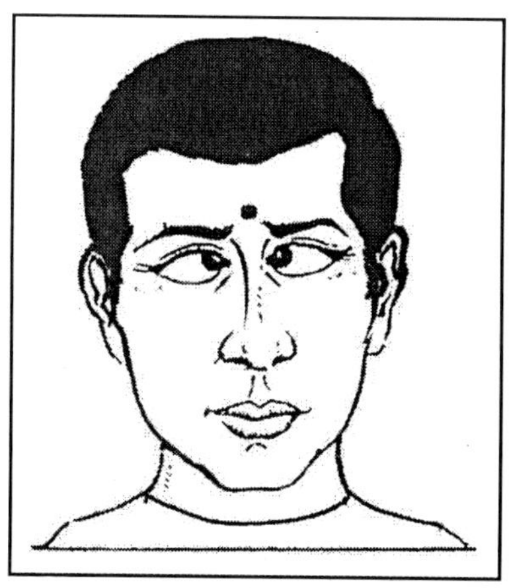

Method: Sit in any comfortable meditative pose. Keep the head and spine erect. Place the hands on the knees in either chin or gyana mudra Close the eyes and relax the whole body specially the face. Open the eyes and look ahead at a fixed point. Keep the body still. Focus on the eyebrow centre for a few seconds at first. Relax the strain. Close the eyes and relax them. Meditate on Chidakash, the dark space in front of the closed eyes. Open the eyes and focus at V shape at eyebrows and coordinate it with the breath. Start with 5-10 rounds. Increase the time of trataka at eyebrows.

Benefits

1. This mudra controls the thoughts and breath.
2. The mind is suspended within a short time and entrance into the psychic world becomes easier.
3. It is a very important method for passing into the astral domain.
4. Insomnia is cured by the practice of this mudra.
5. Shambhavi Mudra strengthens the eye muscles and releases accumulated strain in this area.
6. It calms the mind removing emotional stress and anger.
7. It balances and tones up the working of pineal gland.

Note:

- Release the mudra if any tension is experienced.
- If the nerves are weak and there is strain retinal detachment can take place.

- People suffering from glaucoma, diabetic retinopathy, eye operation should not perform this mudra without expert guidance.
- After mastering shambhavi mudra with open eyes. It may be performed. With the eyes closed. This is a more powerful practice.

7. Nose Tip Gaze

It is called 'Nasagra-Drishti and 'Agochari Mudra' also. It activates mooladhara chakra by gazing at the tip of the nose.

Method: Sit in any meditative pose. Keep the hands on the knees in gyana/chin mudra. Close the eyes and relax he body. Open the eyes and focus them on the nose tip you can see 'V' shaped image. Concentrate on the apex of the 'V'. After a few seconds, close the eyes and relax them before repeating the practice. Continue it upto 5 minutes. Keep the breathing normal. Until the eyes have adjusted to the downward gaze. Later the practice can be combined with antar kumbhaka. Close the eyes and let the breathing be normal. Do palming in the end.

Benefit

1. Nose tip gazing is an excellent method for calming anger and disturbed state of mind.
2. It develops the concentration power of an individual.
3. It awakens Mooladhara chakra.
4. It takes the sadhaka into the psychic and spiritual planes of consciousness.

Note:

- Don't strain the eyes in any way.
- It can be practised at any time of the day but in the morning and before going to bed in the night is beneficial.
- The aim of this practice is to create power of introspection.
- Those suffering from depression should avoid this practice.
- It may be difficult at first to focus the eyes on the nose tip. In this situation, hold the index finger up at the arms length from the eyes and focus your gaze on it. Bring the finger towards the nose slowly keeping the gaze steadily fixed upon it. When the finger touches the tip of the nose the eyes should still be focused on the finger. Bring the focus of the eyes to the nose tip. Afterwards, the practice will be natural and effortless without any strain.

8. Khechari Mudra

The word khechari comes from the Sanskrit roots kha means **'sky'** and **chary** means 'one who moves'. Khechari mudra is associated with amrita the nectar/elixir of life which is recreated from Bindu a point situated at the posterior fontanel and then collected in vishuddhi chakra. This mudra is also called Nabho mudra. In Nabho mudra you have to look at the middle space of the eye brows also. Nabho mudra is complete before when you achieve perfection over Shambhavi mudra and one is able to twist the tongue backwards and touch the soft palete.

Method: Sit in any meditative asana. Padmasana is the best pose. Keep the hands on knees in gyana mudra close the eyes. Relax the body. Fold the tongue upward and backward so that the lower surface lies in sweet contact with the upper palate. Stretch the top of the tongue backward as far as it is comfortable. Practise ujjayi pranayama. Breathe slowly and deeply. Hold the tongue in the state as for as possible. Irritation may be felt in the beginning but with the practice it will be all right. When the tongue becomes tired, relax it and then repeat the practice.

Benefits

1. This mudra has two fold benefits. One is related to spiritual aspect, the other is concerned with physiology.
2. When the tongue is turned upward and the position is maintained for several minutes, the subsidiary glands begin to secrete. This salivary juice is very good for the appetite and maintainance of youth and lusture on the face

3. Khechari mudra stimulates a number of pressure points located in the vicinity of the mouth and the nasal cavity. These points influence the toning of the whole body.
4. A number of glands also get massaged stimulating the recreation of certain hormones and the saliva.
5. This mudra controls the sensations of hunger and thirst.
6. It induces in a striver a state of inner calm and stillness.
7. It is beneficial for inner healing.
8. Khechari combined with Ujjayi pranayama is useful for women in labour.
9. This mudra stimulates the prana and helps in awakening the kundalini shakti.

Note:

- It should be taught right from an early age of 12-16 years. First the tongue has to be massaged with a piece of cloth by gently stretching it, and pulling it from side to side. Cut the tongue thread with a sharp and sterilized blade. Rub the turmeric powder or rock salt powder on the wound. The process of 'milking', i.e. rubbing and stretching, is done every day. Cutting is done on alternative days or every few days by an expert only. Adopting this process the tongue may reach to the eyebrow centre. It takes many years of practice to achieve perfection. This is a Hatha yoga practice.

  Rajyoga practice is very simple—it is done by rolling and turning the tongue backward and of performing Ujjayi pranayama.

- Gradually reduce the respiration rate over a period of months until the number of breaths becomes 5 or 6 in a minutes.
- Practise for 5 to 10 minutes in every sitting.
- During the practice concentrate on the throat or at the vishuddhi chakra.
- If a bitter secretion is tasted, discontinue the practice of the mudra.
- If one suffers from tongue nulcers and other common mouth ailments then don't perform this practice.

9. Kaki Mudra

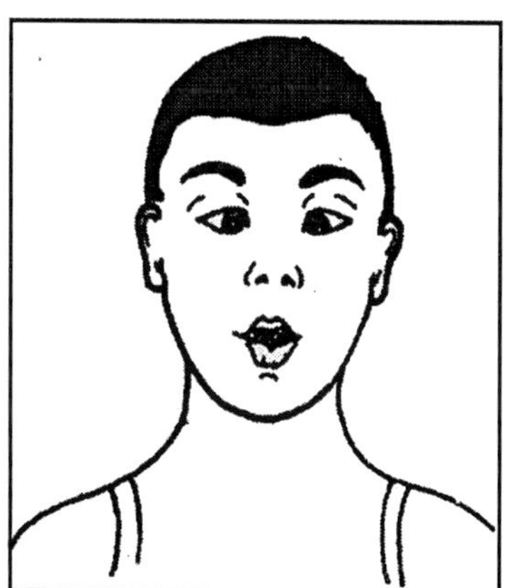

The word kaki means 'crow'. During inhalation the mouth is shaped like a crow's beak. It is said the regular practice of this mudra leads one to a disease free long life. This mudra is a type of pranayama.

Method: Sit in any meditative pose. Put the hands on the knees in gyana mudra or chin mudra. Close the eyes and relax the whole body. Open the eyes and perform the Nasikagra Dristi by focusing both the eyes on the nose tip. Don't blink the eyes throughout the practice. Drink the air slowly through the mouth gradually. The tongue should be relaxed. At the end of inhalation close the lips and exhale slowly through the nose. Repeat the process for 3 to 5 minutes.

Benefits

1. The kaki mudra is an eliminator of many diseases.
2. Kaki mudra cools the body and mind and soothes mental tension.
3. It purifies the blood and controls the high blood pressure.
4. It improves the digestive system.
5. It helps in the development of the mystic vision.

Note:

- Avoid the strain over eyes.
- Be aware of the flow and sound of the breath, and fixing of gaze on the nose tip.
- Perform Kaki mudra after a heating pranayama.
- It keeps the heat balance in the body.
- It can be performed at any time but morning and night time is more suitable.
- It should not be practised in cold weathers.
- This mudra should not be practised in a polluted atmosphere.
- People suffering from depression, low blood pressures and chronic constipation should avoid practising this mudra.
- When eyes get tired, relax them for as long as necessary before recommencing the practice.

10. Bhujangini Mudra

It is called cobra respiration also. Bhujangini means female snake.

Method: Sit in any meditative pose. Close the eyes and relax the whole body especially the abdomen. Push the chin forward and up a little. Drink the air by opening and expanding the mouth a little. Draw it into the stomach, not the lungs, in a series of gulps as through drinking water. Expand the stomach as much as possible. Hold the air inside for as long as comfortable, then expel it by belching. Repeat 3 to 5 rounds, For specific ailments it may be repeated more often.

Benefits

1. All the disorders of the stomach and its chronic ailments are cured by this mudra.
2. Bhujangini Mudra rejuvenates the oesphagus walls and the glands recreate the digestive juices.
3. Retaining air in the stomach enables the sadhaka to float in water for long periods.

Note: This mudra may be practised at any time but is particularly powerful when performed after the Shankhaprakshalana.

11. Bhoochari Mudra

It is allied to nasikagra drishti and Shambhavi mudra, all the three being forms of Trataka. This mudra may be performed as a preparation for meditation or dharana. It is a gazing into nothingness.

Method: Sit in any meditative pose with the head and spine straight and the left hand in gyana/chin mudra resting on the left knee. Close the eyes and relax the body.

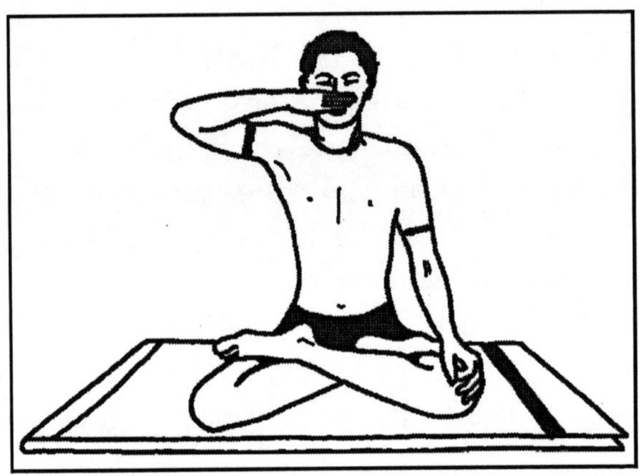

Open the eyes and raise the right hand in front of the face. The elbow should point to the side of the body. Hold the hand horizontally, palm down with the fingers together. The side of the thumbs should be in contact with the top of the upper lip. Focus the eyes on the tip of the little finger and gaze at it intently for a minute or so without blinking or flickering the eyes. Concentrate on the little finger tip. Remove the hand but continue to gaze into nothingness at the place where the little finger was in front of the face. Try not to blink. Be aware any thought space only. Continue the practice for 5 to 10 minutes.

Benefits

1. Benefits are the same as that of practicing nasikagra and Shambhavi mudras.
2. This mudra develops the power of concentration, and memory.
3. It tranquillises and introverts the mind.

4. It is particularly beneficial for people who are angry men and need cooling of mind.

Note: Bhoochari mudra may be practised in any position and at any place, but it would be better to perform facing a blank wall or an open space such as the sky or a still water place. This ensures that there are no visual for disturbances to divert the attention of the practicer.

12. Akashi Mudra

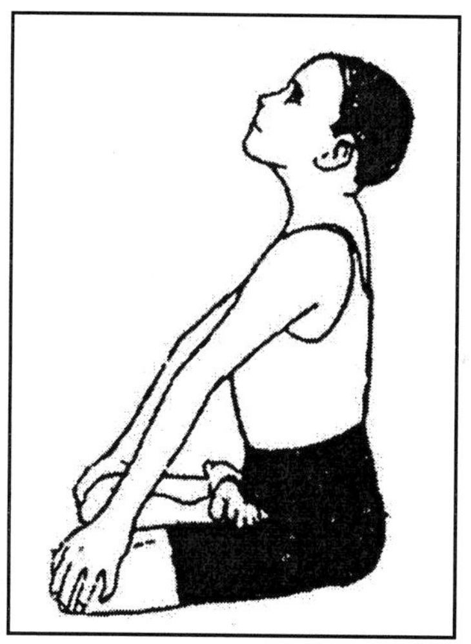

This mudra is also trataka type mudra to achieve Dharana or Meditation with open eyes. The Sadhaka must be completely familiar with the practice of Ujjayi, khechari and Shambhavi before commencing Akashi mudra.

Method: Sit in any meditative pose. Close the eyes and relax the body for some time. Fold the tongue back against the palate in khechari mudrra. Practise Ujjayi pranayama and Shambhavi mudra. Simultaneously bend the head backward at about 45° degrees. Straighten the arms and lock the elbows pressing the knees with the hands. Breathe slowly and deeply in ujjayi. Continue for as long as possible. Bend the elbows and release Khechari and Shambhavi mudras stop ujjayi and raise the head to the upright position. Breathe normally for a few seconds and be aware of the inner space before starting the next round. Begin with 1 to 5 rounds. Maintain the final position for as long as possible. Increase the length interval in the mudra very slowly. Concentrate on Agya (ajna) chakra.

Benefits

1. In this mudra the benefits are manyfold as included in practice of Kumbhaka. Ujjayi, Shambhavi, Khechari and Nasika drishti mudras.
2. It can induce calmness and tranquillity.
3. This mudra bestows controls over the senses.
4. It stops the thought process.
5. It induces higher states of consciousness.

Note:

- If faintness is felt stop the practice.
- This technique must be learned slowly and under the expert guidance.
- One, who is suffering from H.B.Pressure vertigo, brain disorders, epilepsy should not practise this mudra.
- Akashi mudra may also be practised with breath retention.
- Inhale while bending the head backwards. Hold the breath inside in the final position. exhale while slowly raising the head to the starting position.

13. Shanmukhi Mudra

The word Shanmukhi is combined with two words. **Shan** means 'seven' and **mukhi** means gates or faces. In this mudra the seven doors viz. two ears, two eyes, two nostrils and one mouth are closed. This practice is also known as Baddha yoni asana, Devi mudra, prangmukhi mudra the gesture of inner focusing and Shambhavi mudra.

Method: Sit in any meditative asana. Place a small cushion beneath the perineum to provide pressure in this area. Keep the spine and head straight. Close the eyes and place the hands on the knees relax the body.

Raise the arms in front of the face with the elbows pointing sideways, gently close the ears with the thumbs the eyes with the index fingers, the middle fingers on the nostrils, keep the ring fingers above the upper lip and the little fingers below the lower lip together.

Release the pressure of the middle fingers and open the nostrils. Inhale slowly and deeply using full yogic breathing. Close the nostrils with middle fingers. Retain the breath inside for comfortable position. Try to hear any manifestation of sound in the area of Agya chakra or Anahata chakra. After some time, release the pressure of the middle fingers and breathe out slowly. This is one round. Repeat the next rounds. Come back keeping the eyes closed, be aware of external sounds and the physical body.

Benefits

1. This mudra helps in the treatment of eyes, nose and throat infections and alleviates vertigo.
2. Mentally, it balances the internal and external awareness.
3. Spiritually, it induces the state of Pratyahara or sense withdrawal.
4. The mind becomes calm, the nadi becomes clear.
5. It is helpful in awakening of the kundalini.

Note:

- At first there may be no sound or a confused jumble of sounds. This may take a few weeks of practice. As sensitivity develops, another fainter sound will be heared behind it. There are ten sounds you may hear through the right ear in regular practise.
- This is a practice of Laya yoga. Mind becomes silent, pure and clear voiced.
- Those who have been practising nadi shodhana pranayama regularly will find this practice easier.
- Practise for 5 to 10 minutes in the beginning and gradually increase the practise upto 30 minutes.

- Concentrate on Bindu, Agya and Anahata chakras.
- The best time of practice is early in the morning or late in the night.
- People suffering from depression should avoid this practice.

14. Unmani Mudra

The word unmani literally means 'No mind' or 'not thinking' or 'the state of thoughtlessness' or meditation or 'beyond' the world of thoughts.

Method: Sit in any comfortable meditative pose. Open the eyes fully but without straining. Inhale deeply and hold the breath in side. Focus the awareness at Bindu in the back of the head for a few seconds. Breathe out and let the awareness descending with the breath from Bindu to root chakra concentrating on all the chakras in the spine. The eyes should close slowly. Inhale deeply and begin the next round. Continue for 5 to 10 minutes.

Benefits

1. Unmani mudra is a simple method that brings a meditative state.
2. It also calms general stress and agitation.

Note:

- When the eyes are open they should not receive any outer impressions.
- Be in Shunyawastha (Aman state /No mind)

15. Vajroli/Sahajoli Mudra

The word vajroli is derived from the Sanskrit root **Vajra** and **sahajoli** from the root of sahaj, meaning 'spontaneous, oli means 'to fly up'. Vajra nadi connects reproductive organs with the brain.

Method: Sit in any comfortable meditative asana, placing hands on the knees with gyana/chin mudra. Close the eyes and relax the body. Concentrate on urethra. Inhale and hold the breath in and try to draw the urethra upward. This muscle action is like to holding back an intense urge to urinate. Hold the contraction for as long as possible. Exhale, release the contraction and relax. Practise twice more.

Benefits

1. Vajroli/Sahajoli mudra regulates the entire uro-genital system, correcting in continence and recurrent urinary tract infections.
2. It helps also to overcome psycho sexual conflict and unwanted sexual thoughts.
3. Sahajoli corrects urine prolapse.
4. Vajroli balances testosterone levels and the sperm count and gives control over premature ejaculation.
5. It also helps correct impotence by toning the endocrine system and local energy structures.
6. Benign prostatic highpertrophy, a disorder that troubles 80% of men in the later part of life, is prevented.

Note:

- Isolating the muscles of the urethra.
- Begin with 3 contractions and slowly increase up to 10-15 rounds.
- Concentrate on swadhisthana chakra.
- Keep the focus on the genitals.

- Avoid generalized contraction of the pelvic region which occurs spontaneously.
- This mudra may be practised at any time preferably when the stomach is empty.
- Vajroli/Sahajoli mudra should not be practised by those who are suffering from urethritis (infection and inflammation of the urethra) as the rotation and pain may increase.

16. Vipareeta Karani Mudra

Vipareeta means 'inverted' and karani means 'dong'. It is a kriya.

Method: Lie flat on the back with arms straight and close to the body, facing downward. While inhaling raise the legs together and place the palms on the waist, balancing the body on the shoulder blades and the hands. The chest should not press against the chin. Now inhale deeply and slowly with ujjayi pranayama. Feel the breathe and consciousness moving from Manipura chakra to Vishuddhi chakra. While exhaling, maintain the awareness at Vishuddhi chakra. At the end of exhalation, immediately bring the awareness back to Manipura chakra and repeat the same process. Practise 5 to 7 seconds or until discomfort arises. Gradually increase the number of rounds upto 20 over a period of months. Take breathing spontaneously. Come back and relax.

Benefits

1. Vipareeta Karani mudra improves the blood circulation in the abdomen, chest, neck and brain region.
2. It tones up the lungs, cardiac muscles, kidneys, liver, spleen and the inner surface system of the stomach.
3. The digestive system is helped to function better.
4. It is an excellent mudra for varicose veins and piles.
5. The posture induces quietness, stillness, creativity and care as the cooling, soothing effects of the moon is the base of this inverted pose.
6. In this kriya, the energy (shakti) easily flows from the lower centres to the higher meditation centres in the brain.
7. It balances hypoactive thyroid and acts as a preventative for cough, cold, sore throat and bronchial disorders.
8. It stimulates the appetite and digestion and helps to relieve constipation.
9. Regular practice prevents atherosclerosis by restoring vascular tone and elasticity.

10. It relieves prolapse, haemorrhoids hernia.
11. Ida and pingla nadis become vibrant, balanced and active.

Note:

- Vipreeta Karani Mudra should be practised daily early in the morning.
- Concentrate on Manipura, Vishuddhi and breathing movement.
- Perform it before meditation.
- Don't perform after vigorus exercise or for at least 3 hours after meals.
- Do a backward bending asana such as matsyasana, bhujangasana or ustrasana after this mudra.
- The metabolic rate may increase when this mudra is practised for periods of haff an hour or more. If this happens, food intake should be accordingly.
- People suffering from high blood pressure, heart diseases enlarged thyroid or excessive toxins in the body should not perform this mudra.

17. Yoga Mudra

Yoga mudra unites the individual consciousness with the Supreme consciousness, the outer nature with the inner nature.

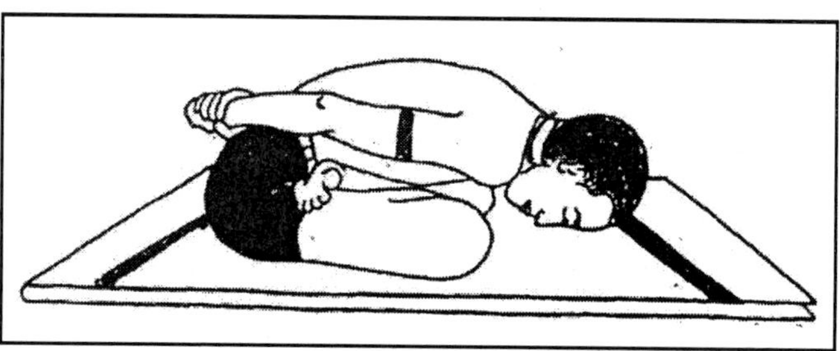

Yoga mudra can be done in any meditative posture. Including Vajrasana, but Padmasana is more beneficial.

Method: Sit in Padmasana keeping the spine straight. Take hold of right wrist with left hand behind the back, concentrate on Mooladhara and perform the Mool Bandha. Inhale slowly and feel the breathe gradually rising form Mooladhara to Agya (Ajana) chakra. Retain the breathe for a few seconds and concentrate on Agya chakra. Exhale slowly while bending forward. Put the forehead on the floor as the air is fully expelled from the lungs. Simultaneously, feel the breathe gradually move downward from Agya chakra to Mooladhara chakra. Retain the breath outside for a few seconds while concentrating on Mooladhara chakra. Inhales, raise the trunk to the vertical position and be aware of the breathe moving upward from Mooladhara to Agya chakra. Remaining in the erect position, hold the breath for a few seconds while concentrating on Agya (Ajna) chakra. Exhale slowly moving the awareness back down the spine with the breathe to Mooladhara chakra. This is one round. Perform 3 to 10 rounds.

Benefits

1. It relieves constipation and balances the vital energy between vishuddha and mooladhara chakras.
2. The extra pressure on the abdominal muscles improves the peristaltic movement of the intestines.
3. It strengthens the prostate glands and reproductive organs.

4. This mudra removes abdominal disorders and helps in concentration.
5. All the parts of urinary system get toned up and their functional capability also improves considerably.
6. Our spine becomes flexible.
7. It eliminates excess of fat from the lower abdomen and the waist line.
8. This practice gives all the benefits of yogamudrasana in addition.
9. It is an excellent preparatory practice for meditation.
10. It calms the adrenal system, engendering a sense of relaxation.
11. It relieves anger and tension inducing tranquillity.
12. It develops awareness and control of psychic energy.

Note:

- The respiration should be as slow as possible without any strain.
- Concentrate on relaxing the back and abdomen along with the breathing.
- Men suffering from sciatica, H.B. Pressure, pelvic inflammatory disease or any other serious abdominal ailment should avoid this practice.
- People who can't sit in Padmasana can sit in Sukhasana or Vajrasana.
- If adopting Vajrasana, bend forward into Shashankasana.

18. Pashinee Mudra

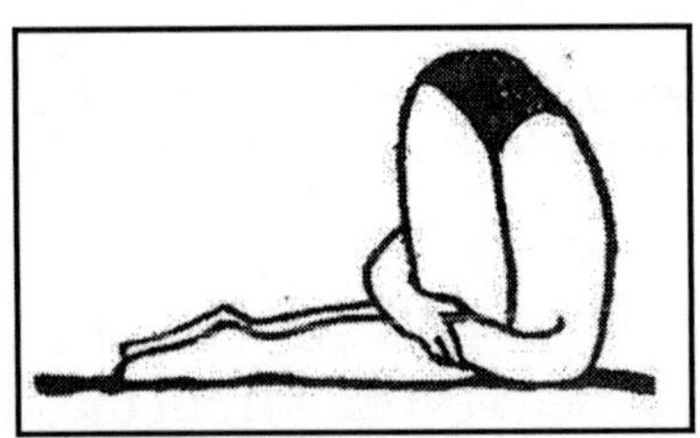

Pash means 'noose'/Bandhan pashini means 'bound in a noose'.

Method: Lie flat on the back with the legs and feet together, arms beside the thighs. While inhaling, raise both the legs together pushing them above and behind the head so as to touch the floor. Bend the knees and bring them towards the face. Keep the knees close to the ears and shoulders as in karnapeedasana. Hold the wrists tightly around the back of the legs and try to bring them closer to the ears. Maintain this position as long as possible and keep the respiration slow and deep. Then return to the starting position and relax in shavasana.

Benefits

1. Pashinee Mudra stimulates and tones up the Medulla oblengata, the nervous system and the vertebral column.
2. It reduces excess fat of the abdomen.
3. It controls diabetes.
4. It improves the working efficiency of liver, spleen, kidneys and intestines.
5. It induces pratyahara, and sense withdrawal.
6. It stretches the spine and the back muscles.

7. It stimulates all the spinal nerves in and around the spine.
8. It massages all the abdominal organs.

Note:

- Concentrate on the stretched neck, Mooladhara/ Vishuddhi chakra.
- This mudra should be followed by a back bending asana.
- People suffering from any spinal ailment should avoid this mudra.

19. Manduki Mudra

Manduki means 'frog'. This mudra is so name because the sitting posture resembles a frog at rest. It is a Kriya.

Method: Sit in Bhadrasan with the toes pointing outward. If it is not comfortable to sit then you can sit in Bhadrasana with the toes pointing inwards. The buttocks rest on the floor. If this is still too difficult, place a folded blanket underneath the buttocks to apply firm pressure to the perineum, stimulating the region of Mooladhara chakra. Place the hands on the knees keep the head and spine erect. Close the eyes and relax the body. This is the Manduki asana.

After some time, open the eyes and perform 'Nasi kagra Drishti'. If the eyes become tired relax them for a minute or so. Continue the practice for about 5 minutes until the mind and senses become introvert.

Benefits

1. This practice affects the brain centres related to mens most deep rooted instrincts and drives.
2. It calms the disturbances and fluctuation of the mind.
3. It balances Ida and Pingla nadis.
4. Perfection of this practice leads directly to meditation.
5. It awakens Mooladhara Chakra. It should be practised in mild light so that the tip of the nose can be seen.

Note:

- The simple method is to swallow the saliva moving the tongue tip around in the closed mouth. It develops the digestion, concentration and bestows peace of the practicer.

20. Maha Mudra

Method: Sit erect, stretch the legs together forward. Bend the left leg and press the left heel firmly into the perineum, the location point of Mooldhara Chakra. The right leg remains outstretched. Perform the Khechari and inhale deeply. While exhaling bend forward and catch the right big toe with both hands. Keep the head straight. Keep the spine also erect. Perform the Shambhavi Mudra and Moola Bandha. Hold the breath inside. Move the concentration from Agya Chakra to

Moola Dhara for 1/2 seconds. Continue the rotation as long as the breath can be comfortably held. Release Shambhavi Mudra and Moola Bandha. Exhale slowly. Return to the upright position. It is one round, Repeat three rounds. Change the leg and complete three rounds with the right leg folded, keep both the legs outstreched. Again practise three rounds.

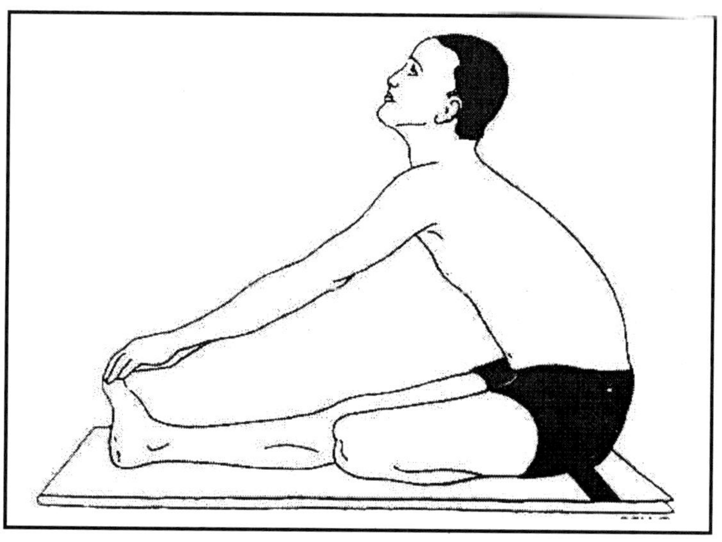

Benefits

1. Mahamudra gives a natural massage to the cardiac muscles.
2. It helps in prostate glands and seminal weakness.
3. By the practice of this mudra the combined benefits of Shambhavi, Moola Bandha and Kumbhaka are gained.
4. The abdominal disorders are removed.
5. Digestion and assimilation of food are stimulated.
6. Mental depression is eliminated smoothly.

7. It stimulates the energy circuit linking Mooladhara with Agya Chakra.
8. The whole body is charged with prana.
9. It is very helpful in meditation.

Note: People suffering from HB pressure or heart ailments should not do this mudra without prior purification of the body.

◆ ◆ ◆

7

The Six Purificational Practices

> "When fat and mucus is excessive, the shatkarmas or six cleansing techniques should be practised before pranayama. Others, in whom the 'doshes' (phlegm, wind and bile) are balanced, need not do them."
>
> *Hatha yoga Pradipika (2/21)*

What is Shatkarma?

The ancient yogis were interested in the matter of personal hygiene and they developed certain techniques to rid the body of impurities. The six main purificational practices of yoga are: Neti, Dhauti, Basti, Trataka, Nauli and Kapalbhati. These all are called Shatkarma. These powerful kriyas should never be learned from books or taught by inexperienced men or women. The six Shatkarmas are as follows:

1. **Neti:** It is a cleansing process of the nasal passage. It is performed in two ways—jalaneti and sutra-neti.
2. **Dhauti:** Dhauti is divided into three main groups: internal dhauti (antar dhauti), head

cleansing (shirsa dhauti) and thoracic cleansing (hrid dhauti). To wash internal part of elimentary canal from mouth to the anus are divided into four parts:

(*a*) Shankhaprakshalana (varisar dhauti) cleansing of the intestines.

(*b*) Agnisar Kriya (vahnisar dhauti), activating the digestive fire.

(*c*) Kunjal (vamandhauti), cleansing the stomach with water.

3. **Nauli Kriya:** It is a method of massaging and strengthening the abdominal organs.
4. **Basti:** It is a method of washing and toning the large intestine.
5. **Trataka:** It is a method of developing concentration power.
6. **Kapalbhati:** It is a breathing exercise (pranayama) for purifying the frontal region of brain to shine the kapal.

Here are given these techniques in details with precautions and advice.

1. NETI

(A) Sutra Neti

Nasal cleansing technique through sutra (thread):

Material required

Sterilization facility, Rubber Catheter No: 3-4

Previous Practice

Kapalbhati, Jalaneti

Technique

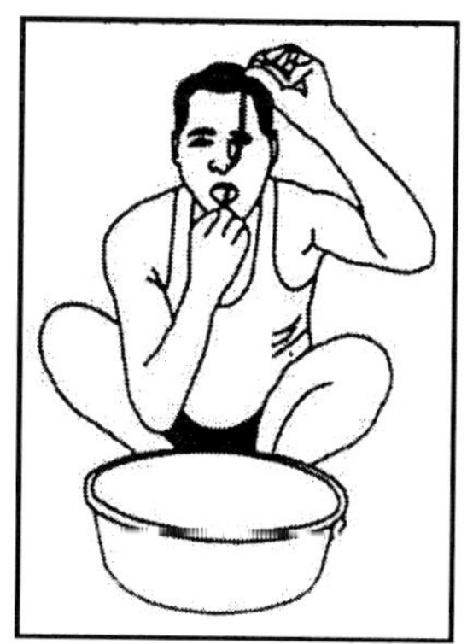

Sutraneti is practised by using thread traditionally. But in modern times a small rubber catheter No. 3 or 4 is used. It can be sterilized and used again. Rubber catheter should be lubricated with butter or mustard oil.

Take any comfortable standing or sitting position, or squat. Relax the whole body. Tilt the head slightly back. Open the mouth and breathe in. Insert the narrow end of the catheter or waxed end of the sutra (thread) into which ever nostril is flowing more freely. As the thread is inserted twist it so that it enters the nostril easily.

Eventually feel for the end of the tube/sutra emerging at the back of the throat. Insert index finger and middle finger or thumb. Catch the end of neti and pullout the blunt end of the neti through the mouth smoothly. Hold the ends with the hands and gently pull the catheter backwards and forwards. So that it gently massages the nasal cavity. Perform this for 5 times and gently remove the tube/sutra neti through mouth. Repeat with the other nostril.

Precautions Sutra/Rubber Neti

1. Check the rubber tube. Don't use the catheter with a cut or damage at the ends or in any other part of it.
2. Sterilize the rubber catheter before use.
3. Practise in empty stomach (to avoid vomiting). Preferable time is morning.

4. Nails must be cut neatly and hands thorougly cleaned.
5. Press the nose upwards and insert the tube parallel to the palate very smoothly otherwise the delicate nasal passage may get injured or the tube may get struck in concha (Shankha).
6. Keep the head in correct direction and mouth open.
7. Inhalation through the nose in which the catheter is being inserted by closing the other nostril with fingers and slight twist of the catheter will help for the practice but never give any jerk or apply undue force.
8. When the catheter is pulled in and out of the nostril and mouth and brought out through the mouth for removing. It should be done smoothly with ones own speed.
9. Persons suffering from blocking of the nose, congestion in nose, swelling of nasal mucosa, nasal polyps, and deviated nasal septum should practise sutra neti under proper guidance.
10. Apply lubricant (like ghee/oil) on the rubber tube or practise jalaneti before practising rubber neti that makes the practice easier. It will be better if the sadhaka drops the one/two drops in the nostrils before going to bed.
11. Avoid spectacles, one may get sneezing when the tube touches the sensitive olfactory mucosa present in the roof of the nose.
12. After the practice if one feels dry, sore and raw in the nasal passage introduce few drops of ghee or milk into the nasal passage by holding the head back.

13. After practice sterilize the tube/thread neti dry it and keep it safe.
14. With a catheter the practice takes less than 5 minutes with a sutra it takes about 10 minutes. Perform every few days or once a week is more than sufficient.
15. Be aware on relaxing the body and moving the catheter or sutra smoothly and slowly.
16. Sutra neti should be performed before jalaneti as the later will flush out all the impurities and particles in the nose which have been dislodged by sutra neti.
17. It is best not to try sutraneti until jalaneti has been perfected.
18. Those people who suffer from chronic bleeding in the nose should not do sutra neti. Any one with nasal ulcers, polyps and severe malfomations of the nasal septum or turbinates should first seek the advice of a Yoga expert or an Ayurvedic doctor.
19. Sutra neti is much better than catheter.

Benefits

- Sutra neti gives purification of nadis and chakras in the region of forehead (Agya) and throat (Vishuddhi Chakra).
- Neti opens the nasal passage and increases the sensitivity of nasal passage which helps to experience the touch, smell temperature and pressure changes of the air in the nasal passage. It is a beneficial practice for kapalbhati and pranayama.

- It helps to balance the breathing in both the nostrils that is important in relaxation, receptiveness and higher awareness in yoga practices.
- Sutra neti removes the asthma, bestows perfect vision. It cleanses the frontal sinuses. The body is brought under control and is free from disorders of phlegm.

(B) Jala Neti

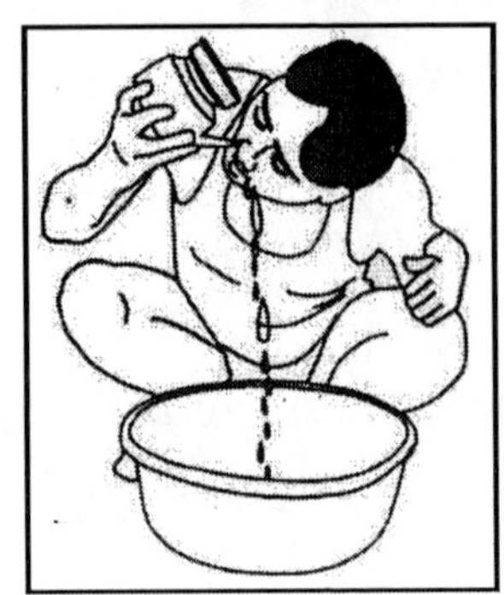

Material Used

Jalaneti pot

Luke warm (salt mixed) water

Towel and tub

Previous Practice

Kapalbhati and forceful fast nasal sneezing (alternate nostril)

Technique

Body Position

Jalaneti can be practised either in sitting or in standing position comfortably. One has to slightly bend forward and sideward especially for Jalaneti.

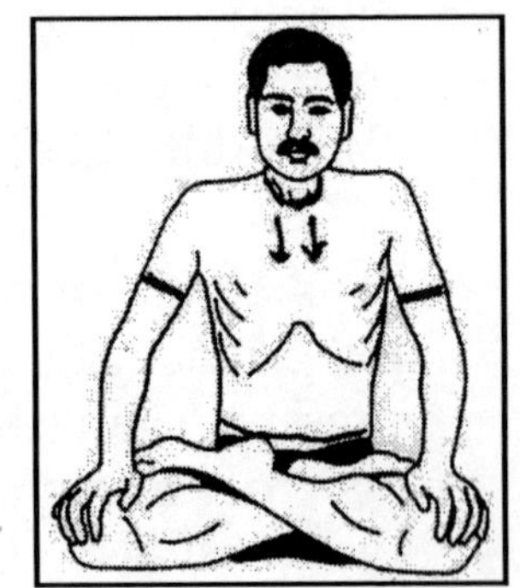

The nozzle of the Jalaneti pot is put in one of the nostrils and the head is gradually tilted to the opposite side till due to gravitational force, water from the neti pot starts flowing through the upper nostril and comes out through the lower. If the head is slightly tilted forward, no water comes in the mouth. Breathing is continued through the mouth during the practice. The same process is repeated through other nostril. Taking the water inside the nose with the help of Jala Neti pot and bring out through the other nostril. The another way is taking water inside the mouth and bringing out through the nose.

After jalaneti kriya kapalbhati (forceful expiration) should be performed. It removes the excess of secretions and water from the nostril passages.

Precautions

1. **Preparation of water:** Water should be clean, fully boiled, then brought into the condition of lukewarm upto 40°C and salt mixed (approximately 5 gram per litre).
2. Clean and check the Jala neti pot before the practice. (Insect, dust or other foreign particles may stick inside).
3. Practise in empty stomach to avoid vomiting sensation. Preferable time is morning.
4. Nails must be cut neatly and hands cleaned thoroughly.
5. **Position of the head:** Nasal passage should be parallel to each other for easy flow of water.
6. Keep your mouth opened and breathe through mouth during the practice; otherwise water may enter into trachea.
7. Mixing of more salt in the water will produce burning sensation and if no salt is mixed in the water it will be painful and difficult for smooth flow of water.

8. Avoid spectacles. One gets sneezing if water touches the sensitive olfactory mucosa present in the roof of the nose. There will be cough if water enters into trachea or bronchial tree.
9. After neti, practise kapalbhati but don't practice forcefully.
10. If Kapalbhati is found not suitable then perform Ujiayi type of breathing (breath in and breath out with slight closure of glottis), otherwise the water remaining behind can give rise to cold, sinusitis and headache.
11. After the practice if one feels dry, sore and raw in the nasal passage introduce few drops of ghee (ghritaneti) or milk (dugdha neti) into the nasal passage by holding head back.
12. The practice should take about 5 minutes. Jalaneti may be practised once daily or as recommended by a yoga instructor/therapist. To relieve severe colds, nasal catarrh or other ailments, it may be performed upto 3 times daily.
13. Be aware of relaxing and positioning the body, making sure no water leaks from nozzle of the neti pot (lota), and on relaxed breathing through the mouth, especially for beginners.
14. Jalaneti is ideally practised in the morning before asanas and pranayamas. If necessary, it may be performed at any time except just after meals.
15. Make sure that the nose is properly dried after the practice, otherwise the nasal passages may become irritated and manifest the symptoms of cold. Don't blow the nose too hard. If force is used, the remaining water may be pushed into the ears.

16. Those people who suffer from chronic bleeding in the nose should not do jala neti without expert advice. If someone is unable to pass the water through the nose he should seek expert advice.
17. Advanced practitioners may suck water up the nostrils directly from a glass or a bowl. It is called ushapan.

Benefits

Jalaneti removes mucus and pollution from the nasal passages and sinuses. It helps to relieve asthma, colds pneumonia, bronchitis, pulmonary T.B. allergies and sinusitis, various disorders of the ears, nose, eyes and throat including myopia, allergic rhinitis, hay fever, deafness, tonsillitis and inflammation of the adenoids and mucus membranes. Mouth breathing in children can be reduced. It increases the beauty of the face. It has a cooling and soothing influence on the brain and is beneficial in the treatment of epilepsy and migraine. It alleviates anxiety, anger and depression, removes drowsiness and makes the head feel light and fresh. Neti helps to awaken Agya Chakra.

2. NAULI

Introduction

Nauli is an abdominal massaging process. In Gheranda Samhita it is called Lauliki. This kriya is related to abdomen. It gives good massage to the abdominal column.

Name

The word 'nauli' comes from the root nala or nali which means a reed or 'hollow stalk' to move hither and thither, rolling and agitation. It rolls, rotates and agitates the entire abdomen and the associated muscles and nerves.

> "With shoulders bent foward one should rotate the abdomen right and left with the speed of fast rotating whirpool. This is called Nauli by the accomplished yogis".
>
> *Hatha yoga Pradipika (2/34)*

Previous Practice

Jalandhara Bandha, Uddiyana Bandha (the raising of the diaphragm) in padmasana, vajrasana, utkatasana, tadagi mudra, vipreeta karani mudra and in standing position.

Technique

Step 1: Madhyama Nauli

(Central abdominal contraction)

Stand with the feet about a metre apart. Take a deep breathe in through the nose and then exhale through the mouth, emptying the lungs as much as possible.

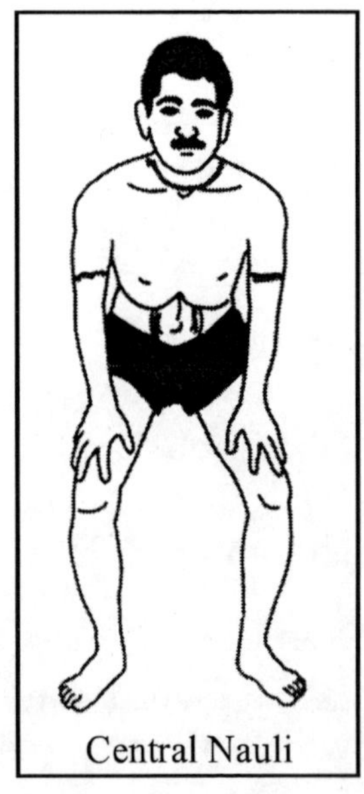
Central Nauli

Bend the knees slightly and lean forward, placing the palms of the hands on the thighs just above the knees. Fingers may point either inward or outward. The weight of the upper body should rest comfortably on this area above the knees. The arms should remain straight. Perform

Jalandhara Bandha while maintaining 'bahir kumbhaka' (external breathe retaintion). Keep the eyes open and watch the abdomen. Suck in the lower abdominal.

Contract the rectus abdomin muscles so that they form a central arch running vertically in front of the abdomen. Contract the muscles as much as possible without straining. Hold the contraction for as long as it is comfortable to hold the breath. Release the contraction, raise the head and return to the upright position.

Inhale slowly and deeply allowing the abdomen to expand. Relax the whole body. This is one round. Relax in the standing position untill the heartbeat returns to normal. Repeat the practice.

Notc: Madhyama nauli should bc pcrfcctcd bcforc proceeding to vama nauli.

Step 2: Vama Nauli

In vama nauli, the left ractus is alone contracted and rolled to the extreme left. At the sametime the right rectus is kept relaxed.

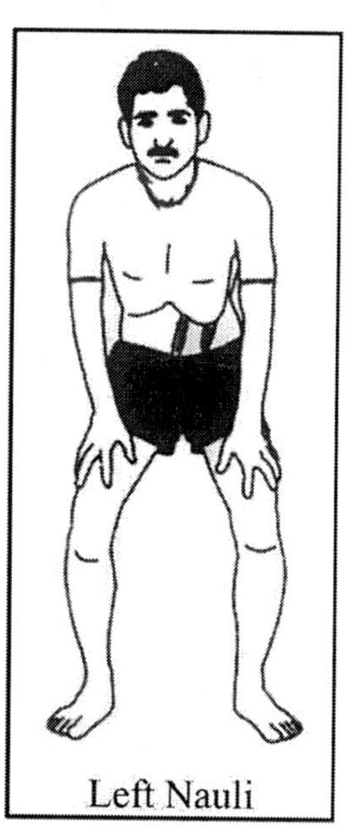

Left Nauli

Step 3: Dakshina Nauli

In Dakshina Nauli the right rectus is alone contracted and rolled to the extreme right while the left rectus is kept relaxed. It is practised from the final stage of Nauli.

Equal weight on both the thighs is given during madhyama Nauli, where as in Dhashina nauli, the practitioner has to bend further forward towards right hand side and slightly stand erect on the left side.

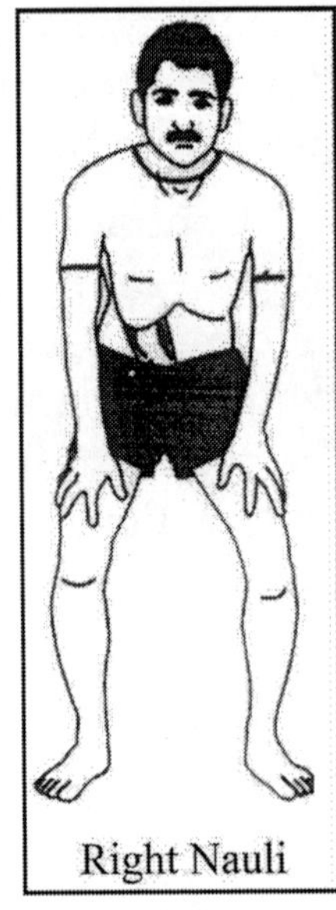
Right Nauli

Step 4: Nauli Chalana

Final stage of Nauli is called Nauli chalana. The abdominal recti muscles are isolated then rolled clockwise and anti-clockwise several times continuously. This requires complete co-operation of abdominal muscles especially the abdominal recti muscles.

Benefits

1. Nauli stimulales the digestive metabolism by increasing peristaltic movements.
2. This is the most effective way of exercising the abdominal organs deeply.
3. It releases deep tensions.
4. It helps to balance the adrenal component of the endocrine system.
5. This practice alleviates constipation, indigestion, nervousness, diarrhoea, acidity, flatulence, depression, hormonal imbalance, sexual and urinary disorders, diabetes, lack of energy and emotional disturbances.
6. Nauli stimulates and purifies manipur chakra, the storehouse of prana.
7. It helps to increase mental clarity and power by harmonising the energy flows in the body.

8. Nauli is a preventive if practised before menstrual cycle to get remedy from dysmenorrhea (difficult and painful menstruation) that occurs due to congestion of blood in the uterus and perineal muscles.

9. Patients suffering from gastric duodenal ulcer, ulcerative collitis, hernia and accute conditions of appendicitis, heart problems, high blood pressure and typhoid fever should not practise nauli.

10. Nauli should not be practised during pragnancy and before the age of puberty.

Precautions

1. Practise nauli in empty stomach.

2. Practise step by step in sequence like doing (*a*) Udd-iyana Bandha (*b*) Madhyama nauli (*c*) Vama and Dakshina nauli (*d*) Nauli chalana.

3. Increase the duration of practice upto the final stage, slowly and very carefully.

4. Whole body is involved during nauli chalana. Don't practise external breathe holding (Bahaya kumbhaka) beyond your capacity.

5. A beginner should not make more than three attempts a day.

6. The excess of practice of nauli may give pain in abdomen and chest. So avoid the excesses.

7. There should be no hurry in any part of the practice including the isolation of recti muscles. Isolation should be complete, easy, painless and without any labour to bring out and withdraw.

8. Relax sufficiently in shavasana after practising kriyas.
9. Take milk to calm down the hunger sensation.
10. Start with 5 rounds of madhyama nauli and work upto 10. Vama and dakshina nauli should be performed together for 5 to 10 rounds each.

    Start abdominal churning with 5 to 10 rotations and slowly increase to 25 rotations gradually.
11. Nauli should only be practised under expert guidance.
12. If any pain is felt in the abdomen during nauli performance, stop the practice immediately. Try again the following day or when the pain subsides.

3. DHAUTI

(A) Vatsara Dhauti

Introduction

It is a cleansing process of intestines with air. This kriya is similar to bhujangini mudra. In bhujangini mudra the air is expelled by belching, whereas in vatsar dhauti it is passed out through the intestine.

Technique

Sit in a comfortable position. Open the mouth and shape the lips like a crows beak. Draw in the air down into the stomach through the open mouth in one sucking action or in a series of gulps, select easy method.

Fill the stomach as much as possible. Then relax completely. Don't try to expel the air. It will come out through the large intestine if its own.

Perform it one/two times a day. This practice may be done at any time during the day but it is most useful just before a large meal. It should not be done during or after meals.

Benefits

- Vatasar dhauti improves the digestive system to work at a more efficient level.
- It removes gas and wind.
- It prevents hyperacidity and heartburn.

(B) Agnisara Kriya

Introduction

It is cleansing process related to abdominal muscles and digestive system. It is called Antar Dhauti also in Gherand Samhita. It gives massage to abdomen and helps for nauli practice.

Name

'Agni means fire' Sara' means essence' 'kriya' means 'action'. Agnisara kriya purifies the digestive system and its associated organs. It is called vahanisara dhauti also.

> " Push the navel against the spine a hundred time. Having, thus, got rid of abdominal diseases, one increases the gastric heat."
>
> *Gheranda Samhita (1-19)*

Materials Required

Peaceful place

Previous Practice

Bahya kumbhaka, uddiyana bandha, kapalbhati

Technique

There are two positions of performing the 'agnisara kriya' as in standing position and vajrasana or padmasana.

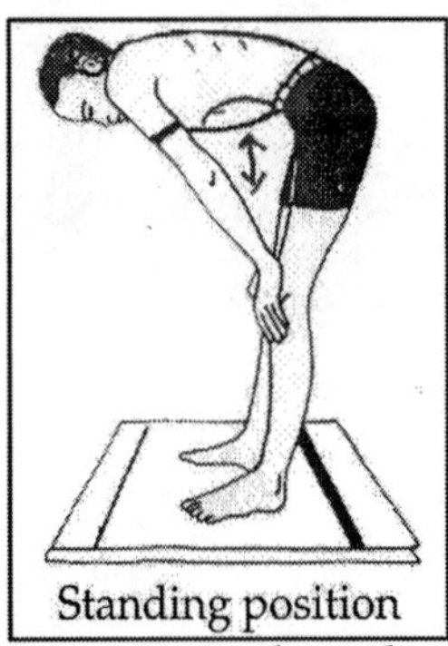
Standing position

Practice in empty stomach either in standing or in sitting position. In standing keep the legs slightly apart, hands on the thighs. Bend forward and breath out and hold it (Bahya kumbhaka). Abdomen goes towards the spine like uddiyana bandha, keeping the abdominal muscles tight move the umbilicus (navals) region forward and backward rhythmically according to the capacity. Raise up and release the abdomen and breathe in. Have few normal breathing like this practice 3 to 4 rounds and increase the strokes upto 100 times gradually.

Siting in Padmasana

Benefits

1. It prevents maladies like constipation, indigestion, hyperacidity, flatulence and sluggishness of liver etc.
2. It increases the gastric fire thus activating the functions of the body.
3. It gives massage to the internal organs viz. liver, pancreas, adrenal glands, kidneys and intestines and improves their efficiency. It relieves constipation.
4. It stimulates the appetite.
5. It stimulates the five pranas, especially the saman and prana.
6. It raises the energy level markedly.
7. It can also alleviate depression, dullness and lethargy.
8. It is used as a preparatory practice for uddiyana bandha and nauli.

Precautions

- Initially practise in standing position then go for practice in sitting position.
- Practise the agnisara kriya with an empty stomach.
- Perfection in Bahya kumbhaka and uddiyana bandha is important.
- Don't perform beyond your capacity.
- Keep the muscle of the abdomen tight during the practise. So that there may be good massage to the internal organs.
- There should not be any pressure in other parts of the body.

- Don't practise if there is any pain in the stomach.
- Agnisara kriya should not be practised during menstrual cycle and pregnancy.
- Contra indicated to heart patients, high blood pressure, chronic asthma patients and old age persons and those who are unable to perform uddiyana bandha (weak persons).
- People suffering from ulcer, hyperacidity, enlargement of spleen and hernia should practise under proper guidance.

(C) Vaman Dhauti

Introduction

Dhauti means cleansing. There are three main types of dhauti Vaman dhauti, Danda dhauti and Vastra dhauti. Vaman means vomiting. As Dhauti means cleaning. So vaman dhauti means cleansing by vomiting. It is also called kunjala or gajakarani.

Material used

Water, salt (after maximum boiling, the water should be filtered).

Previous Practice

Uddiyana Bandha, Nauli Chalana.

Preparation

1. Wash the hands and make sure the nails are carefully trimmed.
2. Prepare about two litres of lukewarm (body temperature) water per person, adding one tea spoonful of salt per litre according to taste.

Technique

Sit in utakatasana. Drink sufficient water about 5 to 6 glasses. So that you may feel sensation of vomiting. Leaning a bit forward, one inserts the three middle fingers into the mouth and tickles the soft palate and pharyngeal wall, water will come out in gushes. Don't take out the fingers till the stomach is totally emptied.

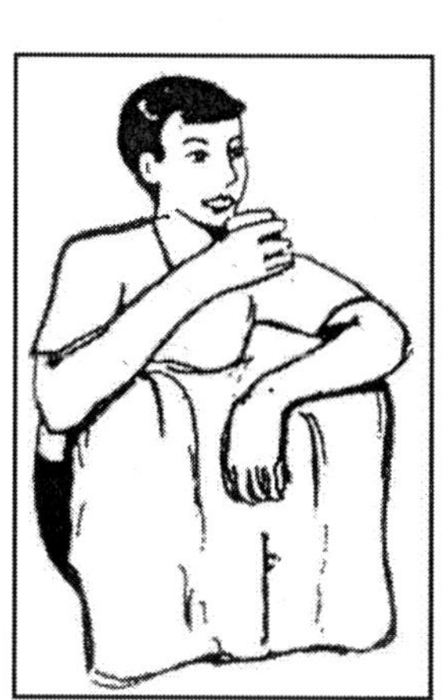

Benefits

1. The problems of indigestion, acidity and gas are overcome.
2. Excess mucus is removed from the body.
3. It helps in removing cough and cold, bronchitis, asthma, and other respiratory ailments.
4. Bad breath is eradicated.
5. It helps to remove heavyness in the heart.
6. It provides purification and awareness of nadis and chakras located in the chest and throat region.

7. It gives concentration to the mind by giving one pointedness and thoughtless state to the mind.
8. Kunjala is helpful in practicing the asanas and pranayama.
9. After kunjala the respiration becomes very smooth and very easy that in turn helps for different yogic practices.

Precautions

1. Water should be clean, salt mixed and used in luke warm condition after boiling it fully. Hands must be clean and nails properly cut.
2. Take proper position, bend forward for vomiting.
3. It should be practised in the morning in empty stomach.
4. Water should not be too cold, as if it would chill the body easily and may hamper the smooth performance of vaman dhauti.
5. If the pressure is created towards down, one will not get vomiting.
6. Ladies should not practise this during menses and pregnancy.
7. Don't practise when there is any injury in pharynx esophagus and stomach.
8. Kunjala should not be practised by those who are suffering from hernia, severe abdominal and chest pains, headache, fever, highblood pressure, heart problems, any serious digestive disorders and acute conditions of any disease.
9. It should only be used to get relief from hyper acidity as it stimulates the gastric juices.

(D) Vastra Dhauti

Introduction

It is a cleansing process related to digestive system, practised with the help of cloth, which is also highly beneficial for respiratory system.

> "One should swallow slowly, as advised by the yoga guru, a wet piece of cloth four fingers (approx 7 cm) in breadth and 6.5 metres long and then draw it out gently. This process is known as vastra dhauti".
>
> *Hatha yoga Pradipika (11/24)*

Previous Practice

Nauli chalana

Material used

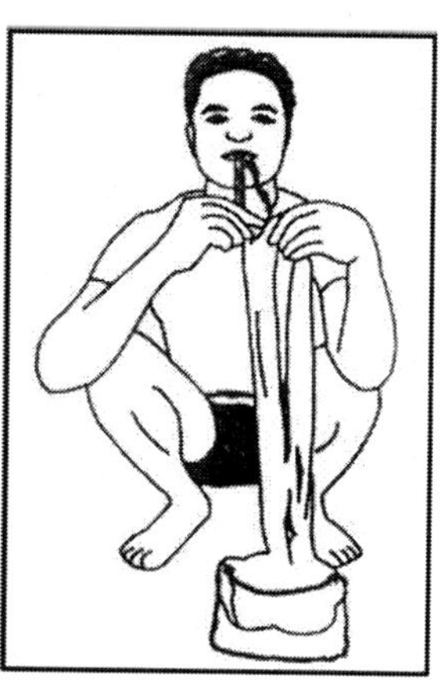

Dhauti cloth; 3 inches in breadth, 22.5 feet in length, a finely woven cotton fabric like muslin (malmal) is suitable. The borders of the cloth are delicately but neatly stitched. Soft white muslin is ideal. Luke warm water, salt, vessel for keeping dhauti.

Technique

Vastra dhauti can be practised either in standing or sitting. Sit in a comfortable position like kagasana or utkatasana. Keep the vastra dhauti pot on the ground about two feet apart.

Take one end of the cloth while the rest of cloth is kept immersed in water and fold (2-3 small folds) forward and backward and place it at the root of the tongue.

The fold should be in such a way that it opens up easily as it moves down the pharynx. Drink a sip of water and swallow the cloth, continue swallowing like food. Don't swallow too quickly because that might induce a vomiting reflex. When the sensation is felt, stop for sometime till the spasm get relieved, then continue swallowing all the more of it.

Swallow till 1 to 2 feet is left out side. Then perform nauli chalana, so that the cloth rubs and massages the stomach.

Stop the practice and pull out the cloth carefully using the fingers. Don't apply force while pulling out the cloth as it may damage the soft parts of the stomach and esophagus.

Time duration for the whole practice should not exceed more than 20-25 minutes. Boil and dry well the cloth for further use.

Benefits

1. The mucus from the chest is loosened and expelled, while the muscles of the bronchial tubes get relaxed.
2. It alleviates the symptoms of asthma.
3. Vastra dhauti induces strong reflexes in the throat and chest region.
4. It tones up the autonomic nervous system.
5. It balances the pitta dosha (bile element) and improves the function of the upper gastro-intestinal tract.

Precautions

- Don't talk while practising.
- Don't try without expert guidance.
- Don't perform it if you are suffering from hyper-tension, heart disease, stroke or general illness.
- Don't swallow the whole cloth; allow at least 30 cm to remain out from the mouth.
- Perform the nauli first right, left and middle for 3-5 minutes to clean the stomach. Beginners should practise for one minute only.
- For removing the cloth sit in squating position and pull it gently and firmly.
- After removing the cloth keep it into the bowl.
- This practice should be performed in the morning before any food or drink are taken.
- Don't use the damaged cloth.
- Cloth should be washed gently by hands using a soft soap. Don't use a brush.
- Boil it, dry it and keep it in a safe place.
- The time allowed for the whole process should not be more than 20-25 minutes in total.
- It should not be practised infront of the public in openness.

(E) Washing of the Intestines

Introduction

It is a cleansing process related to digestive system. Gheranda Samhita describes it varisara dhauti. In 'Shatakarma sangraha' it is called as 'Siddhikarani'. In

'Hatha yoga Pradipika' it is described as 'Shankha prakshalana'. Varisara dhauti means cleansing digestive system with the help of water. Our small intestine is compared to a conch well (stomach) and prakshalana means the act of washing.

Materials Needed

Lukewarm water, salt, glass, towel, toilet facility, lemon etc. Khichari (a plane soft food).

Previous Practice

Practice of Nauli chalana, vipreetakarani (1-2 stages) Tadasana, Tiryaka Tadasana, Katichakrasana. Tiryaka Bhujangasana (1-2 stages) Vakrasana, mayurasana. Padahastasana (1-2 stages) Kunjala, jalaneti, shavasana.

Supplimentary Practice

Kunjala, Jalaneti, Shavasana.

Preparation

- Take a light, semi-liquid meal the night before.
- Plenty of clean, lukewarm water should be prepared and also extra hot water to mix.
- Add 2 tea spoons of salt per litre to the water.
- Prepare special food khichari (moong daal + rice) cooked with 100 gram of ghee. A little turmeric should be added but no salt. It should be semi-liquid khichari should be eaten after 45 minutes of completing the kriya

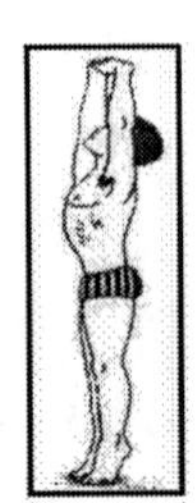

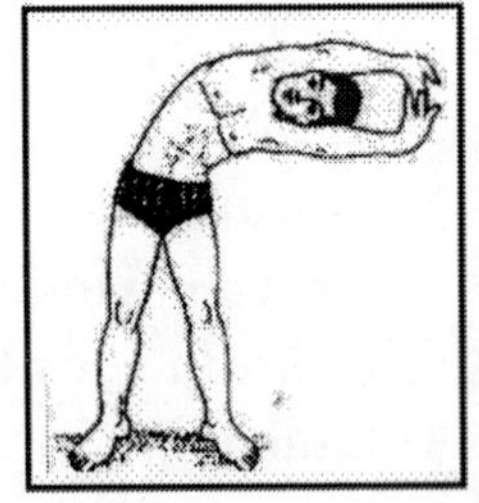

and again later in the day/ evening.

- Wear light and comfortable clothes.

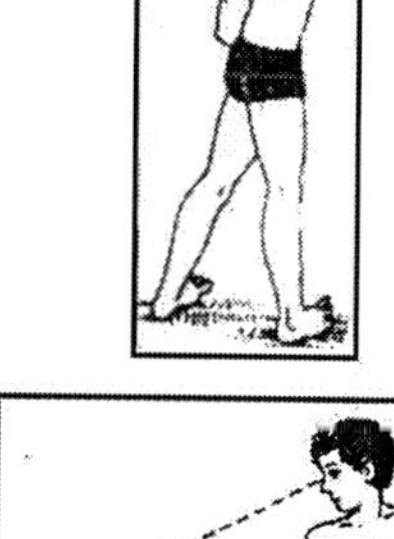

Technique

Drink two glasses of warm salty water as quickly as possible. Perform the five asanas or above mentioned asanas. Tadasana, Tiryaka Tadasana, Katichakrasana, Tiryaka Bhujangasana and Udarakarshanasana. This is a complete set. Perform it. Don't take rest between rounds. Perform 4 to 8 times.

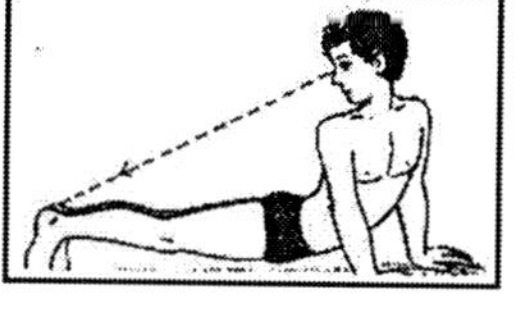

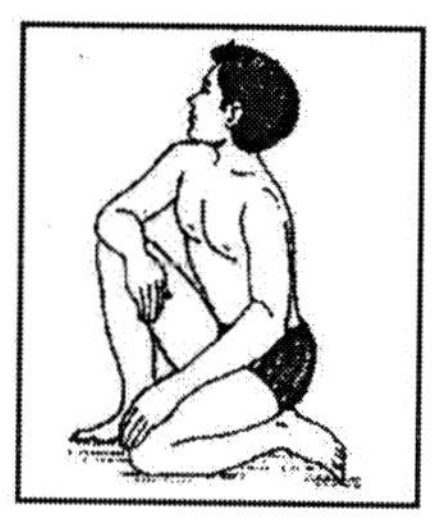

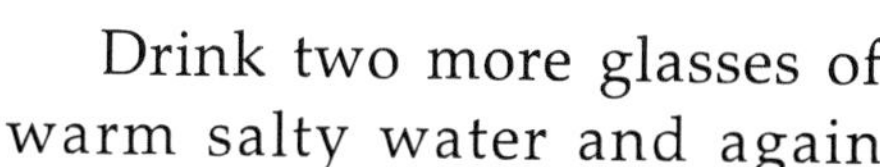

Drink two more glasses of warm salty water and again repeat the five asanas 4 to 8 times. Repeat this process a third time and go for toilet. After a few minutes come out. Drink two more glasses and repeat the asanas. Again go to the toilet but don't use force. Continue the process. Sixteen glasses are generally required for this kriya.

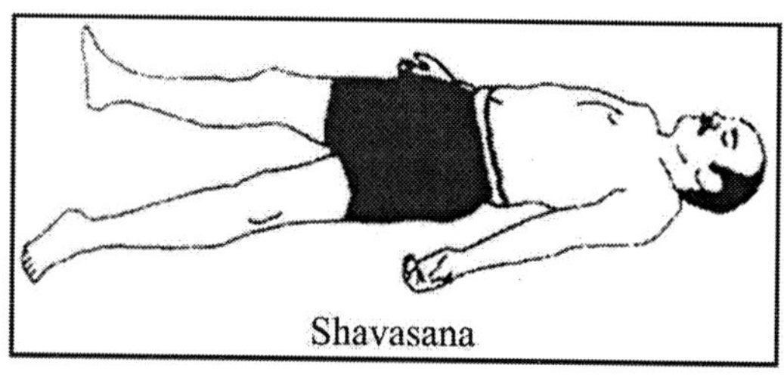

Shavasana

After completing the whole process perform kunjala and jalaneti after 10 minutes then lie down in shavasana and take rest for 45 minutes. Don't sleep, a headache or cold may result. Keep warm during the rest.

Precautions

1. At first take rest after completing the complete process for 45 minutes. Don't sleep during the rest.
2. Take second rest after eating khichari. Complete rest is necessary that day or even the next day.
3. Eat Khichari in late hours and in the evening.
4. Perform shankha prakshalana when the season is warm and dry or in changing season.
5. Avoid the cloudy, windy or rainy season to perform this kriya.
6. Perform this kriya twice in an year.
7. Fans and cool air should not be used.
8. Don't sit in the hot sun or near a fire after doing physical exercise.
9. Don't take milk, butter milk, yogurt, acidic fruits.
10. Practice in empty stomach.
11. Avoid eating after the practice. Don't take oily, spicy and non-vegetarian foods.
12. People suffering from peptic ulcer and HBP should not practise this kriya.

Benefits

- It cures all diseases connected with the digestive

organs. Chronic headaches, diseases of the eyes, nose and teeth.

- Women derive wonderful benefits. Menstrual disorders and barrenness can be cured. It is one of the best exercise for kidneys and urinary system and it also helps prevent urinary infections and the formation of kidney stones.
- Shankha prakshalana makes the body and mind fresh and helps for higher yogic practices.
- According to the Gheranda Samhita the body becomes radiant.
- It removes the waste materials which are poisonous in the body.
- It provides the feeling of lightness.
- It is useful for Asthma, other general respiratory problems, obesity, diabetes, constipation, hyper acidity and many other ailments connected with impurity in blood.
- It helps to train the emotional and behavioural aspect of the practitioner.
- It helps relieve symptoms of arthritis and chronic inflammatory diseases.
- It alleviates from skin problems such as pimples, boils and eczema.
- The harmony of the five pranas is restored and the energy level also gets raised.
- It prepares the way for higher states of consciousness.

4. TRATAKA

Introduction

Trataka is a concentrated gazing of an object. It is related to eyes and different nadis of eyes. This is a cleansing process practised with the help of eyes. There are two types of trataka—external and internal.

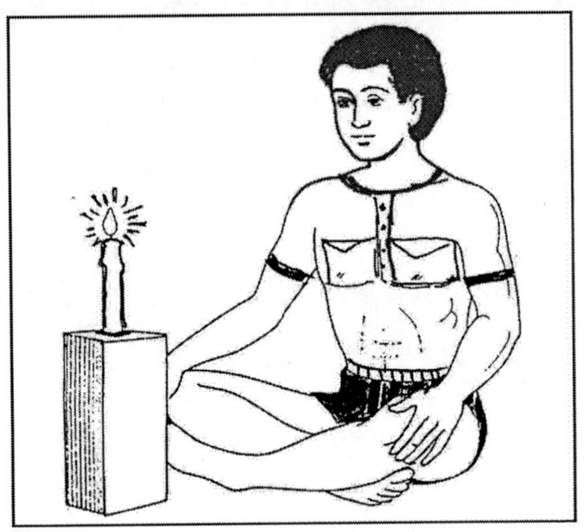

"Keeping the eyes steady, one should attentively stare at a small object until tears come out. This is called Trataka by the yogis".

Hatha yoga Pradipika (11/32)

Material Used

Candle, matchstick, oil, stool, lamp (deepak), picture of God/guru as one desires.

Previous Practice

Any meditative asana. Padmasana is recommended. Vajrasana can be performed. Palming is also good.

Technique

Put the candle/deepaka on the stool so that the flame is exactly at eye level when sitting. Light the candle/deepaka sit in any comfortable meditative pose with the head and spine erect. Candle should be at an arms length away from the body. Close the eyes and relax the body. Be aware of body steadiness for a few minutes.

Open the eyes and concentrate on the tip of the wick. try not to blink or move the eyeballs in any way. Don't strain close your eyes for four seconds. Open the eyes and concentrate again for more time. Increase the stay slowly. After a minute or two when the eyes become tired or begin to water, close them gently. Gaze at the after-image of the flame. It is internal trataka when the image begins to fade then repeat again the process of trataka.

Repeat external and internal trataka 3 or 4 times, After completing the final round, practise palming before opening the eyes.

Benefits

1. Trataka practice makes the eyes clear and bright.
2. It balances the nervous system
3. Trataka relieves nervous tension, anxiety and depression.
4. It improves the memory.
5. It removes the insomnia.

6. It helps to develop good concentration and will power.
7. Trataka activates 'Agya chakra (Ajna chakra).
8. It is an excellent preparation for meditation.
9. It cures eye diseases.
10. The shambhavi mudra is verily facilitated.
11. It improves mental health.

Precautions

- Don't wear spectcles performing the trataka.
- Stop the practice if you get headache during trataka.
- In case of eyes ailments like eyestrain, myopia, astigmatism and the early symptoms of cataract. It is advised to gaze a black dot instead of flame.
- Slowly and cautiously increase the practice of trataka without giving much strain to the eyes.
- Don't practise in front of bright objects or the sun. It can destroy the retina.
- Maximum given time for the practice is 3 minutes.
- Changing the object may give disturbance to the mind.
- The object should be steady and selected according to the need (in darkness-a dim light is preferable).

5. BASTI

Jala Basti

It was traditional method of bowel cleansing.

Method No-1

Stand in a river upto the navel. Lean forward and put the hands on the knees. Expand the anal sphincter muscles and sumultaneously perform Uddiyana bandha and nauli in such a way that water is drawn up into the bowels. Hold the water in the bowels for some times and than expel it through the anus.

Benefits

1. The colon is cleaned and purified.
2. Gas expelled and old stool is removed.
3. Advanced sadhaka who are expert in pranayama use the basti to remove the heat produced during the practice of pranayama.
4. Practice of jala basti invigorates the dhatus, the senses, internal organs and gives a sense of well being.
5. Jala Basti bestows luster, stimulates digestion and completely destroys all the accumulated diseases.
6. Basti provides better digestion, controls nervous system, diarrhoea and strengthens solar plexus.
7. Basti removes the impurities, purifies the blood and increases the blood circulation.
8. All diseases are cured like disorders of the spleen and other glands and dropsy originating from other disorders of vata, pitta and kapha (phlegm).
9. It gives purification of nadis, awareness and sensitivity of chakras located in perineum-mooladhara swadhisthana and manipura.
10. It helps in better concentration in brain functions.
11. It is helpful in appendicitis.

Method No-2: Dry Yogic enema (Sthal Basti)

Sit in the position of paschimottanasana and perform ashwini mudra 25 times sucking air into the bowels. Retain the air for sometime and then expel it through the anus.

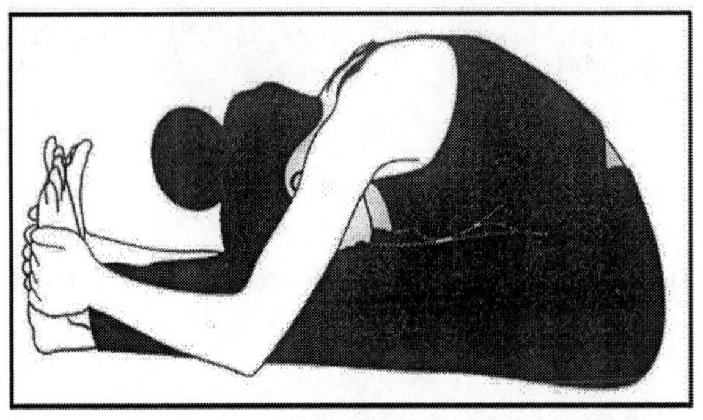

Mdethod No-3: Basti with enema pump/pot

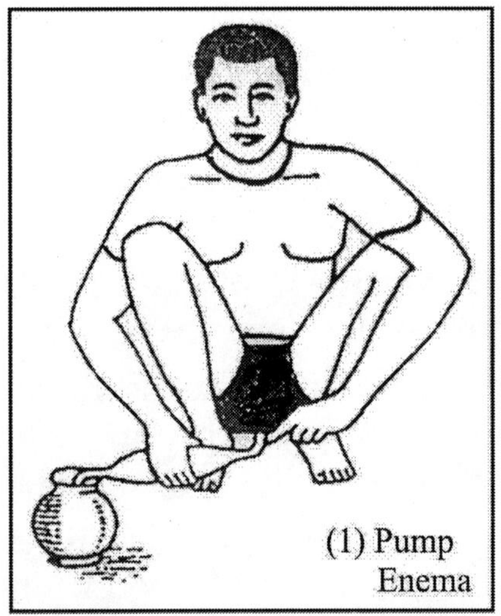

(1) Pump Enema

Privous Practice: Uddiyana Bandha, Madhyama Nauli, Vama and Dakshina Nauli, Nauli Chalana Utkatasana.

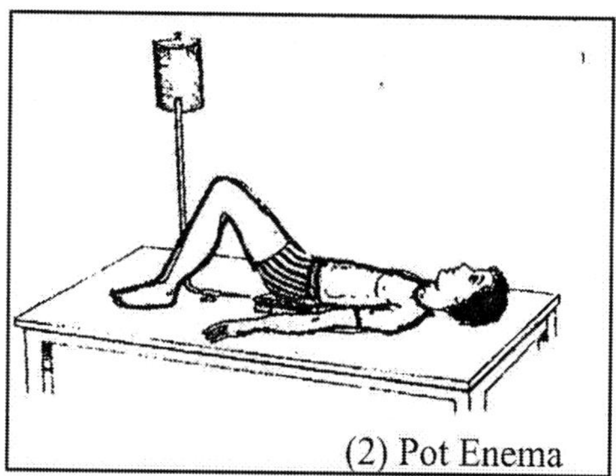

(2) Pot Enema

Materials used: Smooth tube of rubber around 6″, luke warm water 40°C or fresh water 2 litre. Salt, towel, lubricant/oil and soap, enema pump/pot.

Method: Sit in utkatasana/kagasana. Fill the water in the pot. Put one end of tube in the pot and the other in the anus. Press the pump ball several times open the nozzle. The water is sucked in perform nauli and uddiyana bandha in standing position removing the tube. Go for cleansing the bowels.

Precautions

1. Perfection in uddiyana, madhyama nauli, nauli chalana and utkatasana are essential before performing basti.
2. It should be practised in the morning, after normal motion in empty stomach.
3. It is recommended to have light or liquid food in the previous day night.
4. Sterilization and lubrication of the Basti tube must be done before the practice.
5. Inserting and removing the Basti Tube in anus should be done carefully.

6. Clean and enough water should be prepared (luke warm 40°C) with mixing salt for better cleaning of the mucus and stimulate peristalsis.
7. One should take light food (soft food-rice, khichadi) after 1 to 2 round of the practice.
8. One should not practise basti in appendicitis.
9. Care must be taken while treating ailments like collitis and dysentery.
10. Patients suffering from bleeding piles are not supposed to practise basti.
11. Patients suffering from anal fissure should not practise basti.
12. Patients suffering from severe abdominal or chest pain, headache, fever, hernia, high blood pressure, serious digestive disorder and acute conditions of any disease should not practise basti.
13. Ladies during menses and pregnancy should not practise basti.
14. Over eating and practice of basti together is not advisable.
15. It should be practised only when required.

Note: Basti can be performed without salt and fresh water.

6. Kapalbhati

Introduction

This cleansing process is related to respiratory system. In different schools of yoga it is practised as a pranayama. Kapalbhati is predominently on abdominal breathing exercise and cleansing method.

Kapalbhati

Name

Kapal means forehead

Bhati means to shine

Kapalbhati means shining of the forehead.

Previous Practice

- Agnisara (exercise of abdominal muscles)
- Padmasana or any meditative asana.

Materials used

Peacful place

Method of forehead cleansing breath

Sit in any comfortable meditative asana; Padmasana, should be the first choice. Keep head and spine straight and the hands resting on the knees palms down, close the eyes and relax the whole body. Inhale deeply through both nostrils, expanding the abdomen and exhaling with a forceful contraction of the abdominal muscles. Don't strain. The next inhalation should be passive allowing the abdominal muscles to expand. Inhalation should be a spontaneous or passive recoil, involving no effort. Perform 10 respirations to begin with, count each respiration mentally.

After completing 10 rapid breaths in succession, inhale and exhale deeply. This is one round. Perform 3 to 5 rounds. After finishing the practice concentrate on Agya Chakra (eyebrow centre), feeling an alpervading emptiness and calm).

Benefits

1. Kapalbhati helps for the practice for pranayama. It also helps in increasing concentration.
2. It gives the exercise and massage to all the internal organs of chest and abdomen. By this action all the internal organs work smoothly.
3. Kapalbhati increases the lungs capacity and improves the efficiency of gas exchange (oxygen and carbon-dioxide in the lungs.
4. It removes the diseases related to respiratory system, as common cold, cough, rhinitis, pharyngitis, sinusitis, deviated nasal septum asthma, bronchitis, tuberculosis and emphysema.
5. It improves the functions of digestive system.
6. Kapalbhati increases Red blood cells, Haemoglobin and Eosinophils in the blood.
7. It increases heart rate and blood circulation.
8. It reduces obesity and depository fat in the abdomen.
9. Kapalbhati helps for better perfusion and filteration in the kidney.
10. Kapalbhati helps to stimulate the glands, so that functioning of the glands gets normalized.

11. It removes the stress. The brain cells are invigorated continuously during the performance of kapalbhati.
12. The practioners feel light, calm and peaceful in their mind.
13. Kapalbhati purifies Ida and pingla nadis and also removes sensory distractions from the mind.
14. Sleepiness is finished and it prepares the mind for meditation.

Precautions

- Patients suffering from heart disease, high blood pressure, spondylosis, slip disc and hernia should avoid kapalbhati.
- If there is serious injury in the respiratory tract especially in the nose (bleeding) avoid it.
- If there is pain in abdomen or chest, fever, headache don't practise kapalbhati.
- Women during menstrual periods and pregnancy should not practise kapalbhati.
- Kapalbhati is practised according to the individuals capacity.
- Always practise in an empty stomach.
- Kapalbhati vibrates every tissue in the human body.
- Increase your practice very slowly.
- If there is any feeling like giddiness one should not continue the practice.
- Vigour and speed, number of rounds should be determined cautiously.

- Take care that higher force and friction of the air must not lead to any injury in the delicate parts of the mucous membrane.
- In between two rounds take few normal breathing for giving rest to the system and to avoid fatigue, tiredness and giddiness.

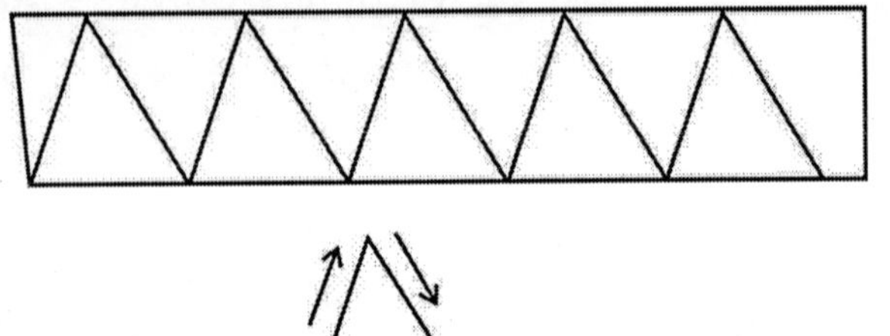

Puraka (Inhalation) **Rechaka (Exhalation)**

- Keep the face muscles in a relaxed manner.
- The numbers of strokes should be two per second that is 120 strokes per minute.

Short Course of Shankha Prakshalana

Technique

Prepare two litres of warm salted water. Drink quickly two glasses of lukewarm water then perform the following asanas eight times:

1. Tadasana
2. Tiryaka tadasana
3. Katichakrasana
4. Tiryaka Bhujangasana
5. Udarakarshanasana.

Drink two more glasses of water and repeat the asanas eight times each. Repeat the process for a third and last time. Go to the latrine but don't strain whether there is a bowel movement or not. If there is no motion immediately it will come later on.

Perform kunjala and jalaneti just after the short course of shankha prakshalana is finished.

Precaution

1. Practise the process in the morning when the stomach is empty.
2. An hour is sufficient for this practice.
3. Rest should be taken for half an hour after the practice.
4. There is no special food required.
5. For general purpose it can be done once a week. In case of constipation it can be done daily until the constipation is removed.

Benefits

The same as poorna shankhaprakshalana kriya.

◆ ◆ ◆

8

What is Concentration?

"Concentration is the focusing of the mind on any point or object internal or external or on any idea", says Maharishi Patanjali.

"The form control of the senses and the mind in concentration." Without concentration, the mind has no strength, no efficiency. Concentrated thinking alone is creative, capable of producing results. Concetration is the basis of every human activity. Through right karma the mind becomes rich in concentration. The state of perfect concentration is achieved, the state of yogaroodha (योगारूढ) is gained. After developing the power the concentration one can hope to enter the seat of meditation.

Concentration (Dharana) is the sixth limb of the eight-fold path of Astangayoga. Once a Pandit asked Kabir, "O Kabir, what are you doing now?" Kabir replied, "O, Pandit, I am detaching the mind from worldly objects, and attaching it to the lotus feet of the Lord." This is concentration. A definite aim, interest and attention are the bases of concentration.

Concentration is the art of reducing the interruptions, attachment and anxiety of the mind and ultimately eliminating them completely so that the knower and the known become one. If we want to develop the mental power we must have concentrating mind. Concentrated mind can influence the health and character and bring peace and harmony. Without concentration our prayer, efforts and endeavour will go waste. There is a story in *Mahabharata* which illustrates the power of concentration. When guru Dronacharya asked Arjuna, "what do you see?" Arjuna replied, "I see only the bird's eye and nothing else."

Develop the Power of Concentration

The secret of sustained concentration lies in the will-power exercised relentlessly at the start of and undertaking. Will power and ability to concentrate are almost the same thing. Concentration is the key to success. Do not realise that they can master this vital force if only they go about it in the right way.

Without concentration, even the greatest of talents will run to waste, squandered in activities begun brilliantly and never finished. Concentration is the act of deliberately turning our attention to a limited section of our environment, excluding the rest from consciousness as far as possible by an act of will.

There are two aspects of concentration, and both are equally important. Concentration is necessary to learn any instrument of music or doing any work. We can get full benefit with full concentration.

But secondly, there must be the capacity to keep it up and improve it day by day and month by month.

Selecting Perceptions

In developing our powers of concentration, the aim must be to learn how to select from among our perceptions of the external world so that we decide rationally which of them shall be "prominent in consciousness." The more salient a perception, the better we apprehend it and the more likely we are to remember it.

Our consciousness is limited in range, and only a small portion of the total field of our perceptions can be salient at any one time. We express this in the common phrase, "I can only attend to one thing at a time." The power to concentrate is the ability to choose this small portion at will, instead of leaving it to our emotions and instincts to make the choice.

What makes a perception silent?

First, its intensity a loud noise makes more impression on us than a quiet one. Secondly, its connection with other preceptions, Thirdly, salency depends on our interest, instinctive or voluntary, in the perception.

The attention which we pay to these salient perceptions may be unified, as when we are absorbed in the sounds of music.

Or it may be distributed, as when we concentrate on several necessary things together. The car driver, for example, must watch the road ahead, and he ready to use eyes, ears, feet and hands at the same time in a controlled process.

Now we can begin to consider ways of augmenting your power to concentrate.

Keep before you a clear, vivid image of your ultimate aim. This will help you to stick at a task or a long period of study extending over months or even years. A strong, emotionally felt incentive is necessary for sustained concentrated effort.

Every day—especially if your resolution temporarily weakens—conjure up in your mind a picture of yourself as you will be when success has eventually crowned your efforts. Hold this mental image before you and see what a small price the effort of today is to achieve it.

Develop an active interest in the matter which demands your concentration. Consider all its aspects. Seek unusual forms of approach and novelty in presentation. Your mind will find it easier to grasp and your attention will be more easily riveted to a subject if you try all the time to give it freshness.

"The natural tendency of attention when left to itself is to wander to ever new things." Helmholtz said. "If we wish to keep it upon one and the same object, we must seek constantly to find out something new about the latter especially if other powerful impressions are attracting us away."

Make out every day an orderly list of jobs to be done. Then work steadily through your list, without hurrying and without giving thought to any other item than the one you are working on.

This rule is most important. A doctor was once asked how he managed to cope up with hundreds of his patients. "I have only one patient," he answered. However many jobs you have to do, however many facts you have to learn, all you need concern yourself with is the one in front of you at this moment.

When it is done thoroughly, go on the next on your list.

Fussing Ineffectively

Without a carefully constructed list, your mind will always be jumping to other matters, wondering what has been forgotten, and generally fussing ineffectively. Observation of this rule produces a steadily increasing number of concrete achievements. It is a practical way of focusing attention on one part of your total field of perception.

To learn to concentrate on several related items at once, as is necessary in those activities like car driving where distributed attention is needed, the secret is long and continual practice, every day if possible. Nerve impulses have a tendency to follow paths they have taken before, so each repetition makes the next one easier.

When the bodily movements become automatic, the mind is free to concentrate on road conditions-which it cannot do if changing gears, for example, is an activity demanding thought. Success in sport, ballet dancing and similar bodily activities requires the utmost concentration on what is going on. This is impossible unless long practice has resulted in utter mastery of the physical elements.

"Sustained in this way by a resolute effort of attention." Says William James. "The difficult objects are long begins to call up its own congeners (its own kind) and associates and ends by changing the disposition of the man's consciousness altogether. And with his consciousness his action changes, for the new object, once stably in possession of the field of his thoughts infallibly produces its own motor effects."

"The attention must be kept strained on that object until at last it grows, so as to maintain itself before the mind with ease."

A great enemy of concentration is fatigue. The attention cannot be fixed on an unchanging object for more than a few seconds, seek means of creating variety, or fresh aspects. Every different facet of any object provides a fresh stimulus to the mind and aids concentration. Without variety tiredness comes quickly.

Look after your physical health and tackle your emotional worries. Concentration is impossible unless you have an unshackled mind and a fit, eager body. Mind and body are inseparable, and as health improves so the power to concentrate will improve with it, on the other hand, failing powers of concentration may be a symptom of some physical weakness.

Whenever possible, give some emotional significance to the subject. Concentration is easy when we are emotionally involved. The things we find dry and difficult to give attention to are usually devoid of any immediate personal application.

Seek always for ways in which what you want to learn applies to you personally. Create some emotional relationship with the facts. This is often difficult, but the attempt is valuable in itself in providing a fresh approach to the subject.

Concentration is easier if the topic is related to other things already known or are of interest to you. A perception's saliency depends on its connection with other saliencies, so that they join together and form a system in the mind. The more you know about any subject the simpler it is to concentrate on it and acquire fresh facts or ideas about it.

It Gets Results

Learning is thus a valuable aid in itself to concentration.

Steady and regular attention to these points will speedily improve your powers of concentration. Work always with the aim of focusing all your attention on one small thing at a time. It takes will-power to have the courage to do this, ignoring all the other matters pressing themselves upon you. But it gets results.

Do not get dismayed by the magnitude of any task. Split it up into stages. Do them or learn them one by one.

A mare ten minutes each day at a slight task will he five hours work at the end of a month, with a solid result to show for your modest daily effort of concentration.

Practice of Concentration

1. Follow the yama and niyama in your life because concentration is of no use without following important rules of ethics, and with control of breath, the mind can be purified. Concentration will become intense.
2. Remove all the negative thoughts and desires from the mind.
3. Interest and attention are the basic requisites in concentration.
4. Observe the object deeply. The power of concentration can be increased by observing silence.

5. In the initial stage of practice of concentration one should focus one's mind and thought on some concrete object like flame of a candle, called Trataka.
6. Sit in any meditative pose. Concentrate on rose-flower. Think of its colour, shape, petals and why it is called the queen of garden. If mind gets diverted bring the mind back to rose flower. Some emotions may disturb you in the process of concentration but these will pass like the pieces of cloud.
7. Keep your mind away from any stress, strain, tension, or depression or worry or anxiety and concentrate on your object.
8. Sustain a keep awareness, don't sleep during the process.
9. Control your breath.
10. Jap can help you in achieving concentration.
11. Read 2-3 pages of a book and think over it and concentrate on the matter.
12. Listen the sound of a clock keeping it three feet away from you.
13. Practice to hear the Anahad Naad in your innerself.
14. Concentrate on the moon in lying pose in a quiet night.
15. Hear the 'om' sound sitting on a bank of a river.
16. Lying on your bed observe the vastness of the sky.
17. Think over any virtue as—truth, honesty, punctuality, regularity, love, forgiveness, happiness, kindness etc.
18. Look at any picture with open eyes. After some time close your eyes and see the picture inside.

19. Sit in padmasana. Concentrate on breath with the mantra-So-Hum for 10 minutes.
20. Sit in any meditative pose concentrate on air and its power.
21. Sitting in your room, concentrate on star/moon's glory with closed eyes.
22. Concentration on Gangavataran: Ganga river comes to Gangotri from Gaumukh, runs through, Uttarkashi, Rishikesh, Haridwar, Varanasi and enters Bay of Bengal. Concentrate for 10 minutes on Gaumukh to Ganga Sagar.
23. **First Week:** Place a clock on a television, playing the news or a serial, etc. try to focus your attention on the movement of the second's hand of the clock for 5 minutes. Don't allow the television to steer the focus of your attention. Try to do this exercise for a week.
24. **Second Week:** Place half of your attention on the second's hand of the clock and the other half on the number series 3, 6, 9.... Juggling both the things in the mind. If you lose the track after a while, just restart the exercise. Do the exercise for 5 minutes. Everytime you do the exercise, change the value of the series, e.g., 4-8, 12, 16... or 3, 7, 11, 15– Do it for a week.
25. **Third Week:** Concentrate on the motion of the second's hand with 1/3 of your attention. With another of the concentration. Sing a song. With the remaining third of your attention, focus on a number series. Do it for a week.
26. **Fourth Week:** Invent your own concentration exercise. Keyword and clock exercise.

◆ ◆ ◆

9

Psychic Centres

Psychic centres are the energy centres. There are deeper secrets in our body which lie beyond the senses and the mind. It is through the 'chakras' that cosmic energy penetrates the body, but such energy is only revealed to those who have developed their latent powers. The psychic centres are also the source of health and vitality.

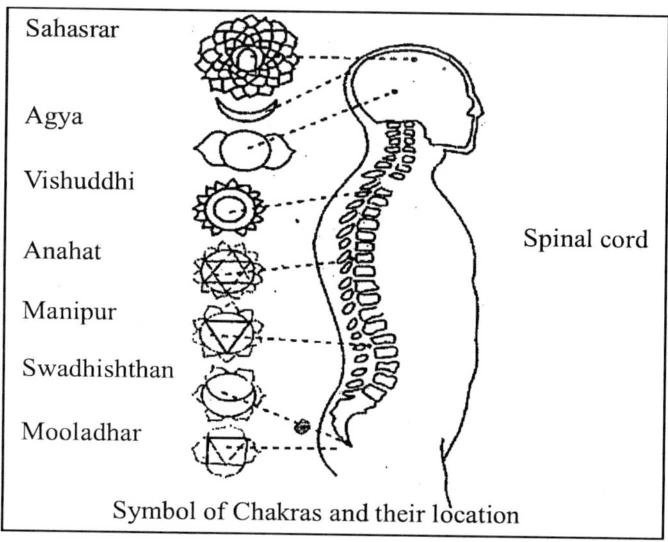

Symbol of Chakras and their location

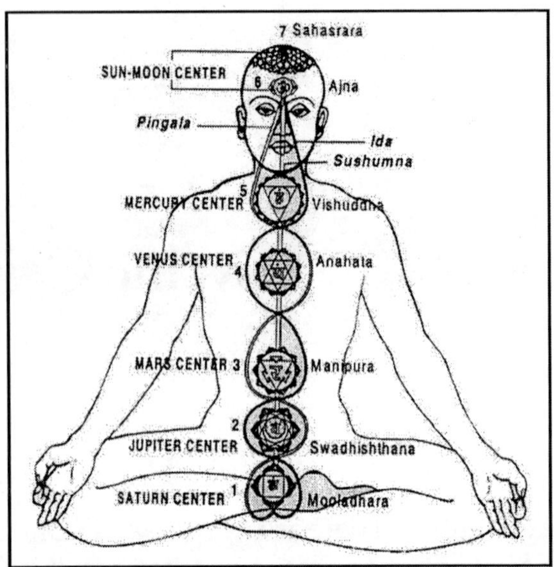

Yogic science states that there are roughly 72,000 'nadis' which transport and distribute cosmic energy throughout the body, carrying it to the psychic centres. The secret of health and growth, both mental and spiritual, lies in the purity, vitality and force of the nadis. They directly influence the body and the mind, helping to maintain the general equilibrium.

The spinal column contains the source of all nervous force. It extends from the 'Atlas' bone to the coccyx and is composed of 33 vertebrae connected by fibrous cartilage pads. The centre of the spinal column forms a hollow through which passes the spinal cord. Holes on either side of the column allow the passage of the spinal nerves to all parts of the body. The cervical, dorsal, lumber, sacral and coccygeal regions of the spine contains astral or psychic centres which form a network of subtle nadis, unknown to medical science, for they disappear at death.

Sixteen of the seventy two thousand nadis are particularly important. They spring from region called kanda, located at the base of the spine, above the anus. Out of these Sixteen, there are three vital nadis; Ida, Pingla and Susumna.

The Ida and Pingle nadis are currents flowing through either side of the spinal column (Ida on the left and Pingle on the right), while the Susumna nadi passes through the centre of the spinal chord. For most people prana only flows through Ida and Pingle because their mind operates. Only on the lower planes of consciousness only highly evolved being, such as the yogis, are able to make prana flow through Susumna and thus awaken the Kundalini Shakti which lies coiled like a serpent at the base of the spinal column in the **Mooladhara Chakra**. Susumna is also called Brahma nadi or the nadi of **'Vigilance'.**

Along the Brahma nadi there are the Chakras (Psychic centres) which correspond to various plexuses and certain glands. They are also called **Padama** or lotus. Each Chakra has its own dominant colour, but according to the various thoughts and emotional states of an individual, many other colours may be seen in them. They are only visible to the psychic gaze as they vibrate and mingle with one another. There are seven main Chakras.

1. Mooladhara Chakra

The first chakra is situated at the base of the spinal column. It corresponds to the coccygeal plexus and the gonads. It represents the Prithivi-Tattva (earth element). It has the symbolic form of a lotus with four red petals bearing the signs Sam, Svm, Sham and Vam. Each corresponds to a mantra. In the heart of the lotus there is a yellow square surrounded by eight spears. The letter **Lam** (लं) is visible in the centre; it is the **Beeja Mantra** (basic mantra) or the secret symbol of this chakra. Brahma, the creator presides over this chakra with the goddess Dakini Devi who dispels fear. They are both seated on the elephant Airavata, the emblem of force and solidity. In the triangle is the Kundalini which radiates a brilliant light and is rolled three and a half times around the lingam, symbolizing creative force.

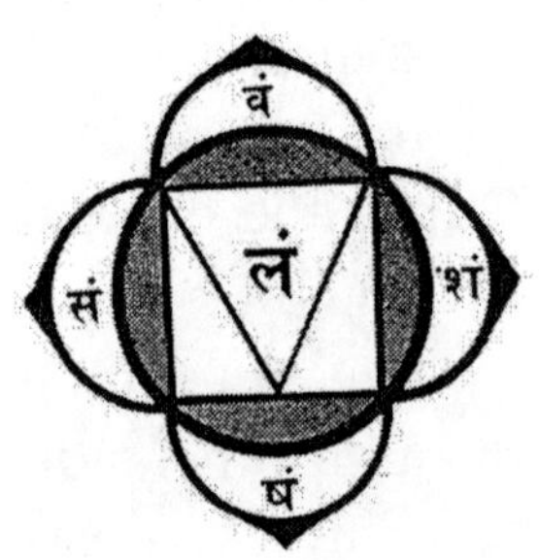

This chakra governs physical consciousness and subconsciousness. Those who meditate upon it become masters of their speech, for their words are full of music and meaning. They are able to undertake all kinds of study and have the power of avoiding illess.

2. Swadhisthana Chakra

This chakra is located in the abdominal cavity, above the genital organs. It corresponds to the prostate gland, representing the Apas-tattva (water element). A vermillion lotus with six petals is its symbol, each petal has a symbolic letter, bam, bham, yam, ram and lam. In the centre of the lotus, there is a white circle with the letter vam (वं). This is its Beeja mantra or secret symbol. The presiding deities of the chakra are Vishnu, the preserver, seated upon Garuda, the golden eagle, and Rakini Devi, who grants all desires.

Swadhisthana Chakra governs all the baser desires. By meditating on it, one is able to destroy one's passions, such as Kama (lust), Krodha (anger), Mada (pride), Lobha (avarice), Moha (delusion) and Matsaya (envy), all of which come from the ego (Ahamkara). One then becomes a maha yogi, supreme among yogis.

3. Manipura Chakra

This chakra is located in the navel. Its corresponding physical plexus is the solar plexus. It represents the Agni-tattva (fire element). The lotus symbolizing it has ten violet petals with the following letters; da, dha, na ta, tha, de, dhe, ne, pa and pha. At the heart of the lotus there is a red triangle which symbolizes fire and bears at its centre the letter Ram (रं), its Beeja mantra or secret symbol. The deities presiding over this chakra are Rudra, the destroyer, and Lakini Devi, the benefactress.

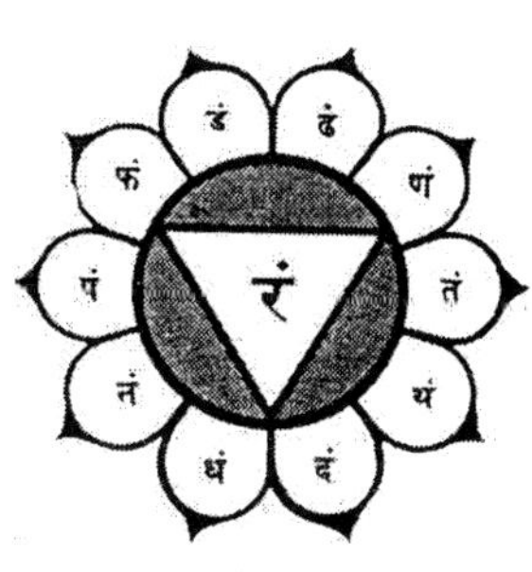

Manipura chakra governs the vital forces. By meditating on it, all fears are dispelled, and one attains supreme knowledge. This chakra brings fulfilment in every aspect of life.

4. Anahata Chakra

This chakra is situated in the heart region. It corresponds to the thymus gland and is represented by the Vayu Tattva (air element). It has twelve pinkish-gold petals each with one of the following symbolic letters, ka, kha, ga, gha, nga, cha, chha, ja, jha, nya, ta and tha. In its centre there are two smoke coloured triangles one on top of the other, one facing up, the other down. The letter yam (यं), in the middle, is its Beeja mantra. The two deities of this chakra are Ishwara, 'God manifested', and Kakini Devi who bestows happiness.

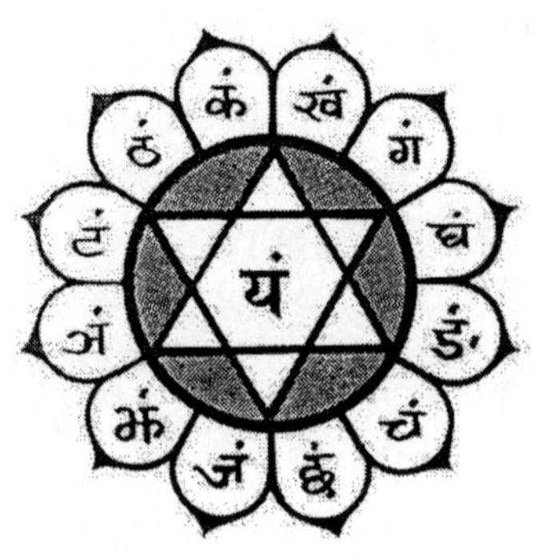

Anahata chakra governs the most noble sentiments. Those who meditate on this chakra achieve complete control over the senses. Their mind is always concentrated on noble deeds and God. Their speech flows like a stream of clear water, inspiring all who listen to them, Universal love emanates from them.

5. Vishuddhi Chakra

This chakra is situated in the throat and corresponds to the thyroid gland. It represents **Akash tattva** (ether element). The lotus has sixteen petals of a smokey-purple hue, each with one of the following a, aa, e, ee, u, uu, ri, riree, lree, lreeri, ae, aai, o, ow, ang, and aha. In this centre of this flower, there is a triangle with a circle symbolizing **Ambara** (sky), the ethereal region. The syllable ham (हं) represents the Beeja mantra of this

Chakra and is placed on an elephant. Its deities are **Sada Shiva**, who enlightens, and **Sakini Devi** who grants beauitude.

Vishudhi chakra governs all the expressions externalizations of the mind. Those who meditaate on this chakra attain complete knowledge of the universe. They enjoy uninterrupted peace of mind, can see into the past, present and futurc, become merciful to all without expecting any reward, are constant, steady, noble, modest, courageous and forgiving.

6. Agya (Ajna) Chakra

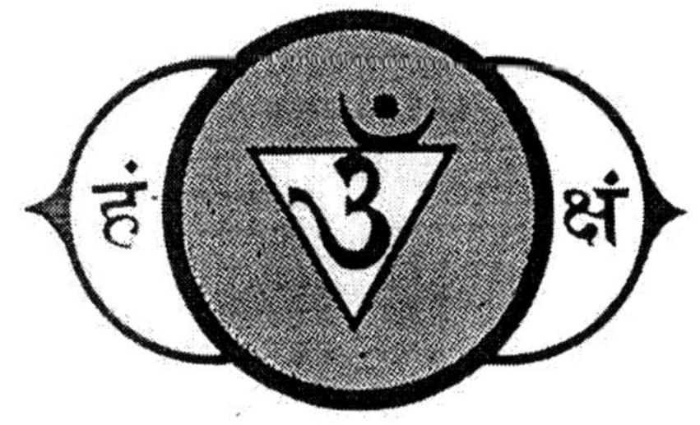

This chakra is located in the middle of the eye brows. It corresponds to the pineal gland. It is represented by a lotus with two white petals, the one on the right carries the symbolic letter **Ksham** (क्षं), and on the left **ham** (हं) and ॐ in the centre. The deity presiding over it is Hakini Devi, who is seated upon another small white lotus situated at the heart of the lotus. She is all-knowing and all-seeing and bestows supernatural powers and pure intellegence. On her left, in a triangle, is a Shivalingam (phallus) representing the creative aspect of Shiva, superimposed on it is the sacred symbol pranva or Aum. Above this there is a crescent moon with a Bindu (dot). Inside the symbolic dot lives Shiva, governing thought, will and vision with his shakti (manifesting power).

If one meditates on this (extremely powerful) chakra, he attains central over all the nervous centres and can thus achieve extraordinary knowledge, spiritual force and will power, Intuition gets awakened.

It is here, in (Agya) Ajna chakra that the rishis and yogis enter their life-breath the pranas before passing into the state of supreme bliss.

7. Sahasrara Chakra

This is seventh and the main chakra. It is situated on the top of the crown, corresponding to the pituitary gland. Its symbol is a lotus with thousand blue petals, surrounded by a golden light. It governs the highest level of thought and enlightens the mind by opening it upwards to intuition. Some have mistakenly identified this chakra with the brain, but this organ is only a channel of communication between the Agya (Ajna) and Saharara Chakras. The aspirant to supreme enlightenment who is able to direct his kundalini as and to this chakra will reach the state of samadhi or super consciousness. This may only be reached in exceptional cases, with the help of a Guru, a spiritual guide and the grace of God.

Once one's sexual drive is controlled, then its sublimated force is transformed into psychic and cosmic energy. In order to achieve this, it is of paramount importance to be pure in mind and heart. When such purity has been attained by controlling the external and internal nature, either by selfless work, worship, psychic control, philosophy, or by all of them, one gets close to awakening the Kundalini. When the Kundalini shakti passes upwards through the Susumna from one chakra to another as a result of will power and concentration in meditation, one experiences the boon of different kinds of knowledge, powers and bliss.

8. Energizing the Chakras

The chakras can be energized by vocalizing the AUM mantra. Begin with a few rounds of digital pranayama, perhaps followed by five minutes of candle gazing. Now close your eyes and see if you can visualize a bright golden light, like a candle flame, at the base of spine at the basic chakra. Breathe steadily in through the nadis and out through the nostrils in a regular and relaxed rhythm. The breaths should be long, deep, and fairly slow. Visualize the Base Chakra beginning to glow and grow in size until it seems to shine like a bright and brilliant sun. After a few moments, or whenever you feel ready, sound the AUM with concentration upon the base chakra. Feel the energy that is generated rising up the spine and entering into the Sacral chakra. Use exactly the same techniques as for the base chakra and sound the AUM in the sacral chakra when ready.

Repeat this process as you move upward into the solar plexus chakra, and finally the crown chakra. At the crown, you may wish to linger a little longer, visualizing the brilliance of the light radiating out from the head as far as you can. Try sounding the AUM at least three times or more at the crown chakra.

This is a very powerful meditation technique, and when you are more experienced it can even be extended to last for a full half hour or so if you feel like it, taking up the whole of an average meditation session. For example, you may wish to begin by sitting for meditation, and instead of candle gazing or breath counting, you might try dispensing with those practices and replacing them with a few rounds of digital pranayama, and then go directly into chakra visualization and resonating the AUM in each of the chakra. Once you have been meditating regularly, your intuition will guide you toward using those techniques that will help you most at any one time. AUM sounded in the chakras has a cleansing and balancing effect, and can be quite a blissful experience. Don't worry of it is not though, just keep practicing.

The mind is the most powerful tool we have, and the body and emotions are directly effected by our constant thoughts. If you continually tell yourself that you are unhappy, it will not be long before you actually feel quite awful inwardly moving from mild upset to deep melancholia. Then even the physical body becomes ill, susceptible to viruses etc. If on the other hand you tell yourself you are happy, then not before long you will actually being to feel happy inside. The physical body of a truly happy person seems to be vibrant and glowing.

In the same way when we visualize light as an energy flowing within us, we draw more of the inner, spiritual light into our psychic, and after sometime, perhaps even just a little time we start to feel that we are changing, purifying at many levels, and becoming more balanced.

◆ ◆ ◆

10

Bhagavat-Kriya of Meditation

Introduction

Bhagavat-Kriya of meditation is a simple but deeply mystic yogic way of meditation. It has been evolved by the yoga sadhana kendra of Sri Srimata Anandamayi Peeth, Indore (M.P.) Main objects of the methods are:

1. To purify, evolve and transform one's consciousness and thus to bring out a change in distorted modern living and values.
2. Silent enquiry into real meaning and purpose of human life.
3. An unfoldment of 'Divine Existence' into human consciousness thus making human life meaningful.
4. To help in leading human existence and consciousness towards perfection.

Better health, increased energy, freedom from psychosomatic diseases, developed will power, ability to face adverse conditions peacefully, calm and quiet mind are some of its definite results.

The method has been designed as to suit the most busy life of modern man only 20 minutes process in one single sitting is needed. The Kriya is practised when taken up as a method, and in due course it starts 'happening' when as a result of constant practice and descent of divine grace it comes out spontaneously from the deep recesses of our own consciousness Sri Sri ma names this process, respectively, '**Karna** and **Hona**', that is 'doing' and 'happening' in this mystic method of meditation one first '**does**' it and then it '**happens**'. The aspirant first meditates and then meditation comes to him. When kriya reaches as the stage of 'happening' it takes the aspirant irresistably and most definitely towards the goal of self-perfection and realisation.

The Meaning of 'Bhagavat Kriya'

The word 'Bhagavat' stands for the Divine, and 'Kriya' for the process. Thus, the term means—'**The divine process**'. Bhagavat kriya meditation means meditation that evokes 'Divine process' in order to save the aspirant from what is unwanted and undesirable. (The Divine Knows Better).

The Constituents of the Process

The process consists of 6 linbs, namely—

1. **Sodhan kriya** (a primal process of purification).
2. **Prana-kriya** (process involving a particular way of breathing enjoined with prana-gayatri).
3. **Hamsa-kriya** (process involving another way of breathing enjoined with an act as that of swan).

4. **Prana-bindu-kriya** (repetition of the 2nd excluding mantra bhavana).
5. **Hamsa-bindu kriya** (repetition of the 3rd excluding mantra bhavana).
6. **Suddha-aham-kriya** (an extension of observation and awareness involved in 4th and 5th applying it in different field of life and behaviour.)

Seven Days Course

One should practise the above mentioned 'Kriya' in the following way (first seven days preparatory course).

The Discipline

For kriya to be effective strictly, follow the under mentioned disciplinary code—

1. Practise kriya 3 times a day (3 meditation sittings each being approximately of 20 minutes only. Time advisable is between 5 to 6 A.M.; 6:30 to 7:30 P.M.; and 8:30 to 9:30 P.M.)
2. Adopt vegetarian diet only.
3. Keep away from all kinds of addiction and undesirable company.

For a more detailed knowledge of disciplinary code see the book **"yoga sadhana and samadhi"** published by Sri Sri Mata Anandamai Peeth, Indore, (M.P.)

First day

1. **Sodhan Kriya:** Slowly and deeply inhale the breath (called puraka) and recite Aum while exhaling 3 to 10 times.

   This simple but deeply effective process purifies out gross-physical, subtle and causal bodies.

2. **Prana-Kriya:** Inhale and exhale (called puraka and Rechaka respectively) deeply and slowly with Prana-Gayatri 10 times. Breath is to be taken with the word **'SO'** and is to be thrown out with another word **'Ham'**, mantra is not to be recited or vocally pronounced but it is to be felt only mentally while inhaling and exhaling.

   This process is related without pranic consciousness evoked.

Second Day

3. **Hamsa Kriya:** This is practised making 3 parts of one deep and slow inhale and retaining breath (called kumbhaka) after each little inhale, exhaling after the last retention, adjoining at every step the Hamsa Mantra. Practise this in the following manner (10 times).

   Take little breath 'in' adding with it the feeling of 'SO'; stop the breath with the feeling of 'Ham'; while retaining breath keep the alphabet 'H' in vishudhi chakra (at throat) and meditate the point (anusvara or bindu) in the sahasrara-chakra taking 'bindu' to be consciousness; this is one part of the first process, repeat this process two times more and then exhale the breath with the word **'sah'** retaining bindu or consciousness in the sahasrrara. Note the while exhaling, breath **'Sa'** and **'Ha'** both the words have been thrown out and what is left is **'consciousness'** or **'awareness'**.

   Vibration existing in these two words viz, 'Sa' and 'Ha' lies at the root of creation and it forms 'mind' and 'matter'. Through the mystic process described above you throw out the physical and mental element from your conscious existence and learn to live.....not with body and mind, but with 'consciousness' alone.

Third Day

4. **Prana-bindu-kriya:** Repeat the second process excluding mantra feeling and add 'observation' of deep and slow breath, inhale deeply and slowly, exhale deeply and slowly; and 'be aware' of this—10 times.

Fourth Day

5. **Hamsa-bindu-kriya:** Repeat the third process excluding mantra-bhavana and adding awareness of the total process involing 3 purakas, 3 kumbhakas and 1 rechaka—10 times.

   See that not a single breath comes 'in' or goes 'out' without your being aware of it. Similarly with 'retention' you must remain aware when the pranic movement is retained.

Fifth Day

6. **Suddha-aham-kriya:** This process is to be practised in two parts: **Part I** asks us to be aware of 3 particular areas forming a circle in fixed sequence or order, **Part II** called 'resting point' may well be compared with 'Shavasana' the last in the practise of postures and asks the aspirant to be with his breath only.

   Practise this process in the following way—

   Part I: (*i*) Be aware of your gross physical body and with this awareness try to develop a distinct feeling that since you can see and know your body 'you' are apart from and have no actual relation with it, try to identify yourself not with body, but with the awareness itself.

(*ii*) Be aware of physical sensory perceptions viz, sound etc. coming from outside, and here too try to develop the same feeling. Make no mental reaction to sensory perceptions. Just observe them in a most detached way.

(*iii*) Be aware of your mental projections and perceptions like memory, imagination, reasoning, thinking and other movements of the mind. Leave all the movements of the mind to it only, do not relate yourself with them, Minutely note that they are not 'yours' but of the mind and you are not mind but awareness only. Just 'see' without any reaction.

Mind has the long, very old habit of immediate judgement and evalution, naming and formation in terms of some fixed codes of culture and civilization philosophy and religion, ethics and morality and vice-versa of modern **carvaka** pattern of living. This 'identifying-perception' is a distorted perception and is detrimental to the practice in hand.

Therefore you are asked to see the things as they are and not as you would like to see them. This non-reactive, unprejudiced 'pure-perception' is called suddha-aham-kriya.

Part II: Reapeat above process 3 to 10 times and then come to the 'resting point' which is the fourth (Turiyam).

Sixth Day

(*iv*) Simply observe natural breathing—with no intention, attitude and expectation.

Since any explanation of this process in terms of 'effect' or 'result' may cause pre-occupation of one's mind thus again starting a new chain of thinking we think it better to observe silence.

This resting point is not to be restricted with time limit. Stay with it as much you like—silently observing natural pranic-movement.

Howerever, few important points need to be cleared:

1. While staying with this process if an urge comes from within to repeat **OM** or any other mantra, do not resist; let it be so. But awareness must be continued.
2. If the great prana-gayatri want's to manifest in inhaling and exhaling, welcome her.
3. If the Divine-gayatri or the Hamsa-mantra out of their sweet will take a new course and movement in your body with a feeling of gratitude leave the way to Her and 'quietly see' the 'happening' and lastly.
4. To resume 'Bhagavat kriya meditation', it is this 'happening' which is called Bhagavat-kriya—the Divine process to discover and unfoled the 'consciousness'.

Seventh Day

7th day is the day of silence, swadhyaya and self introspection. Try to be completely a foreigner to you yourself-whole day.

Note

Remember, "Practise everyday the Divine process intact and preserved keep the Holy thread."

◆ ◆ ◆

11

Yoga in Office

Introduction

If you work in an office, you probably experience physical and mental tension. There are several reasons for this.

1. Office life is sedentary.
2. Office life deprives you of vital oxygen.
3. Office life is emotionally wearing.
4. Office life can generate enxiety.
5. Office life is full of struggle.
6. Office life provides you work load and fatigue.

Yoga can help you to create balance and harmony on all levels of one's being: physical, emotional, mental and spiritual. Yoga practice can help you to become healthier, more relaxed and more content, stronger, active and more disciplined. It can give you greater vitality and optimism, and help you in approach the problems of life in a more positive, more creative way.

How You Sit?

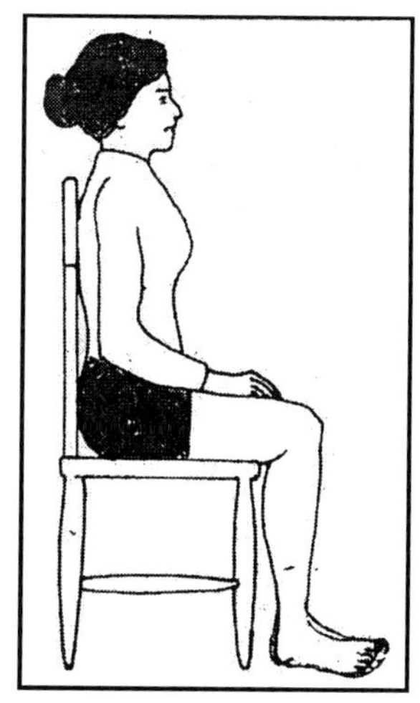

Sit properly, with your spine erect. Sit towards the front of your chair. Place your feet flat on the floor, parallel and about hip with apart. Your knees should also be hip width apart, and a little lower than your hips. Balance the upper body on the sitting bones.

1. The Shoulders

Shoulder Circling

Sit in basic position, with you arms hanging loosely at you sides circle your shoulders gently backwards. Do this slowly and enjoy it.

Shoulder Lifting and Squeezing

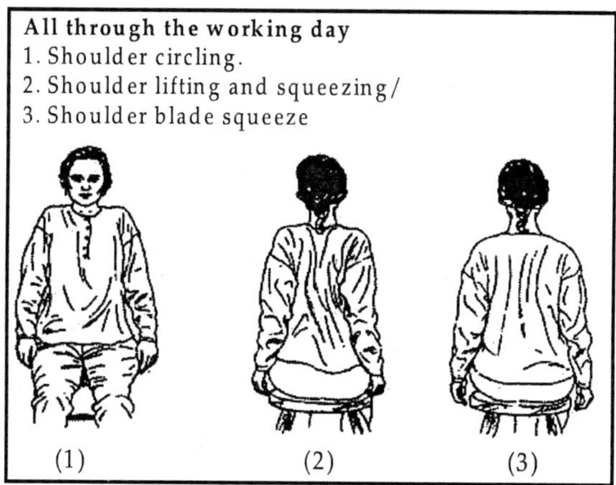

Inhale and slowly lift your shoulders drawing them up towards your ears. Exhale as you draw them back. Squeezing your shoulder blades together. Pull back quite hard to meet in the middle. Imagine that a heavy suitcase in each of your hands is weighing you down.

Shoulder Blade Squeezing

Interlace your fingers behind you at seat level, elbows bent and arms relaxed. Exhale as you slowly draw your elbows towards each other. Squeezing your shoulder blades firmly together. Inhale as you release the squeeze. Repeat this several times with breath.

Arm Rotation

Place your finger tips on your shoulders. Inhale as you bring your elbows together in front of your chest, then lift them as high as possible, keeping them together for a long as possible. Direct them back and then begin to lower them behind you. Exhale squeezing your shoulder blades together, lowering your elbows as far as possible and then bringing them forward and together.

Arm Rotation

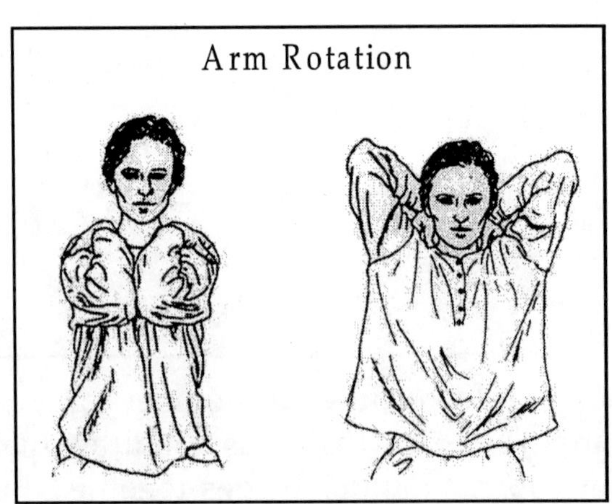

2. The Neck

Head Turing (Brahma Mudra)

1. Inhale as you look forward, and then up towards the sky. Tip your head gently backwards only as far as is comfortable. Exhale as you slowly bring your head up and gently bend it forward, aiming your chin towards the notch in your throat. Repeat twice more.

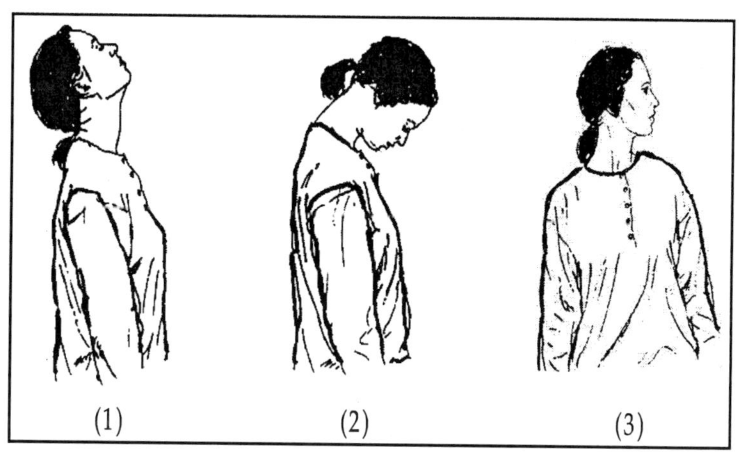

(1) (2) (3)

2. Exhale as you slowly look over your right shoulder, letting your eyes lead your head, keeping the chin level. Inhale as you look to the front. Exhale as you slowly look over your left shoulder. Inhale as you look to the front. Repeat twice to each side.

Stretching Your Neck, Lowering Head Forwards

Exhale as you tuck in your chin and slowly lower your head, aiming your chin towards the notch in your throat interface your finger behind your head. Hold this position, breathing normal. Come back in normal position.

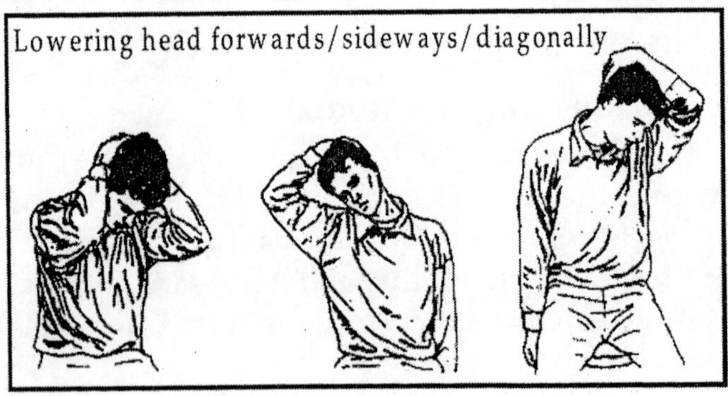
Lowering head forwards/sideways/diagonally

Stretching Your Neck: Lowering Head Side Ways

Tuck in your chin slightly, and exhale as you gently your head side ways to the right, aiming your ear towards your shoulder. Breathe freely as you hold this position. Take your right hand up and over your hand near the left ear, keep the elbow back. Keep your left shoulder pulled well down away from your ear. Hold this position, breathing naturally. Repeat on the other side, circle your shoulders backwards a few times.

3. The Upper Back

The Chest Expansion

Interlace your fingers behind your back. Move your hands outward in a breast stroke movement. Straight your elbows, draw your clasped hands down towards your buttocks and gently pull your shoulders back. Inhale as you lift your arms away from your buttocks. Keeping them straight, lift high comfortably. Squeezing your shoulder blades together. Exhale as you lower your arms, allowing your elbows to bend. Repeat a few times.

1. **Four Upper Back Tension Relievers:** Sit in the basic sitting position. Interlace your fingers infront. turn and your palms outside and exhale as you straighten your elbows. Inhale as you push your palms away from you, raising your hand above your head. Exhale and lower your arms to the front, continuing to stretch and push your palms away from you. Repeat twice more, and then rest your hands in your lap.

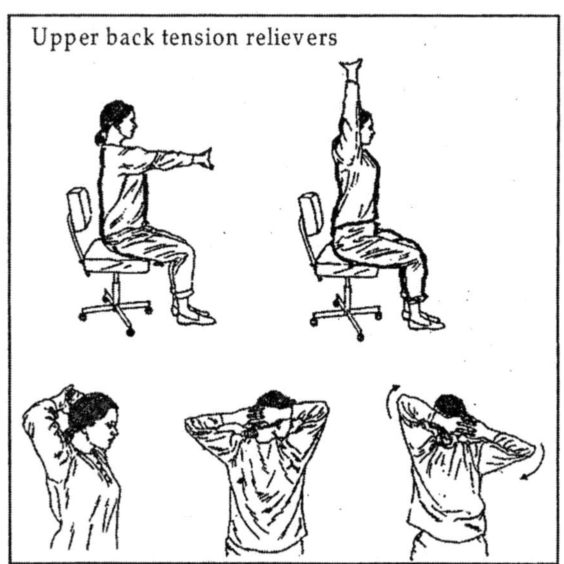

2. Interlace your fingers and put behind your head, but do not touch it. Direct your elbows and shoulders back and feel the squeeze at the top of your shoulder blades. Inhale and stretch your palms towards the ceiling, keeping your elbows and shoulders back, and straightening your arms. Exhale as you lower your arms in front, stretching your palms away. Repeat twice more. Rest your hands in your lap.
3. Exhale as you straighten your elbows. Inhale as you raise your straight arms above your head, palms facing the ceiling. Exhale as you lower your clasped hands behind your head as in exercise 2. This time, rest your cupped palms against the back of your head. Keeping your elbows and shoulders well back, turn your head slowly to the right and then to the left. Repeat three or four more times to each side, breathing freely. Inhale as you stretch your arms up, palms facing the ceiling. Exhale as you lower your arms in front, stretching your palms away. Rest your hands in your lap.
4. Take the position no. 3. Inhale as you raise your straight arms above your head, palms facing the ceiling. Exhale as you lower your clasped hands behind the head, keeping your elbows and shoulders back, and your hands a little away from your head.

   Move your arms in large ovals behind your head, moving your elbows as far out to each side as possible, keeping them as low and as far back as possible. Repeat 3 or 4 times, breathing freely; and then reverse directions. Inhale as you stretch your palms up towards the ceiling. Exhale and lower your arms in front, stretching them and pushing your palms away. Rest your hands in your lap. Circling your shoulders forwards and backwards a few times.

The Shoulder Blade Shove

This is wonderful exercise works directly on the muscles of the upper back, toning, strengthening and increasing circulation to them.

Lift your shoulders up, draw them back and pull them gently. Exhale and empty your lungs. Inhale and slowly raise your arms sideways to shoulder level. Exhale as you form your hands into loose fists with the thumbs curled outside. Inhale as you slowly shove your shoulder blades and arms out away from the middle your body. Exhale as you draw your shoulders blade together. Inhale as you fist stretch your fingers out. Hold the shoulder blade firmly squeeze together as you do this. Exhale as you lower your arms slowly and release the squeeze.

Tension-relieving Massage

Place the right palm on the left shoulder in the middle. Pick up a handful of skin and muscle, and gently begin to knead it. Keep holding your handful of skin and muscle. Then slowly and gently circle it backward a few times.

4. The Spine

1. **Spine Stretching the Spine Forwards:** Interlace your fingers and turn out the palms. Inhale, raise your arms above head. Exhale as you lean forward stretch your palms away from you. Inhale as you come backup. Stretching your spine and arms. Exhale as you slowly lower your arms and relax your hands in your Lap. Repeat again.

At the end of a long session

Neck and shoulder exercises shown opposite

Stretching spine forwards

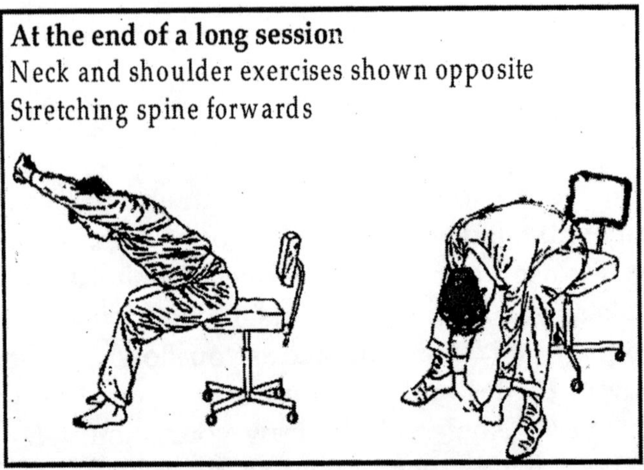

2. Place your feet 45 cm apart flat on the floor and parallel. Exhale and allow your hands to drop forwards the floor and hang loosely. Hold this

pose, breathing slowly and deeply. Inhale as you lift your head and come back up slowly, maintaining the length in your spine.

Stretching the Spine Backwards

1. Place your hands on the lumber region of your back, thumbs pointing forwards. Inhale and lengthen the chest and rib cage upwards. Exhale and stretch the back backwards in a smooth curve. Lift your chest and direct your shoulders back and squeeze your shoulders blades together. Hold this position and breathing naturally. Inhale as you come back slowly to the upright position.

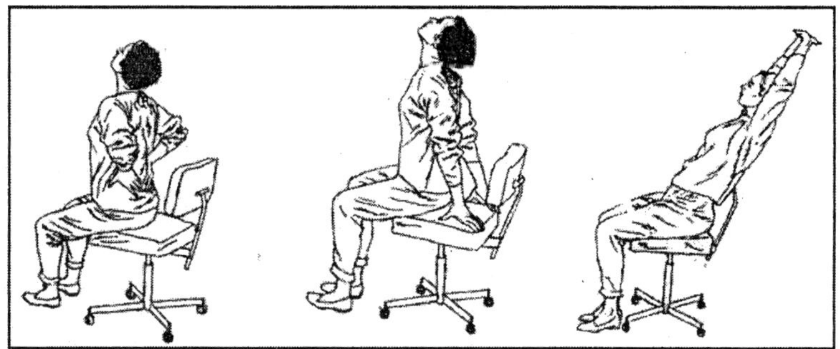

2. Place the palms on the chair behind you. Inhale and stretch the body up and opening the chest and rib cage. Exhale and arch your upper back. Draw your shoulders back and down, and gently bend your neck backwards, to look up the ceiling. Hold this position, breathing freely. Inhale as you come back slowly to the starting position. Repeat twice.
3. Sit to the back of your chair. Legs together. Interlace your fingers. Inhale and strech your arms upwards. Exhale as you stretch backwards over your chair back. Hold the position for a moment, breathing

normal. Stretch on the inhalation, relax on the exhalation.

Stretch the Spine Sideways

Interlace your fingers, turn out and bring them over the head. Keep the arms straight. Inhale and stretch the arms in right side. Exhale as you come back. Repeat once or twice more to each side. Repeat this in the left side.

Spinal Twisting

Cross your left arm and place your palm against the outside of your right thigh. Take your right arm behind you and rest the back of the hand against your left waist. Inhale deeply. Exhale and turn your head to look over your right shoulder. Inhale and lengthen. Exhale and twist your upper body around to the right. Allow your right shoulder to

release and move backwards. Inhale and turn the face forwards. Release your hands. Repeat to the other side.

5. The Arms

1. The Finger and Hands

Stretching and Squeezing

Raise your arms to shoulder height in front, palms facing down. Focus your awareness in your fingers, and breathe normal. Open your hands slowly and stretch your fingers wide. Make fists with the thumbs folded in side. Squeeze your thumbs. Do this 5 times. Flick the tips of your fingers against the thumb one by one. Pull your fingers gentlty. Bend your fingers towards the wrists.

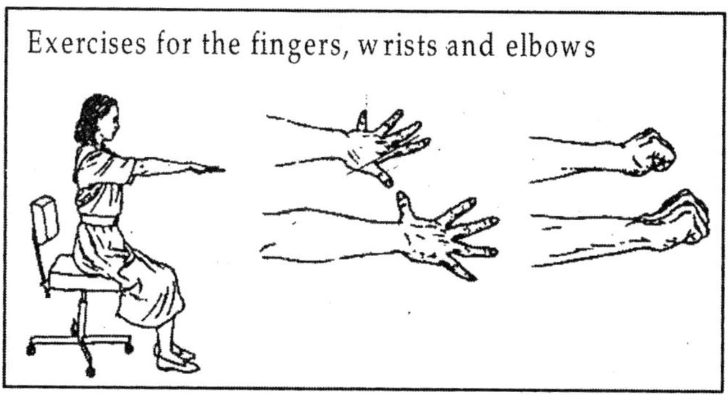

Exercises for the fingers, wrists and elbows

2. The Wrists

Wrist Bending

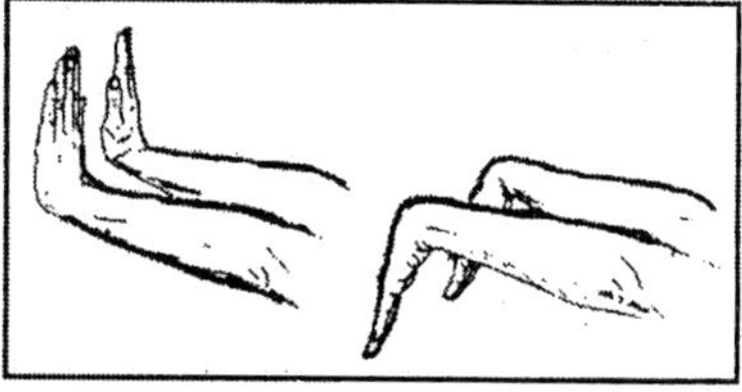

Raise your arms to shoulder height in front, your palms facing down. Focus your awareness in your wrists and breathe naturally. Bend your hands backwards at the wrists. Keeping straight and pointing upward, as if pushing against a wall. Slowly bend your fingers downward. Repeat the movement 5 times. Lower your arms and circle your shoulders backwards.

Wrist Circling

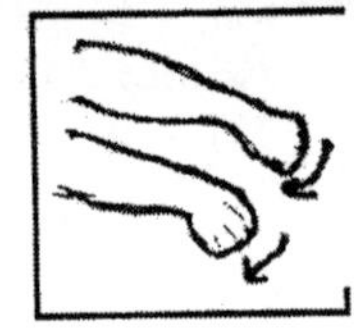

Raise your arms to shoulder height in front. Palms facing down. Make a loose fits and keep thumbs inside. Circle your right first clockwise and anticlockwise 5-5 times, then by left fist repeat 5-5 time.

3. The Elbows

Elbow Bending: Arm Forward

Raise your arms to shoulder height in front of you, with your palms facing up. Focus your awareness in your elbows, and breathe naturally. Exhale as you bend your elbows, bringing your fingertips to your shoulders, Keeping your upper arms parallel to the floor.

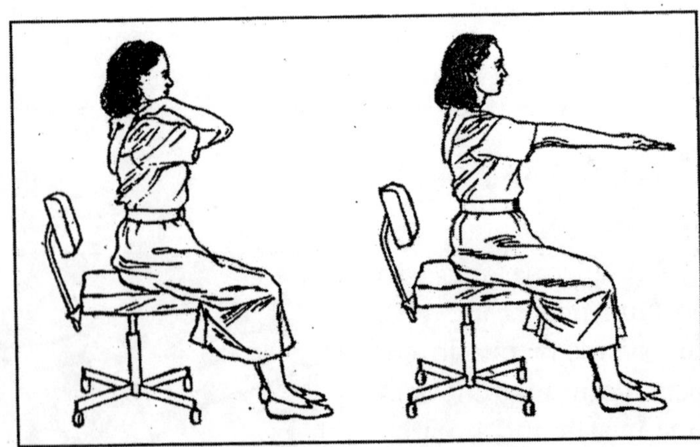

Inhale as you straighten your arms, extending your fingertips away. Repeat, Lower your arms and circle your shoulders back.

Elbow Bending: Arms to the Side

Raise your arms sideways to shoulder height, palms facing up. Exhale as you bend your elbows, bringing your fingertips to your shoulders, keeping your upper arms parallel to the floor. Inhale as you straighten your left arm extending your fingertips away. At the sametime, letting your eyes lead the movement, turn your head slowly to the left. Exhale as you return your fingertips to your shoulder; simultaneously turning your head to look forward. Practise this by the right arm. Do it twice more. Lower your arms and circle your shoulders back.

6. The Legs

1. **Toe Bending:** Repeat five times.
2. **Ancle Bending:** Repeat five times.
3. **Ancle Circling:** One by one clockwise and anti-clockwise.

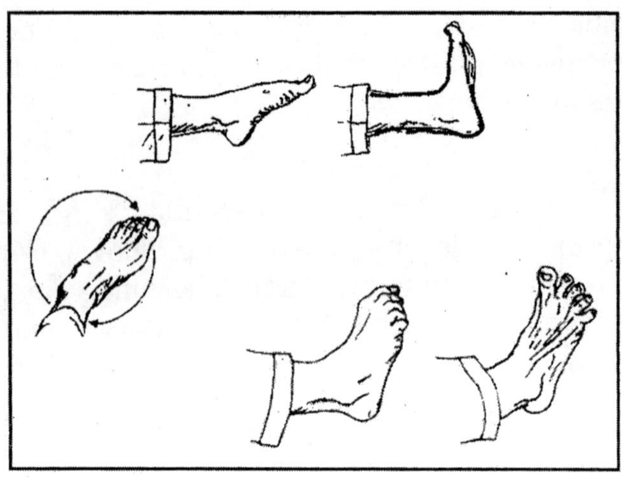

The Knees

Focus your awareness in your knees, and breathe naturally. Raise and straighten your right leg, pushing your heel gently away, and then bend it fully.

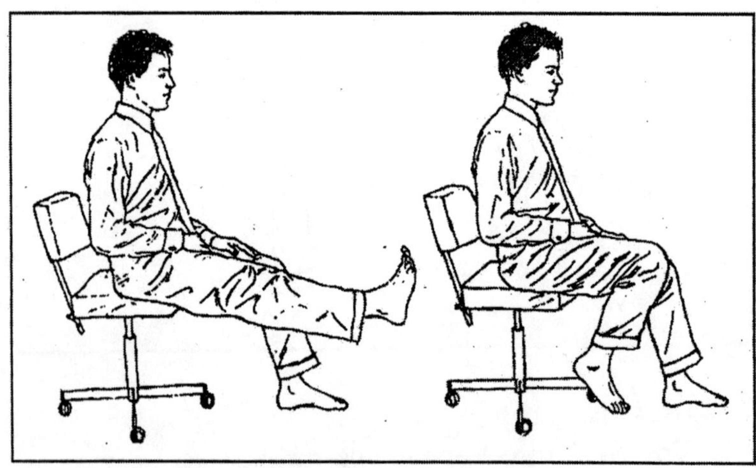

Repeat five times, Repeat on the left.

Note: Do knee circling one by one, in each direction 5 times.

The Hips

1. Place your right ancle on your left thigh just above the knee. Relax your right Leg. Allow your knee to drop towards the floor, and let gravity and the weight of your leg gently open out your hips joints. With your work change leg carefully after 5 minutes or so.
2. Sit cross-legged or Sukhasana.

7. The Eyes

Eye exercise will relax, revitalize and strengthen your eyes. Here are two very simple ones.

1. Watching the Clock

Close your eyes. Imagine that you are gazing at the face of a huge clock on the entire wall. Then open the eyes.

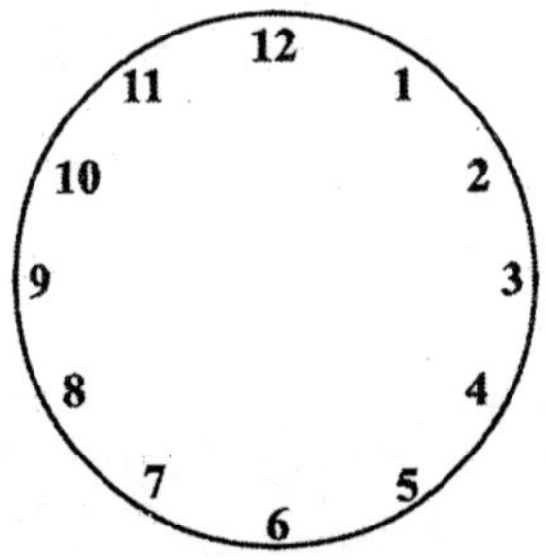

Look up at 12 O'clock. Look down at 6 O'clock.
Look at 3 O'clock. Look at 9 O'clock.
Look at 1 O'clock. Look at 7 O'clock.
Look at 2 O'clock. Look at 8 O'clock.
Look at 11 O'clock. Look at 5 O'clock.
Look at 10 O'clock. Look at 4 O'clock.

Repeat each of these several times in each direction.

2. Palming

Rub the palms very briskly and energetically together. Place them over your closed eyes and sit quietly for a few minutes. Holding then gently. Imagine that your own healing energy is being transmitted to your eye, soothing, relaxing and refreshing them. Breathe softly. Open your eyes behind your hands and gaze softly into darkness. Finally slide your fingertips softly on your forehead, eyelids, nose, cheeks, lips and chin.

While Watching Television

Sitting Exercise

Relaxed Standing Forward Bend

This is a lovely, relaxed movement, marvellous for releasing tension in the whole body, especially upper part of the body. Inhale, Exhale and stretch.

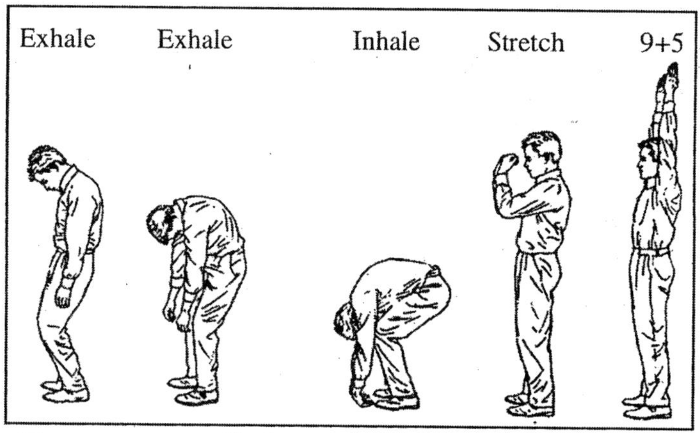

Repeat twice all these exercises.

Full Breath

Stand in balance with your feet apart. Exhale gently emptying your lungs. Turn your arms out from your shoulder sockets. Inhale as you raise your arms to the sides, heels up. Bring your palms over head and together. Exhale bringing the arms and heels down. Repeat 5 times.

◆ ◆ ◆

Other Books on

HEALTH BOOKS

1. A Guide to Your Pregnancy **(New)**
2. Ayurveda for All **(New)**
3. A Guide to Migraine, Airthritis, Cervical Spondylosis, and Backache **(New)**
4. Body and Beauty Care **(New)**
5. Yoga for All **(New)**
6. Child Care and Nutrition
7. Naturopathy Modern Way of Life
8. First Aid How to Handle an Accident
9. Acupressure in Daily Life
10. Complete Book of Yoga
11. Look Younger at Any Age
12. HIV/AIDS - Transmission, Prevention & Alternative Therapies
13. Diabetics and Diet
14. Increase your Height & Loose your Weight
15. Make Fitness A Way of Life
16. Common Problems of Children
17. Handbook of Nutrition & Dietetics
18. A Guide to Massage Therapy
19. A Guide to Family Medicine
20. A Guide to Digestive Disorders
21. Complete Book of Child Care
22. A Guide to Homoeopathy

23. Life Begins at 40
24. Alternative Therapies
25. How to Overcome Stress
26. Yoga Therapy
27. Obesity
28. Self Motivation
29. Yoga for Health and Relaxation
30. Women Disorders and Pregnancy
31. A Guide to Body Pains
32. Sex Education
33. Common Diseases and Cure
34. Pranayama for Better Life
35. Herbal Home Remedies
36. A Guide to Beauty & Skin Care
37. A Guide to Heart Care
38. A Guide to High Blood Pressure
39. Cancer Causes and Prevention
40. Nature Cure for Common Diseases
41. Good Health Through Food and Regimen
42. A Guide to Allergies
43. A Guide to Aging
44. Ayurveda for Health & Beauty